THE REAL
MUSSOLINI

THE REAL
MUSSOLINI

by Rachele Mussolini
as told to Albert Zarca
translation Christine Hauch

 SAXON HOUSE

First published in the United
Kingdom by Saxon House,
D. C. Heath Ltd., Westmead,
Farnborough, Hampshire, in
1974.

Saxon House,
D. C. Heath Ltd.,
Westmead, Farnborough,
Hampshire, England.

L.C. 73-10624
ISBN 0 347 00011 8

CONTENTS

CHAPTER 1

Mussolini and Roosevelt

"Remember Napoleon, Benito, since you admire him so much. True he was powerful; he mastered Europe and even ruled countries further afield. But what did he really do? As soon as he won one victory he looked for more. After each conquest, he still wanted a bigger empire. And what happened to him, Benito? He lost the lot! Everything crumbled under his feet. Don't be like him. Remember thàt song we sang when we were children: 'Napoleon with all his superb . . . wound up on Elba'."

"What do you want me to do? Resign? Raise chickens in Romagna? You must be joking, Rachele."

"No, I don't want you to raise chickens in Romagna. I want you to stop in time, to become part of history while you're still alive, to devote 10 or 15 years of your life to your wife and children after giving 30 to politics. Political life is too dirty to be good all the time. So far you've been lucky, you've known only the good times, but watch out from now on."

This conversation occurred in May 1936 when my husband, Benito Mussolini, and I were staying at Rocca delle Caminate, our home in Romagna. A few days earlier, he had stood on the balcony of the Palazzo Venezia, announcing to the ecstatic crowd the creation of the Empire after the Abyssinian conquest. Now we were alone and nobody heard me entreating him to abandon power.

On the surface, there was nothing to warrant such a

step. At the time Benito, who was not yet 53 (he was born on July 29, 1883) was in perfect health. And in a political sense he had never been so strong either in Italy or abroad. Our armies had crushed the Abyssinians completely. The lira flourished as one of Europe's most stable currencies and the League of Nations' sanction – imposed after the Abyssinian adventure – had failed. With patriotic fervour, the Italian people had themselves contributed to this failure by giving their gold to the government. In Rome, for instance, the Queen and I were among the 250,000 women who cast their wedding rings into a brazier on the marble base of the Tomb of the Unknown Soldier. And in 1935, numerous Italians domiciled in the United States, had ingeniously sent the tons of copper which Italy so badly needed – inventing a special copper post-card engraved with Christmas greetings.

Even such prominent opponents as the philosopher Benedetto Croce or the former Prime Minister Vittorio Emmanuele Orlando had acted with my husband whom, as head of government, foreign powers hailed as a "realist", "influential", or "wise".

There were no black clouds to darken the horizon, yet I could not resist the urge to persuade my husband to quit the political scene – a desire doubtless fostered by the marvellous weather which enhanced our family holiday at Rocca delle Caminate. Our happiness sprang. from the fact that two of our children, Vittorio and Bruno, who were pilots, had returned safely from combat in Ethiopia.

I seized my chance one afternoon after a long drive through the Romagnole countryside. Soon after lunch, unescorted by secretary, prefect or security police we'd gone out alone in our Alfa Romeo "Spider". With Benito wearing a beret pulled low over his head and I with a scarf knotted round mine, we enjoyed ourselves like twenty-year-olds.

We'd stopped several times at peasant houses – as was Benito's habit in Romagna – and, as always happened, after the first few moments of surprise and emotion,

Benito and the locals were chatting about the crop, the cows, the house and the children. To the people of Romagna he was still "Muslen", the son of Alessandro the *fabbroferraio*, or blacksmith. I'd had to tug at his sleeve to remind him of the time.

So, for the moment, he was alone with me in the garden, his sleeves rolled up, splitting logs, while I pottered about in a bed of roses. Occasionally I glanced at him and seeing him with his tanned skin, and a hint of gentleness in his expression that had matured with age, I could almost understand why women fell on his neck, at his feet or into the sea when he went bathing.

Once he had chopped the logs, Benito called: "You know what the King suggested the other day? He wanted to make me a prince."

"I hope you didn't accept."

"Are you joking? Can you see me arriving somewhere with the usher announcing 'His Excellency Prince Mussolini.' "

"And I'd be Princess Rachele Mussolini! Lord, what an idea!"

"Don't worry. I kept a straight face, though the thought of my head beneath a crown made me want to laugh out loud, and I answered: 'Majesty, I'm touched by this gesture, but I cannot accept. I was born Mussolini and I'll die Mussolini, without title.' "

"And what did the King say?"

" 'You could at least take a dukedom.' Again I refused." Then, pretending to look upset, Benito added: "You won't be Princess Mussolini or the Duchess of Rocca delle Caminate. You'll stay Rachele Mussolini."

And we began to laugh. I could scarcely believe this story and had to make Benito swear it was true. Then he went on: "I know someone who'd dearly have liked to be made a duke – your 'cousin', the Marquis of Sabotino."

"Badoglio? He already has the Collar of the Annunziata and a marquisate. Isn't that enough?"

"Apparently not. We are happy with the Collar of the Annunziata but some people still want more."

Perhaps I should mention that the Collar of the Annunziata was the highest distinction the King could confer. My husband had received the honour some years before and it made us honorary "cousins" to the King – just as we were "cousins" of Marshal Badoglio, another holder of the decoration.

These relaxed moments offered too good an opportunity to let slip. "Tell me, Benito. Supposing you went further. Supposing you said to the King, 'Your Majesty, you summoned me to govern when the country was in chaos. I have restored peace and prosperity at home and made Italy great and powerful abroad. Now the Italians aren't all "ice-cream sellers" any more. They're proud of their country. Before me you were King of Italy. Now you are Emperor. Everything is going well, so I am putting Italy back into your hands and I'm resigning.' "

"In fact, you want to pension me off, do you?"

"No, Benito. You'll write articles, your memoirs. You've your newspaper in Milan. It's going so well, we're even living off it. I'm not asking you to retire completely. But think of all you've done already for Italy. What more do you want to do? Our country has never been so great or well-respected. Look back 15 years. There was civil war then. And what have we now?"

My husband stayed silent for a while. He listened, frowning slightly, more surprised than annoyed by my outburst. I had stopped because I was scared I'd already gone too far. But etched in my mind was the warning of a gypsy woman when I was sixteen. She'd enlightened: "You will receive the highest honours. In fact you'll be the equal of a Queen. Then everything will crumble away and there'll be a time of mourning." I was aware that the first part of this prediction had already come true. I'd been loaded with honours and was by now "cousin" to the Queen. But what about the other part of the prophesy? Suddenly I felt frightened. "Think, Benito," I said. "Our children have grown up. We're happy but we could be even happier. I know I'm selfish, but I'm also thinking of you. When you left for the royal palace in 1922 and later telephoned to tell me

4

everything that happened, what did I say to you? I told you that you were now the people's servant even though you were your own master. Now you can be what you were before, with the added weight of your success. You could be the arbiter, the man the people consult when there's a national problem. You could become part of history while you are still alive.

"No more decisions to be ratified, no more pitfalls to avoid, no more tensions or fears for yourself and the children. There are men waiting for you to make your first mistake so that they can scoff and say: 'Mussolini has fallen.' Cut the ground from under their feet."

I stopped, breathless. I'd put everything into my plea for the first time in twenty-six years of anxiety, tears, joys – and love. For once I'd spoken my true feelings.

Benito took me tenderly by the arm, as if to protect me, his expression a trifle vague. Perhaps he was looking back over what he'd already achieved. I began to feel that I might succeed, that my dream might conceivably become reality. I put my hand on his and murmured: "Try, Benito, please."

"I'll see," he replied, his voice faint with emotion, as it was to be nine years later, during the final tragedy, when he called to ask me to take care of the children. "I'll think about it. Don't upset yourself over it, Rachele."

We went back to the house. On the steps I turned my head. The smell of burning wood was mingling with the scent of pine and flowers; the countryside was settling down for the night. The sunset over the misty hills of our Romagna had never seemed so lovely.

Some days later my husband left for Rome. We had not discussed his retirement again. I was waiting for the summer holidays at Riccione to do so. Besides I knew that he was extremely busy and it would have been a tactical error to press him for a decision.

But, on this occasion, time was against me and the success of my own initiative was my undoing. As soon as he arrived in Rome Benito told Achille Starace, the secretary of the National Fascist Party, about it, and even asked him to look into the practical aspects of his leaving.

Starace, frantic at the idea of Mussolini resigning, alerted various officials of the regime. He and several others were loyal and decent. In their eyes the Duce's work was not over; he had to continue in government. But there were also the opportunists whom Mussolini had brought out of obscurity, who confused Italy's interests with their own financial gain, and who were the first to desert him at times of trouble. Everyone agreed that Mussolini must be prevented from resigning, whatever the cost. They'd plenty of arguments in their favour – among them Communist penetration in Spain which had been behind the Duce's decision to send help to General Franco.

Finally, my husband agreed to stay in power. Apart from political reasons, there were several factors working against me. First, Benito had made known the proposal too soon, when I was not there and could not even balance the scales with my own side of the argument. And then I'd forgotten how difficult it is for a man to give up what he has fought so hard to win. After years of hardship, Benito Mussolini was now savouring the delights of triumph and the heady wine of glory.

Some days earlier, on the balcony of the Palazzo Venezia, he had watched the frenzied crowds yelling "Du-ce! Du-ce!" to show the total support of the Italian people. It seems amazing that I had not remembered it, for I'd been there too – an anonymous face lost in the crowd, holding Romano and Anna-Maria, two of our children, and listening to his speech amplified through loudspeakers. With a lump in my throat, I'd been carried away by my own thoughts. "Supposing all these people knew that you were the wife of the man who is speaking, the man they are cheering – knew that this evening, at home, he'll ask: 'Well, what did you think of my speech?' "

A year later, in October 1937, my husband had another opportunity to change the destiny of both himself and his country.

My son Vittorio, then a film producer, considered the American market – the most important in the world – as one which would provide a profitable outlet for Italian films. At that time, the box-office revenue from American films shown on Italian screens was frozen in the banks. He planned, therefore, to use this capital to make films in Italy on, say, poetic subjects, and distribute them in the United States. By exporting Italian culture, this would allow the Americans to make good their losses and bring work to our own industry. After preliminary approaches to the Americans, he planned a trip to the United States.

Vittorio feared his father would oppose the idea since relations between the two countries were somewhat cool. Italy was helping General Franco to fight the Communists in Spain – tactics which the American Government, if not the people, freely criticised.

But Benito enthused over the idea, agreed to it and Vittorio left for America. There he had talks and visited studios, and in general did what he had gone to do. Shortly before his return, he was told that the President and Mrs. Roosevelt wished to entertain him at the White House. This in itself came as no surprise, for Benito had welcomed the Roosevelt's son, John, at the Palazzo Venezia on a visit to Rome. Vittorio therefore thought that Roosevelt was merely being polite.

The invitation was for October 13, 1937. Also present were Fulvio Sulvich, the Italian ambassador in Washington, and Philips, his American counterpart in Rome. My son was received in the chimney room, famous – as he told us – as the setting of Roosevelt's radio talks to the American people. Mrs. Eleanor Roosevelt served tea during a dull, formal chat about Vittorio's journey to the United States and John's to Italy. When Roosevelt joined them, he welcomed Vittorio warmly, asking him to prolong his stay and making flattering remarks about Italy.

Then, suddenly casting pleasantries aside, he said: "Will you please give my regards to the Italian Premier and tell him that I would dearly like to meet him. I would like to have a personal conversation with him so that we can get better acquainted with the problems of our two countries. Italy is the only country with which the United States can maintain the closest relations without compromising its democratic traditions. This is because of its history, its geographical position and because the seat of the Catholic Church is within its borders. Signor Mussolini is the only man who can keep a balance in Europe. Germany and Russia are at opposite poles from America and we can do nothing with them.

"I know that Signor Mussolini cannot leave his country for long. I'm in the same position. So could you tell him that I suggest we meet in neutral waters – say, in a boat on the high seas. And I would be glad if we could meet next spring at the latest."

On his first evening back at the Villa Torlonia, Vittorio told us about his amazing conversation in Washington. To seek the meeting with my husband, Roosevelt told Vittorio that he'd chosen less conventional channels because he thought them better. The diplomats could deal with the details later.

Benito would have given thought to the proposal, even if he found the novelty of it American in flavour, but he doubted Roosevelt's sincerity; he would have preferred talks with a different President. He thought that under his democratic exterior, Roosevelt was in fact, running a dictatorship. Besides, he believed Roosevelt was making the same mistakes about Europe as his predecessor. I remember how, in 1919, when Benito returned from the banquet given for Wilson in Milan – which he'd attended as editor of the *Popolo d'Italia* – he told me he'd been disappointed in the President and his self-centred politics.

In any case, Roosevelt's invitation came a month too late. At the end of September Benito had returned from his triumphant five-day visit to Germany and his relations with the Führer were by then too close for a change of sides.

And yet, if Roosevelt hadn't attacked Italy so fiercely

for aiding France, had not linked Fascism with Communism and Nazism as the three scourges – thus dismissing Mussolini's restraining influence – something might have come of it, especially as Benito was on excellent terms with the American Press and respected in the United States.

Indeed, as long ago as 1910, a Socialist weekly had invited him to settle in America and edit the paper's daily edition. We had almost gone, but Benito gave up the idea because I was expecting Edda; he was afraid I would be ill.

When I was in a concentration camp at the end of the war, I told an American officer that my husband had been offered the chance to live in the United States. He replied: "You realise we could have had Benito Mussolini as President."

In fact, Benito Mussolini had other chances to change the course of events – perhaps even of history. But later his fate was often linked to the exigencies of war – to luck.

On the other hand, in the instances I have mentioned, Mussolini held all the cards. He was in a position to decide, totally independent of others. And each time, the head of government gave way to the man; the qualities and defects of the man took precedence over political considerations. Whether he was wrong or right, it is not for me to judge, but I thought these episodes merit a mention.

I can give another instance of the man, at a crucial time of his life since it was the end, when he was true to himself by thinking first of others. This was on April 25, 1945, three days before his death, when he could have saved himself, taking refuge in Spain and perhaps meeting a different fate.

Years after the war, Vittorio told me that he'd worked out a plan which was complete save for one detail – his father's consent. On April 25, Vittorio outlined a plan to Air Marshal Bonomi to fly my husband to Spain. Bonomi confirmed that some three-engine planes were ready to leave Ghedi aerodrome, near Brescia and guaranteed to get Benito to Spain provided he left quickly.

That same day, Benito was in Milan. Now in control of the Prefecture, he had convened a succession of meetings to decide on future action. Incidentally, I shall return to these last days of his life, but meanwhile, I would stress that my husband, as Vittorio confirmed, was quite indifferent to his own fate.

When he arrived at my husband's office in the morning, Vittorio found his father alone. Outside, the yard and corridors seethed with nervous activity; everybody searched madly for some idea which they thought would solve the insoluble problem. Benito asked Vittorio what he wanted, and my son, fearing a sudden interruption, quickly described his plan. He said that once safe in Spain, Benito could treat with the Allies and thus help Italy in her terrible dilemma. In fact Vittorio tried every means to persuade my husband as I had done when I appealed to him to resign in his hour of glory.

Benito listened, not reacting at all until Vittorio had finished. Then, smiling and pointing to the door through which came excited chatter, he asked: "You think that's the right solution? Fine. And have you a plane for all those Fascists outside and the Fascists in the north?"

To serve Italy, he had remained in office nine years earlier. Now, true to himself, he thought it his duty to stay with his followers in that fateful hour. I do not think he considered his attitude heroic, but – as we had said in conversation some days earlier – simply logical.

CHAPTER 2

Mussolini's stormy courtship

In Italy and elsewhere, reaction varied strikingly when it was learnt that I proposed to write my memories of Mussolini. Some people claimed that I'd portray him in a false light, trying to excuse his mistakes and persuade the world to forgive him.

Such people have scant knowledge of myself. Intimates know me as being objective and untainted by politics – a reputation that must have some basis, for in 1945, when my husband was dead and I in prison, a partisan secretly told me: "Donna Rachele, do not worry. We have received official orders from Moscow not to touch a hair of your head."

When Benito was at the height of power, I once even threatened to shout "Down with Mussolini" under his window in the Piazza Venezia – a public demonstration seeking to open his eyes to the treachery of followers whom he blindly trusted.

I have never looked for forgiveness for Mussolini because I do not recognise that he did anything wrong. He made war, but was he the only head of government who ever did this? His sole crime was to have lost. As for the other military and political leaders of his time, they hardly dare examine their consciences without misgivings. True, he entered into an alliance with Hitler, but somewhere there are secret archives proving how strenuously he tried to safeguard peace.

I want neither forgiveness for Mussolini nor pity for myself. Despite the tales that I was an abandoned wife, submissive to Benito and resigned to his infidelities, I can look back over eighty years and say that I have lived the life I wanted. At one time my private intelligence network, backed by police officials, made me the best informed woman in Italy. My husband's liaisons were my own problem. I admit that three women caused me great unhappiness – Ida Dalser, Margherita Sarfatti and Clara Petacci. But where is the man who does not deceive his wife at some time or another? Anyone in the Duce's position was bound to attract more attention.

If I was a boastful person I would say that of all the women Benito held in his arms, I'm the only one qualified to write about the real Mussolini. I say this because I was the only one who really knew him. I'd known him since I was seven years old. We first met in 1900 when Benito was seventeen – ten years older.

He was the eldest of three children. His mother, Rosa Maltoni, who taught me at school, was as gentle and retiring as his father, Alessandro, was well-known in Romagna and even outside Italy. The Mussolinis lived in Dovia, a little village in the Predappio district deep in Romagna, where Alessandro eked out a living as a blacksmith. But his fame sprang from his activities as a Socialist revolutionary and many evenings in Romagna passed in recounting his exploits. Alessandro's notoriety rested partly on his skill at smashing ballot boxes and as the terror of the Royalist police – not that they ever missed a chance to march him off to prison under armed escort.

From his earliest years Benito gave his mother cause for concern. As a child, for instance, it was a long time before he even talked. Finally, she had him examined by a doctor who immediately put her mind at rest. "Don't let it worry you," he assured her. "He will talk. He may even talk too much."

Later, his father exerted strong discipline, never hesitating to add blows to words when he wanted to make his point. In fact, Benito learnt as much about life at the forge as he did from his father's conversations, which he scarcely understood. From the earliest moment, Alessandro was keen to instil the rudiments of Socialism in his son. He'd even christened his children Benito, Amilcare and Andrea in memory of revolutionary heroes – Benito Juarez the Mexican, and the Italians Amilcare Cipriano and Andrea Costa. He wanted his son to be properly educated. So Benito was sent to the primary school in Predappio, where he left scars on the heads of any school fellows who disagreed with him.

Then, at the age of nine, his parents sent him to Faenza – to a boarding school run by the Salesian Fathers. Benito told me later that his record there was deplorable since he objected to the seating arrangements in the dining hall, where there was one table for the lower classes at 30 lire, another for the middle classes at 45 lire and the top table for the nobility at 60 lire. He never accepted his place at the lowest table. He fought more than ever and inflicted two blows for every one he received. In the end the college principal was compelled to send him home.

In October 1895, he attended the Royal Normal School in Forlimpopoli. Although he was involved in various escapades, he did well there. During his later years at school, he began to hold political meetings with some success. At the age of seventeen he even wrote some articles for Forlí and Ravenna newspapers. As he had a good voice, the head master once arranged for him to speak at a commemoration of Verdi in the municipal theatre. To the surprise of his audience, he delivered a speech about the prevailing social conditions. *Avanti*, the Socialist daily paper to which he was appointed editor some 12 years later, mentioned it briefly.

Meanwhile, I was in the second class at the primary school in Dovia. Although their land was sunny and fertile, the peasants of Romagna were continually in revolt against the establishment as seen in the monarchy and the Church. It was not unusual for the driver to hold up a whole train if he saw a priest stepping on board. Generally speaking, apart from the great landowners, the peasants were poor. My parents worked on one of the vast estates stretching along the slopes from Salto, where we lived, to the outskirts of Predappio-on-the-Hill. My family consisted of five sisters. We were all fairly lively, though I suspect I was the sharpest. Nicknamed "Fearless", I was slim, with blonde hair and small, mischievous blue eyes. No one was better at climbing trees or catching birds than I.

When the time came round for school, I was the only sister who decided to attend classes. I wanted to learn, to increase my knowledge, to know everything. My parents would rather have kept me at home but I persevered and stormed until they agreed. I was even prepared to walk the five miles to school every day.

Because his mother was ill, Benito had returned home to take over her job. He noticed me on the first day, not for the reasons which drove him to threaten suicide ten years later, but because I was wild in class – never still for a moment. I was so intent on tomfoolery that I did not notice the ruler descending on my knuckles. Half hurt and half angry, I put my hand to my mouth. Then I found myself staring into huge, black eyes which expressed such willpower that, without really listening to the teacher's remarks, I immediately calmed down.

After this show of strength, I didn't see him again for nine years. However, I still heard talk of Mussolini – Alessandro Mussolini that is – and altogether a kind of aura seemed to surround the name.

When, in 1901, my father died suddenly leaving us destitute, we were forced to move to Forlí where the family broke up. My mother went into service and we were all put out to work.

And so at the age of eight, I earned my first wages of three lire a month. But it was purgatory; the vegetable sellers who employed me were hateful people, giving me an old sack full of crushed straw to sleep on in a small hut so cold it was used as a wine store. A young woman with tuberculosis had slept on the sack before me. But the worst torture was seeing the children of the house laughing round the table at meal times while I was made to sit on the terrace with a cracked plate and an iron spoon. Blinking back my tears, I discovered the meaning of social inequality at a tender age.

I was only too glad to leave and work for a fencing master. His daughter and I used to enjoy watching his lessons and playing "musketeers" with sticks of wood. I did not stay there long, however, as his wife's morals were none too strict.

My next employers, the Chiedini family, were the best. Although they were rich "conservatives" – the name we give the wealthy in Romagna – they were kind and affectionate to me. The future began to look brighter. My mother had finally found a permanent post at the little inn for which Alessandro Mussolini had left his blacksmith's trade after his wife's death in 1905. Besides, I was sixteen by then and at that age life always looks rosy, especially as I was pretty. I had too much good sense to lose my head over the compliments that came my way, but I enjoyed them.

The handsome young son of the Chiedinis' neighbours even proposed to me while walking through the vineyards one day. He swore to make me happy if I accepted him, adding persuasively that I was too beautiful to be a servant; I ought to be a princess, he said. But because he never lifted me on to his horse, I refused him.

Some days later a gypsy woman told me my fortune, astonishing me by predicting that great things were in store for me. She gave me a small stone, saying: "Keep this, but give me a bag of flour." I could hardly refuse, and though my employers scolded me for it, with such promises for the future I didn't care. One day I would be the equal of the Queen.

One Sunday in 1908, while leaving the Church at Forlí with my employers' little girl, someone called my name. It was Benito Mussolini. He'd grown a moustache and a small beard and wore a loose neck-tie, a big black hat and a threadbare suit with newspapers sticking out of the pockets. But what struck me most of

15

all was the gleam in his eyes, which now seemed larger than ever. Considering his later skill as an orator, his opening gambit was scarcely original: "Hello, Chiletta, (a diminutive of Rachele) you've grown. You're a young lady now." I should have replied in the same vein, but the expression in his eyes disturbed me.

As we walked on that sun-drenched day together, in Forlí I proudly noted how deferentially the passers-by greeted Benito, and felt that some of their respect was reflected on me. Although we walked all the way back to the Chiedini's house, I was careful not to tell them of our meeting for I remembered the delight Signor Chiedini had taken in describing all the details of Benito's arrest a few days earlier.

Before he left, Benito asked: "Why don't you ever come and see your mother at my father's inn?"

"Because the Chiedinis have forbidden me to visit the house of a revolutionary," I replied. "But I'll ask the Signora's permission."

Each time we met on subsequent Sundays, our affection for each other grew. Not that Benito ever played the great lover, but his very presence told me much. We went for long walks through the countryside, hardly speaking. Now and again, Benito would kick a stone out of the way as if he were dismissing an idea or an opponent, then turn to me and say: "We'll get rid of them in the end. We'll chase out the bourgeois, the rich landowners who get a good living from their estates without even bothering to cultivate them."

I had my own revolutionary ideas but his forcefulness made me uneasy. I said: "They'll put you in prison, Benito, as they did before."

"So? I'm not ashamed to go to prison for reasons like that. I'd be proud. I'm not a murderer or a thief."

One Sunday Signora Chiedini gave me permission to visit Mussolini's inn. I went in the morning, helped to wait at table and, after lunch, Benito and I went dancing. He was a fine dancer. As we said goodbye, he asked, "Why do you stay with the Chiedinis? You ought to be at the inn with your mother and my father.

Listen, in a week's time I'm going to Trent to work on Cesare Battisti's newspaper. I'd like you to be settled at the inn before I leave."

"I'll see," I replied. But everything had already been decided. Three days later I knocked at the door of the inn and Alessandro Mussolini had a new servant. He didn't regret it, for within days his customers were clamouring to be served by the "little blonde".

To celebrate the occasion, the evening before Benito's departure his father opened several bottles of wine. Benito played the violin and we danced. I discovered then what a fine musician he was. After the guests had gone, Benito took me to one side, telling me that we'd be married on his return. There was no proposal, no question of seeking my agreement; he simply told me that he'd decided for both of us. In the circumstances, I saw no need to reply. Silently I determined that I would not even think about his proposal in his absence, and by the time I retired to bed I'd forgotten all about matrimony.

Suitors danced attention on me again, while, more carefree than ever, I devoted myself to my work at the inn. I was particularly skilful, so they said, at serving a local dish consisting of fish from the Adriatic. For a third time my hand was sought in marriage – this time by a young surveyor from Ravenna, called Olivieri, I think. I refused him much to my mother's disappointment and even more to Alessandro's. He realised that I was fond of Benito, but was familiar enough with his son's politics to know that it would breed unhappiness for me.

Two months later, a postcard arrived from Trent. Beneath his signature Benito had written: "Give my best wishes to Rachele and remind her not to forget what I told her." Clearly he still had his own ideas, but Alessandro advised me not to wait however much his son persisted.

"My wife was a victim of politics," he confided. "Benito won't make you happy, Rachele. You mustn't wait for him. If you find what you're looking for, then grab it with both hands."

Stark in my memory were Rosa Maltoni's tears as her husband was dragged off to prison. I had no desire to follow in her footsteps, but I was still undecided.

Eight months elapsed before Benito returned to Forlí – expelled by the Austrian authorities in Trent, he told us, for having inflamed Italian nationalism with a provocative article in the *Popolo*. He had argued that the frontier did not stop at Ala, a small town on the existing Austrian-Italian border, and proudly explained that the Trent Socialists had called a strike in protest against his expulsion.

He'd shaved his little beard, but other than that, he returned looking much the same – his pockets still stuffed with newspapers, his violin tucked under his arm. The reputation he'd acquired in Trent followed him to Forlí where he was promptly appointed secretary of the local Socialist branch.

Politics engrossed him, yet Benito now put his private life in order. Having learnt of a particular male companion, he made me burn his letters. Then, in a brief encounter he tersely ordered him not to liaise with me again. He, Benito Mussolini, was back on the scene. His meaning was all too clear, and the Mussolini reputation did the rest; never again did I see the young man.

I was extremely put out by this behaviour. I might have been fond of Benito, but solitary confinement was quite another matter. I fought back, emphasising that the reason why I could never marry him was because of his politics, that a man who spent all his time at political demonstrations or in prison was no husband for me. His father rallied to my support, advising Benito to leave me alone. "You're not short of girls," he said.

Though protesting, I was confined to the inn. I was even debarred from serving the customers, let alone go out dancing. Benito had rented a room in Forlí but came each day, taking over my job as waitress and washer-up. The customers didn't take to this at first – a little blonde has more appeal than a moustache – but soon became reconciled when Benito played the violin. But his father was distraught.

"What a dreadful state of affairs," he lamented. "A trained teacher serving in a restaurant!"

But Benito shrugged it off replying that he considered no job degrading. He was so jealous he would have done anything to keep me away from others.

Matters came to a head one evening in the autumn of 1909. Benito had organised a Socialist meeting, and Alessandro asked: "Would you care to come with me? You can hear Benito speak then stay on for the dance." Much as I wanted to go, I was scared of offending Benito for he'd forbidden me to go dancing and attend political meetings. My presence, he told me, paralysed him when he got up to speak.

Nevertheless, I accepted the invitation, and managed to hear Benito without being seen. I felt proud when the enthusiastic cries of "Viva Benito! Viva Muslen!" greeted his speech.

Now came the dance – alas, a catastrophe. I remember the band playing the Red Flag before the opening waltz. No sooner was I partnered than the trouble began. Suddenly I came face to face with an enraged Benito. Angrily he snatched me from my partner's arms, we finished the dance, his great eyes glaring. Then, hauling me outside he called for a taxi. Benito sat in silence during the drive home, refusing to be calmed by a friend, the lawyer Gino Giommi, who was sharply rebuked. But once we reached the inn the scene was terrible.

My mother and Benito's father had caught up with us by then. At once Benito attacked them, bitterly reproaching them for allowing me to go to the dance, boorishly ignoring their explanations. To change my mind, his tactics had varied over the weeks, alternating from gentle persuasion to threats of suicide. "If you don't want me, I'll throw myself under a tram," he would say. Indeed, if I refused him he threatened to take me with him.

By now my mother, who was normally patient and gentle, decided that it was time to intervene. We were sitting in the kitchen, I remember, my mother and I on one side of the table facing Benito on the other.

"I warn you," she protested, "Rachele is still under age. If you won't leave her alone, I shall lodge an official complaint against you and you'll be sent to gaol."

"Right," said Benito, and left the room. But he was back within moments, pointing his father's revolver at my mother's face. "Now it's my turn to warn you," he shouted. "You see this revolver, Signora Guidia, it holds six bullets. If Rachele turns me down, there will be one bullet for her and five for me. It's for you to choose."

Within two minutes it was all decided. I was engaged to Benito. I was glad, really, for I suspect I'd been in love with him since I was seven. I just needed a final nudge to send me over the brink.

Benito returned to his lodgings in the centre of Forlí but by morning he was back to announce his plans. I was to go to the home of Pina, my sister, at Villa Carpena, some five miles from Forlí, and there I was to stay.

Benito came to see me each evening, sometimes on foot, sometimes on a bicycle. He said the journey gave him time to think. When he arrived he would take from his pocket a bundle of newspapers and sheets of paper covered with his precise handwriting. After reading his article for the following day's paper to "Chinchin," my sister's father-in-law, we would walk in the countryside. Naturally, we held hands and kissed, but we did none of the gazing into each other's eyes and rolling in the grass that so many lovers do. Even if we'd been inclined that way, it was December and too cold and wet for such pleasures.

Practical by nature, Benito soon realised that the situation could not last. So, one afternoon in January 1910, he came earlier than usual. To my sister he calmly remarked: "Pina, I have found an apartment for Rachele. I want her to come and live with me and be the mother of my children. Tell her to hurry because I have other things to do."

While Pina tearfully broke the disquieting news to me, Benito sat confidently downstairs reading his article as usual to Chinchin. It took me five minutes to reach a decision. "We'll be going then," I said.

My humble trousseau comprised a pair of shoes now three years old, two handkerchiefs, a blouse, an apron and a few lire. We walked the five miles to Forlí in torrential rain, with an escort of dogs barking as if they were outraged by what we were doing.

I was pleasantly surprised to find that Benito had reserved two communicating rooms at Forlí's best hotel. Grandly, he ordered the porter to run a bath for the Signora. "I believe that's already been attended to," he replied, wiping up the puddles from our dripping clothes.

The next morning, Benito took me to an old building in the via Merenda. It had been beautiful once. "That's it," he said. This was our home – a top floor apartment at the end of a corridor that was rife with gloom. To reach it, we'd to climb a stairway so narrow that when I was expecting our first child, Edda, a few months later, I could hardly pass. Benito had already installed some furniture – a bed, a table, two chairs and a charcoal stove. My mother supplied us with our other needs and our 36-year union began.

I should point out that, legally, we were not married. The Socialist doctrine forbade it. In those days the Socialists took such exception to bourgeois practices that any member who contracted a civil or religious marriage was promptly expelled. So Benito and I had not appeared before a registrar or a priest. Events impelled us to do so some years later. In 1915, Ida Dalser embarrassed me by pretending to be Signora Mussolini. A civil wedding was the only solution. Then we waited fifteen years for the religious ceremony which occurred on December 29, 1925, in Milan – this time to please Pope Pius XI. Another five years went by before we had a honeymoon.

CHAPTER 3

The birth of our children

Throughout his time in office, Benito rarely drank a glass of wine. Now and again he might wet his lips, since it was inconceivable that the head of government of a wine-producing country did not appreciate the national drink. From this was born the legend of the Duce's temperance. True, he was abstemious, but few people are aware that this now worthy virtue originated in something many a family has experienced at least once: an unforgettable night on the tiles.

It happened in 1911. We had been living together for a year and were not at all rich. Indeed our income totalled no more than 120 lire a month – Benito's earnings as secretary of the local branch of the Socialist Party and then as editor of the party weekly, *Lotta di Classe*, which he had founded in January that year. From his wages he gave 20 lire to the party and the rest to me. Obviously after spending 15 on the rent not much remained for us to live on.

All that we owned were the few items of furniture which Benito had bought and his wardrobe – a black suit which I'd seen him wearing for two years, a wide-brimmed Romagnol hat, a threadbare neck-tie, two shirts greying with age and a pair of shoes. My belongings comprised what I had brought in my bundle.

From the beginning, Benito's day fell into an almost fixed routine. Rising early, he washed, shaved, ate a breakfast of bread and coffee and left the house – the whole operation taking twenty minutes at the most. Stopping at a kiosk on the Piazza Saffi, he scanned through all the newspapers at breakneck speed. Not once was he made to pay, for the owner not only knew him but stood entranced by this daily marathon. Next Benito carried on to the tiny office where he edited his journal or held long conferences which were accompanied by wild gesticulations.

Around midday he came home for lunch, gulping it down within minutes, and reading a newspaper propped against a bottle as he ate. He didn't even notice what was on his plate – usually tagliatelle, fresh vegetables (which he loved) and fruit. When I urged him to eat more, he replied that as a child he'd never been accustomed to eating big meals. He once said: "On weekdays we had soup at midday and chicory in the evening. Then on Sunday my mother would make broth from a pound of mutton for the five of us – father, mother, my brother Arnaldo, my sister Edwige and me."

Sometimes he spent the afternoons at home writing his articles. He would cover sheet after sheet of paper in his small, rapid handwriting, crumpling up a sheet and throwing it on the floor when the words refused to flow, or he'd get up and stride about the room seeking inspiration.

In the evenings his headquarters moved to the "Macaron", Forli's main cafe, at the corner of the Serrughi building on the Piazza Aurelio Saffi. This was a focal point for the Socialists, Benito's friends, and on occasions the police, who came to search or make arrests. Young people often enlisted Benito's help with their homework for both young and old still looked on him as the teacher he was trained to be. Benito would sit at a table, working out the problems in pencil on the marble itself, then move to another table as one was covered with notes and calculations.

These Socialist gatherings sometimes went on far into the night, usually on market days – Mondays and Fridays – when a tense atmosphere was so charged with political venom that mounted Carabiniere, their truncheons drawn, occasionally scattered the crowd. Strategically, Benito made political capital at such times by inciting the peasants from the neighbouring countryside with his inflammatory speeches. Then he returned home with his clothes torn and muddy, his body bruised – but quite happy. Triumphantly, he used to say: "What a fight, Rachele." //

When he was not battling with the forces of the law, it was with the Republicans or even with fellow Socialists. Local branches outside Forlí held more moderate views and strongly rejected Benito's extreme attitude to overthrow the monarchy, Church and the existing régime.

So eventful were our two years in Forlí that I didn't notice the time passing. It was only at night that I counted the hours, straining my ears for the sound of Benito's footsteps or his voice. I was sure that, sooner or later, he would be brought home bleeding and critically hurt, or that I would never see him alive again.

Such were my fears and sentiments one night after I'd waited up for him till dawn. My head in my hands, I was sobbing my heart out, utterly convinced that Benito was either in prison or dead in the morgue, when I heard shuffling on the stairs. Trembling, I cautiously opened the door to see two strange men supporting my husband whose face was ashen and wild-eyed.

"Don't worry, it's nothing," the men said. "He talked a lot tonight and didn't realise he drank an incredible amount of coffee laced with cognac." Then they left him to me to deal with him as best I could, and went.

As I struggled to undress him, he stared at me with a curiously blank expression. Then without warning he burst into life, shouting and raving like a lunatic obsessed with the madman's craving to smash. He began to break up the apartment – furniture, our few pieces of china, even the mirror. Desperately I woke a neighbour and we called Doctor Bofandi (whose son became Prefect of Forlí in 1940, and was still in office when my husband was arrested in 1943). Between us we tied Benito to the bed and, to my relief, he gradually calmed down.

On waking the following afternoon Benito was quite bewildered, refusing to believe my account of what had happened. "Look," I shouted, pushing a pile of rubbish towards him, "you've broken everything. It'll cost a fortune to replace it." He said nothing but just stared at the fragments of glass, china and wood. "Get this into your head," I said. "I'll never agree to be married to an alcoholic. When I was little I had an aunt who drank and that was enough trouble. I admit you have your good qualities – and I'm even ready to forget about the other women – but if ever you come home again in that state, I'll kill you."

Benito heard me out without saying a word. Then taking my hand he led me to the bed where one-year-old Edda lay sleeping. "I swear to you, on her head, that I'll never do it again," he said.

I knew he'd keep his promise because Benito was devoted to his daughter. He would rock her, spend hours watching her sleep and, to wake her, he would sometimes play the violin over her bed. Indeed, apart from the times when he could not avoid sipping a little wine, Benito never again drank alcohol. That memorable night was the start of the Duce's legendary temperance.

My husband's undoubted affection for his children amazed even his own father who had never thought his son capable of such feelings. The birth of Edda, the eldest, put him in a fluster. He insisted on buying the cot for her himself – though usually he was disinterested in domestic matters – and actually carried it home on his shoulders. Like all babies, Edda would sometimes wake and cry in the night. Whatever the time, he would play his violin until she went back to sleep.

Later, when she was just three, he took her everywhere – even to his newspaper office. So by the age of four, she already knew the alphabet and used to write it proudly with chalk on the kitchen floor. And Benito, who was equally proud, did not want me to wipe it away.

26

It was then, too, that Benito got hold of the idea that if hair was cut short it would later grow more beautiful. He cut Edda's. But the first evening there were tears because the lock of hair she had wound round her finger as she went to sleep had gone. Even the violin now failed to help. Thus the next day the ever-practical Benito, buying a ball of linen, unravelled the ends and hung them on the bed behind her head. And when she was sleepy, Edda had merely to catch hold of the ball.

Later, when Vittorio was born, we had the same routine in Milan. The neighbours were treated to a concert every time he woke in the night.

When they were grown up my children derived great delight by comparing their birth dates. Apart from Bruno, who was born on April 22, all – Edda, Vittorio, Romano and Anna-Maria – arrived in September. And every time they talked about it, they asked the same sly question (which infuriated me): "Mummy, are we really Christmas babies?"

When Edda and Vittorio were born we had celebrations, but at Bruno's birth it was different. We were then living in Milan where Benito edited the *Popolo d'Italia*, a flourishing daily paper which he himself had launched. On April 22, 1918, Benito, finding it imperative to go to Genoa, looked sternly at me with his great eyes before catching the train. He said: "I hope you're not going to take advantage of my absence by giving birth to our son (he had already assumed it would be a boy). I don't want to be the last to be told again, as I was with Vittorio."

"Don't worry, you can go," I replied, as I cleaned the floors. "You'll be there when he's born."

That same evening Morgagni, the manager of the *Popolo d'Italia*, greeted him at the station with a broad grin and the words: "It's a boy. Rachele's doing well."

Benito leapt into a taxi, dashed up the stairs and before even looking at the baby, said severely: "I told you to wait for me. Why didn't you?"

Men are like that. They want to be in charge all the time. So that he could be involved, he determined to take my mother's place and cook for me during the following days. From the bedroom which adjoined the kitchen I gave him instructions but I soon realised it was useless. Benito had burnt all the saucepans and now I could not even boil an egg. Moreover, he'd spent the month's housekeeping money in two days. As a result, after twenty-four hours I got up to prevent even worse havoc.

Just over nine years later, Romano's birth – on September 26, 1927 – was almost disastrous. Endless precautions were taken because by then I was the wife of the head of government and had the services of a midwife and a well known gynaecologist. The latter annoyed me so much with his new techniques – and reminders that I was the Duce's wife – that one day I burst out: "You know, when a woman's in labour, the pains don't change with her social status. A peasant and a queen both feel the same way."

But the crisis came with the actual birth because my husband, who was in Rome, heard that the baby was about to be born. Once again, so confident was he that it would be a boy, he announced through the Stefani News Agency that I had delivered a son, adding that he had been called Romano in honour of Rome. But after driving madly to the Villa Carpenia, where I was confined, Benito was horrified to discover that the baby had still to be born. The time was five in the afternoon. "Well, what are we going to do?" he asked me. "Stefani's office have already announced the birth and all the details."
"What can I do? You go and sleep. I'll send someone to tell you what is happening."

He was a simple man at heart. At about midnight, Cina, our maid, knocked at his door. "Duce, it's arrived. It's a boy," she told him.

My husband threw on his shirt inside out and, rushing into my room, took the baby in his arms, kissed me and began to shout, though he usually spoke so quietly: "It's marvellous, Rachele, really marvellous. You've made me very happy." I never knew whether he was more pleased to have a boy or confirmation of news he had broadcast too early.

When our last child, Anna-Maria, was born on September 3, 1929, Benito and I were both taken by surprise. Learning from my experience with Romano, I had told him that the baby was due on a date later than was really expected. So, dispensing with the gynaecologist (who had begged to be mentioned in the Press report) and with the midwife (who had asked for the same publicity because she reckoned she had taken part in the proceedings), I went through the confinement on my own and called Benito in Rome.

"She's been born," I said calmly.

"Who?"

"The baby."

"What baby?"

"Ours. Now you can find a name."

I hung up, delighted at having played such a trick on him. I fully expected him to call back, telling me what he wanted us to call her, but no call came. The following day I read in the papers that I'd given birth to a baby – Anna-Maria. Benito had outwitted me, but even so I was glad, for Anna-Maria was my mother's name.

When we became grandparents, Benito enjoyed playing with the little ones. He only asked them not to make a noise because it gave him a headache. But they had such fun. Duce or no Duce, my husband was down on the carpet playing horses and racing about like any other parent or grandparent. One day, when Edda and Galeazzo Ciano invited us to lunch, Benito vanished with the children before the meal. Suddenly a maid, hearing shouts from behind the drawing room door, opened it and was horrified to see the Duce on the floor. She thought he was ill or hurt, but he was just playing a game with Edda's children – Fabrizio and Raimonda, nicknamed Cicino and Dindinna.

Benito always worried about the children's shoes. They had to be one size larger than necessary. He used to say to me: "I suffered so much as a child. I had to wear my shoes even when they didn't fit any longer because my parents couldn't afford others. And later I couldn't even pay for them myself. So now I don't want my children to suffer the same tortures. Their shoes must be comfortable."

I remember another story about the children. On the back of his head, near the neck, Benito had a wart. Count Pulle, a doctor friend, wanted him to have it removed.

"It's nothing, Duce," he told him. "It'll only take a few minutes. Have it removed. It's not nice to look at."

"Nice or not, I don't care," replied Benito. "This wart is a great delight to my children and grandchildren. My great-grandchildren will find it too, if it stays where it is."

In fact the children – especially Guido, Vittorio's eldest – made a game of climbing on my husband's shoulders. As they pressed on the wart with their index finger, he would go "Dring – dring" in a shrill voice and join in the children's laughter.

CHAPTER 4

Mussolini becomes a Fascist

In December 1912, when Mussolini was appointed editor of *L'Avanti*, the daily newspaper of the Italian Socialist Party, we went to live in Milan. One evening in October 1914 – the 19th, I think – Benito returned from Bologna bitter and depressed.

"We'll have to start all over again, Rachele," he said. "They've sacked me from the paper."

"What happened?"

"The Socialist Party is totally opposed to my campaign for Italian intervention on the Allied side. The executive committee considers the paper's attitude contrary to party policy, so they've dismissed me."

"What are we going to do now?"

"First, we shall need enough money to live. Then we must think about starting another paper. I'm lost without an outlet for my ideas. I must have a paper of my own."

"Surely they're going to pay you some kind of compensation. They owe it to you."

"I know, but I refused to take anything. I don't want anything more to do with them. I told them I'd work on a building site if I had to, but I wouldn't touch their money."

I was extremely upset – more for Benito's sake, for he had driven himself hard during the past two years. When he took over as editor from Claudio Treves, the daily circulation had been only 20,000. In less than two years he built up that figure to 100,000. I had watched him writing his articles and editorials until far into the night. Sometimes – while waiting to check the proofs – he would take me to the theatre, then spend several hours in the office.

I was all the more unhappy because, with his usual unselfishness, he refused to accept the full salary as editor. While certain colleagues earned 1,000 lire a month, he preferred to take half that sum to pare down *L'Avanti's* expenses. It had incensed me when he came to tell me of his decision in Forlí. I had asked: "Why should others get what's due to you? How do you know if we can live on 500 lire? Who does the shopping and who knows the cost?" Benito had difficulty in pacifying me.

When we left for Milan, we had to sell our belongings to pay for the fares and our lodgings in the first few days. But as the months passed, it looked as if everything was working out. In a working-class area we'd found an apartment at 19 via Castel Morrone and made it fairly comfortable. I began to think we had left the dark days behind forever. Now, suddenly it was different. I didn't wish to add to my husband's worries, but I wondered how we were going to pay our monthly rent of 80 lire. And what were we going to eat when our money ran out? Fortunately, Benito's first impulse was always, blessedly, to consider his family, even at the end. He understood what I was thinking and borrowed money so that we would at least subsist.

The next task was to find enough capital to start a newspaper. At our home Benito convened a "council of war", bringing together political friends and others interested in the idea of a new paper edited by Mussolini. Among them were Filippo Naldi, the editor of the *Resto del Carlino* of Bologna, Manlio Morgagni who later ran the *Popolo d'Italia*, Nicola Bonservizi, Sandro Giuliani, Lido Caiani, Gino Rocca, and Giacomo di Belsito. The 200 lire Naldi had in his pocket formed the basis of the paper's assets.

Luckily Morgagni secured an advertising contract for which 4,000 lire was to be paid in advance. Then a subscription scheme was launched and I became treasurer, recording payments and issuing receipts. Benito and his friends combed Italy for funds and with Naldi's help formed a team consisting of a printing technician and two sub-editors who gave signed agreements in exchange for advance payments. The *Messageria Italiana* were to deal with the launching and with sales and a new advertising agency willingly agreed to take over the publicity side.

My husband at last published the first edition of the *Popolo d'Italia*. He had won a great victory over the reformist Socialists (then in the majority), over everyone who had tried to ruin him, and over his own lack of confidence. November 15, 1914, was a momentous day. I didn't see Benito at all the night before. He had stayed at the presses checking the whole paper, line by line and word by word, and had subtitled the paper a "Socialist Daily" – indicating that he was still a Socialist at heart.

Pale, unshaven, exhausted, he was jubilant all the same. But he knew that the hardest task might still lie ahead, in defending the *Popolo d'Italia* against Socialist Party opposition. So he rallied us all – my mother, myself, our women friends – to make a daily tour of the news vendors, checking that the paper was well displayed and how it was selling.

Our home was in a permanent state of chaos, and people I had never seen wandered endlessly in and out. Subscriptions arrived from all over Italy. Sometimes there would only be four or five lire at a time since people paid what they could afford. But there were also larger sums of 500 or 1,000 lire. Soon Morgagni took over the advertising and the number of contracts increased.

One Sunday, Benito and I were out walking with Edda. We stopped by a news kiosk and Benito, questioning the man in charge, asked casually: "Does this paper sell well?"

"Not bad," came the reply, "but if that 'brain' Mussolini wrote an article every day it'd sell a hundred times better."

Benito remained inscrutable.

The creation of the *Popolo d'Italia* spawned many rumours about Benito: that he had received money from abroad, that he had been paid to persuade the Italian Government to enter the war against Germany and Austria on the Allied side. Mussolini always told me that at the outset of the First World War he'd thought Italy should remain neutral, but that after the Battle of the Marne he believed that neutrality would bring Italy nothing; she would not benefit by any postwar settlement.

He had never forgotten the reason for his expulsion from Trent in 1908. Any opportunity to revise the Austrian-Italian border should be grasped with both hands. Benito was convinced, furthermore, that the Italian people would not see the need for a great social upheaval until after they had fought a war. In his mind war was half way to social revolution, as proved to be the case.

At a riotous Socialist meeting in Milan soon afterwards, he explained why he had changed his attitude towards the war. He had not taken his decision lightly, but after lengthy consideration and after realising that there was no alternative. I remember being struck by what he said when he came home. "They hate me because they still love me," he claimed. "But they won't take away my Socialist beliefs or stop me fighting for the revolutionary cause by tearing up my card."

As to the accusations that Mussolini accepted money from abroad, I was unaware of any such dealings while I was in charge of the finances. Indeed, if there had been financial backing he could have paid his colleagues and the printing bills slightly more often. Later, in 1915, Marcel Cachin, a French Communist, did in fact come to our house. I remember him well because he neither spoke nor understood Italian and we had difficulty communicating when Benito was not there.

Cachin had several conversations with my husband, but – as far as I knew – he never brought the money he is supposed to have done. Besides, apart from Cachin

Mussolini was in contact with other Socialists and Communists and Lenin himself saw him in Milan, soon after he founded the *Popolo d'Italia*.

Lenin had journeyed from Switzerland to try and induce him to rejoin the Socialist Party, but Benito would have none of it despite his liking for Lenin. They had met in Switzerland when Mussolini was working and studying there. I found Lenin a kind, likeable man with his little beard and academic spectacles. Much later Benito commented: "Lenin's great good fortune was to have died before Stalin could have him killed."

After the excitement of creating the paper I had to bear the agonies of Benito's "duelling period". Indeed, life with Mussolini held many surprises. The night before his first combat, I couldn't sleep for fright and when he and his seconds left at dawn, I was convinced he would never return alive. Everything else apart, there was the stark fact that his opponent was an officer. Although Colonel Cristoforo had deviated from the party, this did not detract from his skill as a swordsman. As for Benito, he was full of quiet self-confidence, trying his best to comfort me with the remark: "Don't worry, Rachele. I've had good coaching from Camillo Ridolfi." But I was sure that however brilliant an instructor Ridolfi was, the worst was bound to befall.

I'd bought him the new shirt he'd asked for the day before and now lay awake all night listening to low voices as he discussed tactics with his fencing master and seconds in the adjoining room. The clashing of swords sounded so ominous that I blocked my ears, certain now that Benito was about to die. I saw them leave at dawn, decked out in black like undertaker's men, top hats in their hands.

Despite my fears Benito returned without a scratch, carrying in his arms a little cat. "I found him on the way there," he told me. "He brought me luck, we'd better keep him." That cat must have had an endless supply of luck for all the duels that followed. Each time Benito disagreed with anyone – a political opponent or even a friend – the argument had to be settled on the duelling field, strictly following the correct code of conduct. My husband must have fought a dozen times, against all types of people – including a Socialist, an anarchist and even Claudio Treves, his predecessor as editor of *L'Avanti*. That was one of the fiercest fights, for Benito came home without the bottom of one ear and with his shirt soaked in blood. Treves, however, was in a much worse shape with a deep wound in the armpit.

That particular duel stirred me to action. So often had Benito returned unscathed that I no longer worried for his life. But the cost of his duelling had begun to irritate me. He had to pay the fencing master and the doctor and find something for his seconds – only a gift, perhaps, but it still cost money. Also – I'd almost forgotten – there were the look-outs to engage to warn them if the police were coming; for duelling carried severe penalties, by royal decree. Indeed, my husband was brought to trial several times for this reason.

That a new shirt should be ruined in a couple of hours infuriated me. I tried to wash off the blood, but in vain. So I told Benito: "I've had enough of this. Your shirt can stay as it is and I'll keep it for the next time. You don't imagine I'm going to throw money down the drain every time you disagree with someone. Either you stop fighting duels or you can go in this shirt."

My husband kept the shirt and carried on fighting. Eventually the duels became so much a part of our lives that we worked out a code in which to discuss them, so as not to alarm my mother who couldn't bear them. First thing in the morning, Benito would say: "Today we're making spaghetti."

Immediately I'd pack a little bag for him with everything that he needed. After the fight he'd call me. If everything had gone well, he would bellow: "You can throw out the spaghetti." We used to celebrate in the evening by going to a puppet show, one of his favourite forms of entertainment.

I must confess I enjoyed my husband's tales about his duels, for he had a great sense of humour and a fine eye for the twists of fortune which added spice to an adventure. One day, for instance, Benito and his opponent were earnestly crossing swords in a field when they heard loud weeping. A group of women, coming to wash their laundry in the river, had accidentally stumbled across the fight. They took to their heels in a mad rush, shrieking: "Help, help, they're killing each other." The duellists had to stop and finish the fight elsewhere – under a bridge, I think.

One other time they'd rented a room, locking the door to avoid being disturbed. Having pushed the furniture to one side, they were in the thick of the fight when the look-out warned that the police were coming. Grabbing their top hats in one hand, they ran out still brandishing their swords. With the police in hot pursuit, they leapt into a car – in true gangster film style – and drove off to the station. There they boarded a goods train and the fight that had started in a room ended in a little village.

Much later, after Benito's arrest on July 25, 1943, I remembered the code language we'd used for the duels and thought I might be able to apply a similar system. I was allowed to write to him, though I'd no idea where he was, and so my letters had to go to the Carabinieri. I knew that my mail would be censored. Consequently, to let him know that everyone in Romagna keenly awaited his return, I wrote: "Everyone here is waiting for the water to flow in the river again." When Benito replied that he was sorry to hear that there was a drought in Romagna, I gave up all attempts to use symbols.

Our life in Milan also had its amusing side; our visits to the theatre, for example. One evening, possessing complimentary tickets sent to the newspaper, Benito suggested that we should go to the theatre before he visited the printers to check copy. Within minutes I was sorry he'd persuaded me to go. Every time he disapproved of anything, Benito broke into peals of laughter and volubly criticised both the play and the actors. When angry eyes turned in our direction I shrank back into my seat in embarrassment, but Benito so disliked the show that he felt entitled to poke fun at it. In 1911, he had himself written a play called *Claudia Particella, the Cardinal's mistress* which, published in the *Popolo* of Trent, had boosted its circulation considerably.

I pointed out how inconsiderate he was being but Benito thought that no management had the right to bore the public with such appalling plays.

"Write about it in the paper, then," I admonished him, "but don't draw attention to yourself like that."

"You think I care if I'm attracting attention. I go to the theatre to be entertained. If I'm not entertained, I say so. That's all."

Our next theatre visit was to see an opera – *Parsifal*, I think. To my great relief, Benito slept from start to finish.

From then onwards he tended to doze off during theatrical performances; he was so tired. When, as head of government, he was obliged to attend a theatre, or if he had gone simply because he liked the show, he began to feel sleepy whenever he sat down. He would then push his chair to the back of the box and sleep steadily to the end.

That wasn't just peculiar to Benito. Indeed, many eminent people take similar discreet cat naps. At least they fulfil their obligation to be seen by the public when the performance is over. Not that my husband really fell into this category, for I know that he genuinely enjoyed plays and concerts.

When he first came to power he often went to the theatre. But the people's hysterical reaction soon forced him to minimise these visits. He therefore organised recitals at the Villa Torlonia. The children above all still remember them, for no excuse to absent themselves was tolerated. Their father made them attend – even though they found it a torture.

To return to our outings in Milan, if Benito was not the ideal theatre-goer, he had an almost childlike enthusiasm for vaudeville and variety acts. As he watched, he became totally oblivious to his surroundings. This was typical of him to the end of his life.

When we watched a film at the Villa Torlonia or at Gargnano, I knew in a flash when the titles appeared whether Benito would stay till the end; if it was a sad, poetical or romantic film he was bound to get up and go. But if it was a Laurel and Hardy comedy or had a historical basis, Benito would then be almost child-like, showing such unsuppressed pleasure and applauding every custard pie which hit its target.

Once I'd established which plays provoked him, I decided not to accompany Benito to see them. Instead my mother agreed to accompany him, but after just one evening she swore she'd never go again. I must admit that the experience was traumatic. That evening, to express his annoyance, Benito had taken off his shoe and thrown it at the actors. My mother was still stammering with fright when she came home, whereas Benito laughed gleefully.

After that, understandably, she thought up any conceivable excuse not to go to the theatre with him. Because he never wanted to go alone, we had to find a solution to the problem. I therefore engaged a young lady for the ticklish mission as his female companion. That didn't last long, for I'd taken the precaution of picking someone too plain for Benito's taste. He decided he would rather go on his own – and we were all happy.

CHAPTER 5

How Mussolini came to power

One day, in Edda's history text-book, I read some fine words attributed to my husband when King Victor-Emmanuel III received him at the Quirinal on October 30, 1922. "Majesty, I bring you the Italy of Vittorio Veneto."

The authors must have meant that Mussolini was bringing a victorious Italy, like Vittorio Veneto's. In 1922, the country was in the shocking state it had experienced after defeat at Caporetto during the First World War. The riots and chaos – which were the prelude to the March on Rome – had been subdued, and Italy enjoyed unity in victory.

I told my husband that his words rang like a clarion call and were appropriate to the occasion, but, to my astonishment, he answered that he had never uttered them. History may have to be re-written, but I must reveal that Mussolini never spoke these words.

This in no way diminishes the importance of the occasion, for if there had been no March on Rome, our fate might have been strikingly different. Whatever his position in 1919, my husband never imagined that he would be the head of government three years later. For us, 1919 was a black year. If I'd made a New Year wish for 1920 – perhaps I actually did – it would have been that the coming year should be completely unlike the last.

We'd experienced all kinds of difficulties in 1919, both on the political front and within the family. While still nursing Bruno, I succumbed to Spanish 'flu – that epidemic which killed over 500,000 people in Italy, more than the total of our victims of the First World War.

In that same year Bruno caught diphtheria, his illness affecting Benito far more than any political success or defeat, though perhaps defeat would be more accurate, since he'd suffered grave setbacks in this area. My husband and I spent whole days at Bruno's bedside, watching his breathing, his slightest movement – indeed, the faintest sign that he was getting better or worse. Benito hardly ate anything and left the house just long enough to see the newspaper to press. Even then he 'phoned from the office for reports on Bruno's condition. We didn't think he would ever recover, and for hours on end I held him in my arms, weeping silently. Finally, the doctors pronounced him out of danger and when I told my husband his eyes filled with tears of joy.

However, no sooner had he recovered than Bruno suffered a bronchial complaint and by the time he'd got over it his weight had reduced to about fifteen pounds.

These sharp fluctuations between hope and despair left us jaded. Benito was affected the most for he hated sickness in others as much as in himself, and seeing the children ill depressed him. He felt so helpless that he would have summoned doctors from the four corners of the earth if he'd thought it would help their recovery.

The political scene was equally gloomy. On March 23, 1919, Benito created the "Fasci di combattimento" – the Fascist movement – but when he came home that evening, he wasn't particularly elated. He'd announced in the *Popolo d'Italia* that sympathisers could join his new party by enrolling at a meeting at the Dal Verma, a theatre in Milan. Depressingly, in spite of the public notice only 147 people responded – a meagre turn out which caused Benito to transfer the meeting to a small hall in the Piazza San Sepulcro, so that it wouldn't look too ridiculous. It now seems odd, but when appointing the executive committee, he merely chose at random from the first row of enthusiasts.

...olini in 1904, a revolutionary syndicalist ...Switzerland. (Syndication Inter-...onal.)

(left) 1917, in the Bersaglieri during the War, (right) 1922, in dress uniform as Prime Minister, (below) at London conference 1922 with (l. to r.) Poincare, Bonar Law, and Theunis. (Syndication International.)

Even so, some months later, at a general election in November 1919, my husband stood as a Fascist candidate with other men of importance under his banner, including two well known figures – Filippo Tomaso Marinetti, the founder of the Futurist movement, and Arturo Toscanini, the orchestral conductor.

That evening, at about eleven, Benito 'phoned me. "It's a total fiasco," he said. "We haven't a single seat. In the Galeria [the central district of Milan] the people are rioting against us, the Socialists most of all. I'm afraid some of them may come to the house. Don't worry about it, but, to be on the safe side, you'd better find shelter for the children."

Desperately my mother and I looked round for a hiding place. Finally we decided that the attic, under the roof, which we could reach by an inside stairway, offered the only safety. I wrapped Edda, Vittorio and Bruno in blankets and settled them up there as best I could. Vittorio, who was nearly three, asked: "What's the matter, Mamma, is the house on fire?" And Edda, who was just nine, answered: "Be quiet. If they hear you they'll cut your throat."

Then I went down into our apartment and mounted guard behind the shutters. Since the summer we'd been living in new quarters – on the top floor of 38 Foro Buonaparte. It was a pleasant building, not far from a park, but equally close to the offices of the Socialist Party. It was from there that I feared the greatest danger – more so because an uproar rose from the street below and from the areas held by our opponents.

After an hour or two I saw a curious sight – a strange procession in which men bore coffins. At first I thought it was a trick of the eyes, for at night the street lamps barely pierced the mist, and torches carried in the cortège made the macabre scene look even more eerie. By the time the crowd had reached our house the coffins were clearly defined and sinister, as were the faces of men brandishing their fists and shouting: "Mussolini is dead! Mussolini is dead! Here is his corpse and the bodies of his friends."

By now I was totally engulfed by panic, even doubting the state of my mind. Half of me was convinced that my husband was dead, while the other half wanted to rush at the men in the street and snatch his body from them. But I couldn't leave my mother and the three children.

Much later, in 1945, I was to endure the same terror when, hearing gunfire, I saw from my window young Italians – both Fascists and non-Fascists – falling under the fire of the pursuing partisans.

This unbearable agony lasted all night until morning. Contrary to his practice, my husband hadn't called me once, which seemed to confirm the piece of play-acting I had witnessed. Worse still, the caretaker, in great distress, came to me in the morning. According to *l'Avanti*, he said, a corpse identified as Benito Mussolini's had been pulled from the river. The news almost left me demented until a compassionate policeman, putting an end to my torment, asked the caretaker to tell me that Benito was safe. He'd been arrested, the man explained, during the demonstrations in the night and was now in the San Vittore prison. Rather strangely, Benito was freed during the course of the day. Toscanini and Luigi Albertini, the editor of *Corriere della Sera* – the most important paper in Italy and one fiercely opposed to my husband – had obtained his release. This gesture of Albertini's would save his paper from extinction three years later.

From my account of what I'd seen the night before, Benito learnt his lesson about the family's safety. Reminding me of the hand grenades he'd brought back from the front in the First World War, he explained how they worked and, relieved, I put them on top of a wardrobe. "This way," I said, "they'll get one in the teeth before they hurt us."

I completed my arsenal with a revolver which Benito brought me. During the day I kept it in my handbag and at night I put it under Vittorio's bed since he slept in our room. Benito never liked weapons, but I was determined to defend the family to the death. I'd always enjoyed shooting and hunting and I think that, of the two of us, I would have been the first to fire had it proved imperative.

Luckily for everyone, there was no need to use the revolver and 1919 came to an end with a few, less serious accidents – though one of them might have cost Benito his life. Driving my husband home from a Fascist congress, Leandro Arpinati, a supporter, passing over a level crossing crashed into a barrier which suddenly came down and though hurled for some yards, Benito escaped with bruises and shock. The injury to Arpinati was much more serious.

It would be misleading to say that 1919 ended without any further incident, for in September Gabriele d'Annunzio embarked on his adventure in Fiume – a town on the Adriatic which, following the agreements signed at the end of the war, wasn't part of the Italian-occupied zone.

This had led to skirmishes with the French, which had excited public opinion in Italy and re-awakened Italian nationalism. An international commission was probing the situation when d'Annunzio decided to act. With a group of loyal supporters he seized Fiume without further ado.

One evening – September 11, I think – my husband and I were leaving a theatre when a man handed Benito a note. It was a message from d'Annunzio. "The die is cast," he wrote. "I am leaving now. Tomorrow morning I shall arm myself and take Fiume. May the God of Italy come to my aid."

This operation, which by its impulsiveness was in character with the famous poet, was an open insult to the Italian authorities. Though my husband thought Fiume should be Italian, he found himself in an embarrassing position. Still, he helped d'Annunzio, never dreaming for one moment that the venture would succeed. Yet that is what happened, but after a surfeit of parades and ceremonies in Fiume, d'Annunzio's friends took him less and less seriously. On Christmas Eve 1920, the Italian marines stormed Fiume, and d'Annunzio quit four days later.

Even then my husband didn't desert him. He realised that by occupying Fiume, d'Annunzio had fired the spirit of Italian nationalism. He had proved that the basic feeling was waiting to be inflamed.

Besides, all the men the poet had gathered round him, the Arditi, or legionnaires whom d'Annunzio had armed, now turned to my husband, injecting new blood into the Fascist movement.

The ceremonial that appealed so much to d'Annunzio, or its less exaggerated aspects of it, suggested many ideas to the organisers of Fascist demonstrations.

All this earned Benito's gratitude, and he never forgot d'Annunzio even when he was leading the government. Apart from his qualities as a leader of men – for which some people even thought to make him Duce of Italy rather than Mussolini – Benito admired d'Annunzio, the poet. They remained close friends.

I did not, however, always share these sentiments, particularly after 1922 when I saw how d'Annunzio was exploiting Mussolini's friendship and admiration. His whole way of life irritated me. For example, he never sent letters by post. If he was writing to someone in another town, he would send his correspondence by messenger. If he wanted to communicate with someone abroad, he would send a telegram. And as the telegrams were as lengthy as letters, they cost a ludicrous amount of money which he never paid. Indeed, my husband finally had to instruct the Minister of Posts and Telecommunications to stop charging d'Annunzio for his telegrams. It worked out cheaper for the State than having to increase d'Annunzio's pension.

More than once I asked Benito: "How can you admire someone like that? You've always paid your debts, aren't you shocked by his offhandedness?"

Benito tried to placate me. "Come now," he smiled, "you don't measure talent in terms of debts."

I remember when Edda was married, d'Annunzio did something we found very amusing. He sent a "winged messenger" with a present from the Commandant at Lake Garda to the Duce's daughter. Such a ceremony was made of the whole affair that Edda and I were sure that the parcel must contain some treasure. Instead, we were surprised to find red pyjamas beautifully embroidered with dragons and lotus flowers, like the ones peddled to tourists as "Made in China". I made an outfit of shirt and trousers out of them to go cycling in.

Benito began to weary of the eccentricities of his brilliant friend after spending a short holiday at his house on Lake Garda. He had hoped to rest, but returned more exhausted than before and, moreover, astounded by what he had seen. All the servants, he told me, bore names taken from mythology, novels and d'Annunzio's poetry. And every time they encountered their master they had to bow deeply and fold their arms. Whatever they were carrying was allowed to drop and there were frequent breakages.

Benito could never get used to being wakened at five every morning by cannon shot from the little warship *Redipuglia*, which d'Annunzio had installed in his garden. "Mind you," Benito explained, "I was almost glad to get out of that bed. There were two stone archangels guarding the foot of it, life-size too." To his amazement, my husband discovered that d'Annunzio himself slept in a coffin – to get used to it, so he said, as a foretaste of his approaching death. In fact, d'Annunzio died soon after, still managing to shock us even from beyond the grave.

D'Annunzio died on March 1, 1938. Benito went to his house to pay his last respects and had a strange adventure there, which he decribed to me on his return. After meditating for a while before d'Annunzio's remains, Benito was retiring to bed when he learnt that, under a clause in the deceased's will, he was expected to fulfil an unusual ceremony. Furthermore, it must be carried out at once.

To his amazement a surgeon solemnly presented Benito with a sharpened sword on a velvet cushion, explaining that he was to cut off one of the poet's ears

– "the loveliest and purest part of the body" – which d'Annunzio had left him as a token of their friendship. And Benito was to bring this legacy home with him. He had never been in such an embarrassing situation.

We were sitting at table with Romano and Anna-Maria as he told this story. (Bruno, an officer in the air force, was at Guidonia aerodrome and Vittorio was already married and no longer living at the Villa Torlonia.) Romano and Anna-Maria, looking slightly queasy, put down their forks and stopped eating, and Romano, who was eleven, asked his father: "Did you cut it off, Pappa?"

The boy looked so scared I dreaded his father's reply. But Benito said nothing. Instead he put his hand in his pocket and, with deliberate slowness, brought out his large handkerchief.

When he opened it out, Romano gave a strangled cry and Anna-Maria covered her eyes with her hands. I was choking. None of us could relax. Then all at once he blew his nose noisily as if he had a cold. "You think I'm a cannibal?" he grunted. "I was in a real predicament, but I managed to make them see that I couldn't accept my legacy. But," he smiled, "I must have caught a cold at Gardona."

Apart from these colds, 1920 was a rather uneventful year, compared to 1919 and 1921. We led an ordinary life and, politically, luck began to turn in my husband's favour.

There was also an important family event. Benito bought our first car, a Bianchi torpedo – a fourseater with folding seats. It was white or grey, I don't remember which, but I do remember how glad we were to have it. On Sundays we went out driving with the children in the back and Benito and me in the front. At that time we made a handsome couple. Benito had become very elegant after his return from the front in 1917 and wore a black or grey suit (he always wore dark colours), with a stiff-collared shirt and a fine neck-tie. I was a follower of fashion and had lovely dresses with wide hems and pinched-in waists. I loved the buttoned boots which gave me an elegant nineteenth-century look.

Later we had a chauffeur and looked like any other middle-class family in Milan.

In the evening we often went to the operetta at the nearby Fossati Theatre. I had even reached an agreement with Benito that he should cause less disturbance when he disliked the performance. It was then that I began to grow really fond of Milan. We were happy. The children had their own friends, and Edda was attending school. And, like every father who feels he has missed his vocation, Benito decided she must study the violin. But both Edda and I were against it – she because the idea had no appeal and I, because the lessons cost me ten lire a time.

Journalism and politics consumed much of Benito's time. This meant that I saw far less of him. As a newspaper editor and a politician he was extremely active. He travelled a great deal, but when in Milan his headquarters were the "cellar" – a room he'd furnished in the offices of the *Popolo d'Italia* on the via Paolo de Cannobio. During the next two years there was much telephoning from and to our house – as during the royal investiture in 1922 – but the nerve centre of what became the March on Rome, was Benito's "cellar".

As always in Italy, the Galeria, or central district of Milan, near la Scala (where well known establishments like Biffi's and the Savini restaurant still stand) was a recognised hub of political activity. Benito used to drink coffee there and have long discussions with his friends. Altogether, he led the same sort of life – but on a loftier plane – as he had at Forlí when he ran the *Lotta di Classe* and the *Macaron*. Now, however, he owned an influential daily paper and led a party which he'd founded and was growing in power.

In 1920, Fascism seemed to gather momentum. At the autumn municipal elections the Fascists won four seats in the Socialist stronghold of Bologna and the Socialists themselves only held Milan with a tiny majority. During this period Fascism probably waxed in power – after a grave incident during the inaugural session of the municipal council of Bologna on November 21, 1920. In a riot Giulio Giordani, a Fascist councillor, was shot dead.

When Benito arrived home, bad tempered and angry, he related what had happened, then immediately after dinner left the house, I had a confused feeling that we were about to go through yet another harassing time.

From that day onwards, there was a pitiless struggle between the Fascists and the "Reds" who outnumbered them; for all divisions – into Socialists, Republicans, Popularists and so on – had broken down. Now there were only the Reds. Benito agreed to organised reprisals, but before that he'd written a stern article in the *Popolo d'Italia*. He warned that, although he hated all forms of war – especially civil war – he intended to answer extremist violence with force.

The small landowners and industrialists, haunted by the spectre of the Russian Revolution of 1917 and disturbed by the unrest erupting all over Italy, began to join with the war veterans and Mussolini's supporters. It was a time of political change in Italy – a time too, when a change came over Benito.

The would-be social revolutionary of 1908, 1912 and even 1920 became the defender of law and order. Or rather, the Reds and Communists, whose infiltration into Europe had made Mussolini increasingly apprehensive, had become the creators of disorder. And the Mussolini who'd incited the masses to revolt now looked for social revolution within the legal structure. He was fighting on two fronts – against the Reds and against government weakness.

My husband also realised that he could achieve nothing without the army's basic support. In that he showed the beginnings of the leader, the man who holds his friends in check while keeping up the troops' enthusiasm. Later, Benito was accused of double-dealing, but he found it much more difficult to restrain men than to give them their head. If he'd given them complete freedom, he might have avoided many subsequent troubles with the King and his aides. He could have eradicated these problems at source by dispensing with the King in October 1922.

At home, fearing a search by the police, Benito asked me to get rid of our hand grenades. For this I enlisted the aid of my sister Pina, then staying with us. She'd been seriously ill, a critical period when – unknown to me – Benito had been sending her money. Secreting the grenades in her bodice, and looking furtively like a thief, she set off to throw them into a ditch at the nearby Sorze castle. Afraid of an explosion, she was certain it was her final hour – or at the least she'd be arrested.

As I'd expected, 1921 was more eventful both at home and on the political front. In March, I had a premonition in a dream. For some time Benito had been taking flying lessons with Cesare Redaelli, an excellent instructor. One night I dreamt that my husband was trapped in the aircraft's cockpit by a wall of flames. When I woke up, I told him about it and begged him not to fly.

"Don't worry," he said, "I promise."

As further assurance, he left his leather flying coat at home. But soon my peace of mind was shattered. The telephone rang and before I'd even answered it, I told my mother: "I'm sure it's Benito. He's had an accident. He's refused to take my advice."

I was right. While taking off from Bresso, there had been engine failure and the plane had crashed. When eventually I saw a car from a window, I dashed down the stairs. Benito, supported by a doctor, came hobbling towards me with a broken knee. I didn't bother to ask if he was in pain, but burst out angrily: "Well done. I'm very glad." Then I broke down, sobbing, while he murmured kindly: "Calm down, Rachele, it's nothing. I shall even have to stay quietly at home."

Quiet he was not, for he had a very high fever, but at least he stayed at home for three weeks.

On May 15, 1921, Mussolini became "onorevole", or deputy, for the first time, having been elected in

Bologna-Ferrara-Ravena-Forlí and in Milan-Pavia. The Milan results pleased him most of all because he'd received 124,918 votes as opposed to 4,064 in 1919. It was then that he forged closer links with the men who later became the Quadrumvirs of the March on Rome – among them Italo Balbo, Michele Bainchi, De Vecchi and De Bono.

Throughout this period Benito strove to avoid violence. In July 1921, at a meeting of the National Fascist Council, he won approval – despite some internal opposition – of a plan by Bonomi, the Prime Minister, seeking a truce between the Socialists and Fascists. Totally against the wishes of his own party members, he signed such an agreement in Rome on August 2, 1921. The matter didn't rest there. Opposing his action, a motion was carried at a congress of Fascists from Emilia, Romagna, Mantua, Cremona and Venice on August 16. Some of those who voted against him, but later helped him were men like Italo Balbo and Farinacci.

Again, the man gained the upper hand over the politician. As he had done in 1914 – and was to do in 1943 when he accepted a decision made at a higher level – Benito agreed to resign, quitting his seat on the Fascist executive committee. I remember what he said that day because I'd wondered if we were going to have to start again from nothing. "The matter is settled. The man who has been defeated must go. I'm leaving the top rank. I remain and hope I shall be allowed to remain, an ordinary soldier in the Milan Fascio."

Fortunately, everything was put to rights on November 21, when 4,000 Fascist delegates assembled from all over Italy. It's worth noting at this juncture that Benito's status had changed since the time the Socialist Party expelled him. Now he owned a thriving newspaper and was independent. And, although he'd been a member of both the Socialist and Fascist executive committees, he didn't leave the party in 1921. Moreover, a number of leaders – including Cesare Mossi, the associate secretary – continued to support him. This meant that Benito hadn't committed an irreparable act and Fascism was, after all, Benito's "son" – to quote his own words.

In the midst of these political anxieties, I was confronted with a further disturbing prospect – another duel. His latest opponent was a one time Socialist friend, Francesco Cicotti, editor of the *Paese*, who'd challenged my husband after he'd been criticised in the *Popolo d'Italia*. Due to relentless police surveillance, Benito had to use the cunning of a fox to arrange the fight in a villa at Livorno. Swords clashed until the fourteenth bout when the doctors, who were worried about Cicotti's heart, ordered him to stop.

On November 22, 1921, in an article in the *Popolo d'Italia*, my husband hinted for the first time that there might be a change of régime. But he didn't see it happening until much later – after ten years even.

I shall not describe the organisation and the political aspects of the March on Rome, for the subject has been adequately disposed of by the historians, judging by the amount of material written about Mussolini. But apart from that, there is now a law in Italy against attempts to vindicate Fascism.

From my own experience, however, I can say that we did not have time to fritter away at home. Benito was travelling all over Italy, for he was anxious to prevent political clashes getting out of hand. In order to reach trouble spots more quickly, he used a fighter plane of the First World War, but this only added to my worries. I believe he was the first politician to travel by private plane.

Italo Balbo, the architect of the first major operation to threaten State authority, planned in April 1922 to kidnap the Minister of Agriculture on a visit to Ferrara, accompanied by the Prefect of Bologna. Having asked the Minister for a report on the condition of local agriculture, Balbo took the Prefect of Ferrara aside and coolly told him that he'd decided to kidnap the Minister unless Fascists who'd recently been arrested in Bologna were released at once. The Prefect assured him that the arrests had been purely a precautionary measure; they would be set free within two days. He obtained a promise to this effect from his colleague in Bologna.

In August, the Fascists managed for the first time to compel government forces to obey their orders – an incident which took place in Parma. Again it involved Italo Balbo. Local party leaders had asked him to prise out the Reds who were entrenched in the town. Balbo summoned Fascist detachments, known as the Squadre from several towns, then the following day he saw the Prefect, who received him in the presence of General Lodomez, the garrison commander. Balbo fiercely attacked the Prefect for his complacency towards the Reds and gave him 12 hours to allow government troops to tear down the barricades and disarm the Socialists. If the Prefect failed he, Balbo, and his forces would seize authority from the State.

The Prefect asked for two hours grace, after which the troops destroyed the barricades. But because they did not disarm the Socialists Balbo told the Prefect that, in the circumstances, he'd have to use force. Intervening, Michele Bianchi, the party secretary, pleaded with Balbo to avoid a clash. Balbo therefore returned to the Prefect and asked that the army should take over. The Bishop of Parma now offered to mediate between the Socialists and Fascists – a proposal which was flatly rejected, though he was treated with respect and given a guard of honour.

The impasse was resolved at midnight on August 5. Coming to the hotel in which Balbo had set up his headquarters, General Lodomez told him that a state of siege had been declared and that the power invested in the Prefect was now in army hands.

In September, two months before the March on Rome, a similar operation took place in Bolzano. The Fascists thought the situation there ridiculous, for in effect the province was a State within the State. Any signs of Italian authority there were so slight as to make one wonder whether the power of the State was not merely provisional. The uniforms of the militia dated from the Austrian Empire, the Alto Adige had its own laws, and so on. Bonomi, a former Prime Minister, had even allowed the Mayor of Bolzano, Perathoner, to make a speech in German when the King visited the town.

Backed by the Fascist Party hierarchy, de Stefani, Starace and Giunta soon settled matters. Leading the Squadre from Trentino, Venetia and Lombardy, they occupied the town hall and the German schools (which were much more handsome and comfortable than the Italian) before setting out their conditions. The Mayor was to be dismissed immediately, the civil guards in Austrian uniforms were to be disbanded and the Italian schools transferred to the German buildings. After some hesitation, the Rome government finally approved these measures, even agreeing to the Mayor's dismissal.

After Bolzano, there came Trent, where the Fascists wished to dismiss Credaro, the Commissioner for Venetia and Trentino, because of poor administration. The government hung fire, but once again agreed to Fascist demands and Credaro was dismissed.

All these operations, which Benito's supporters carried out so skilfully, led Italians to believe that at last there was an organised force in the country to deal with irregularities. And as the months passed, it became clear that Italy now possessed two authorities: the official one – the government in Rome; and the other exercised by the Fascists in the provinces.

This peculiar situation could not last indefinitely since as the one became weaker the other grew stronger. Mussolini could have taken power on August 22. The garrisons were rallying to his side, the generals were openly lending their support. He had the means, and one forceful manoeuvre would have tipped the scales. But although Mussolini had ambitions to lead Italy, he wanted to do so legally, with the army's support, which he thought was vital for a successful revolution.

I was not in the capital to see the effects of the March on Rome, and so I never saw my husband arrive at the station at 5.30 on the evening of October 30. On the telephone he jubilantly explained how wonderful it had been to stand with the King on the balcony of the Quirinal and watch the procession of Black Shirts. It was not until he had closed his eyes for some seconds then opened them that he knew it was not a dream. He Benito Mussolini, was really head of the Italian Government.

As for myself, I'd stayed on the sidelines until Benito left for Rome on the night of October 29, 1922. My job was to record and forward to my husband the telephone messages arriving from all over Italy.

On October 16, the whole business had got under-way. With Benito presiding, the Fascist leaders met in Milan at the via San Marco, reviewing the situation and setting up a quadrumvirate composed of de Bono, de Vecchi, Balbo and Michele Bianchi. I remember we'd nicknamed de Vecchi the "little drum" and that de Bono already had a white beard. Later I valued the honesty of Bianchi.

People came in what seemed an endless stream to the house: men of all ages, some with a semblance of uniform, others quite simply in civilian clothes – all carrying bundles on their backs, with bread, ham, salami, cheese and potatoes, and wood and paraffin for the camp fires; for, to avoid arrest by the police, they were to sleep in the open countryside.

Some slept under our roof to guard my husband whenever he returned for a few hours' rest. For we expected trouble any moment – as much from the police as from the Reds. To reduce the danger to our home, the Fascists even rented the apartment opposite ours so that nobody dangerous could take it over. That way they could also maintain a better watch on the street from its windows. Each time an emergency seemed imminent, they gave the alarm by singing the song (which I still find myself humming sometimes): "L'ardito è bello, l'ardito è forte, piace alle donne, paura non ha" (The ardito is handsome, the ardito is strong, women like him, he knows no fear . . .). From our apartment we kept a constant vigil on a palm tree growing in the courtyard. We were afraid that someone might climb its trunk and hurl something into our home.

On October 22, Benito left for Rome. He feared that certain party extremists, obsessed by their desire for total revolution, might themselves seize power. In the circumstances, he wanted to be on the spot – to take the necessary precautions. I had seldom seen him so strained, for once more he was trying to stem the tide to stay as close to the law as he possibly could.

From Rome, where he spent some hours, Benito went to a party congress in Naples. It was here that my husband nearly began the March on Rome. Indeed, some could have started from Naples and my husband very nearly gave the go-ahead to the 40,000 Fascist enthusiasts who awaited his signal to do so. Instead, he merely finalised the details of the March. Among the salient points, there would be secret mobilisation on October 27, the prefectures and other big buildings would be occupied on the 28th when – in the morning – three columns would converge on Rome. They were to avoid any confrontation with the army and the towns were to display the national flag.

Back in Milan, Benito continued to follow by telephone the negotiations his representatives were conducting with possible heads of government. Right up to the last minute, the only prospect seemed to be that of Fascist participation in the government and not a government led by Mussolini himself.

In the evening of October 27, Benito to my annoyance, suggested that we should see the *Merry Widow* at the Manzoni Theatre. "How can you go and see the *Merry Widow* with so much on your mind?" I asked. He did not answer straight away but, fastening his shirt collar, he began to whistle. This was even more surprising since he hated whistling, and woe betide the children or the maid if he caught them at it. Not until we were on our way did he explain his reasons for going. "Everything," he revealed, "is ready for the March on

Rome. My presence at the theatre will mislead the police. They'll think that there can't be anything in the offing if I'm going to a show."

Actually, after we'd made certain that he, Edda and I had been noticed as a little family group, we discreetly left the Manzoni after some 20 minutes.

The next day Benito confided that he feared that Luigi Facta, the Prime Minister – who had resigned but had consented to the proclamation of a state of siege – would try force if he thought he, Mussolini, was about to take action. Clashes between the Fascists and those sections of the army which had stayed loyal to the government would have been inevitable. That's why Benito wanted to appear so relaxed in the theatre the evening before – to put the police on the wrong track.

On October 28, the first round went to the Fascists. The King – a skilful politician – refused to sign the proclamation of a state of siege. Throughout that day Benito was phenomenally calm – a characteristic of his after he'd taken a decision. Both at the "cellar" and at home, the telephone calls were unceasing from his supporters in Rome. Salandro, a former Prime Minister, offered him five ministries in the government he was trying to form. But Benito drily refused, conscious that power was now within his reach – and only a matter of hours away.

Naturally, excitement mounted at home, but my husband ate lunch and dinner ostensibly indifferent to dramatic events. He even glanced at Edda's homework, and after dinner returned to his office, preparing the edition which contained his last article as a journalist. I remember some phrases, which I re-read recently: "A tremendous victory is in sight, with the almost unanimous approval of the nation. The government must be clearly Fascist. Fascism will not abuse its victory but is determined that it shall not be diminished. Fascism wants power and will have it."

A furore greeted the paper's publication on October 29. At home, while Benito was still asleep, his chauffeur Cirillo waited for him, playing the piano and singing *(above)* Visiting wheatfields with the King (Radio Times Hulton Picture Library), *(middle)* with German ministers Bruning and Curtius during their visit to Rome in *1931*, *(below)* with Cardinal Gasparri at the formal signing of the Lateran Treaties. (Syndication International.)

Mussolini with his daughter Edda when she was seventeen. (Syndication International.)

"We have taken power" as if he'd achieved it all himself. Edda and Vittorio took the opportunity to miss school.

As soon as he rose, Benito, closetting himself in a room with me, told me to instruct the Milan Fasci that on no account must they set fire to the *Corriere della Serra*. When the editor called some moments later, I set his mind at rest. Then Mussolini left for the *Popolo d'Italia*.

It was about ten o'clock when I received a call from Rome. A man's voice said: "We wish to speak to Mussolini in person."

"He's not here," I replied. "You'll find him at the *Popolo d'Italia*."

"He's not there. We've already tried."

About half an hour later, there was another call from Rome and this time I learnt from where it came. "It is very urgent. We want to know where to find him. This is the Palace speaking."

In fact I had the King's aide-de-camp on the line telling me that the King had decided to entrust the formation of the new government to Benito Mussolini. Provided they manage to find him, I thought.

Some minutes later Benito called.

"Benito, the Palace is looking for you everywhere," I said. "Where have you been?"

"I know, I know. I've been in contact with the Quirinal. I must leave for Rome. Pack a bag with a suit and the usual things. But don't say anything to anybody."

Stubbornly, Benito had declined to leave Milan until he'd received a telegram officially confirming the King's desire that he should form a new government. Shortly before midday a first telegram had arrived, signed by General Cittadini, requesting my husband to go to Rome for consultations with the King. But Benito had refused to leave, insisting on a telegram that asked him specifically to form the government. This arrived at midday, again signed by Cittadini. Then Benito uttered words which may have become legendary but were certainly true. "If only our Father was still alive," said Benito, showing the telegram to his brother Arnaldo.

As there was no train to Rome, Benito went to his newspaper office in the afternoon. He settled his affairs, prepared a special edition of the *Popolo d'Italia* and made arrangements for the editorship to pass to Arnaldo. He then met Cesare Rossi, ensuring that the news was passed on to the Fascist militia and to the general headquarters at Perugia, with a demand that they should not forget discipline in their enthusiasm.

In the evening, he came home to an atmosphere of intense excitement. He took his case, said a brief good-bye – we had never been very demonstrative in the family – kissed the children and left for the station – reminding me once again, to make sure that the *Corriere della Sera* was not burnt down.

There was a crowd of people on the station platform and I heard from Cirillo, who was carrying his case, that he said to the stationmaster: "I wish to leave exactly on time. From now on everything must work perfectly."

At home calm was gradually restored. I went out for a little while and astonished myself by entering a church. I knelt down and said a prayer (which I kept to myself for a long time): "Lord do not let us change. May my husband stay as he is and may I never give way to pride or vanity."

CHAPTER 6

The first steps of Mussolini the dictator

We suddenly discovered when my husband became head of the Italian Government an incredible number of friends, of people who at some time had rendered us some service and who – with varying degrees of tact – reminded us of the fact.

One day in Milan, I was accosted by a man who told me that he'd lent my father-in-law, Alessandro, a wheelbarrow wheel which he had never returned. When I expressed my amazement – seeing that Alessandro had been dead for twelve years – I learnt that the incident dated back nearly twenty-seven years. Without further question, I paid him for the wheel.

From another man I received an enormous bouquet of flowers with a message begging for an interview. When I agreed to see him, he simply said that he was an ardent Fascist upon whom Mussolini could count for liberal support. I remembered having met this visitor two years before on a train between Forlí and Milan. During a discussion about politics, he'd explained at length to fellow passengers that Mussolini was a nobody. Much to his annoyance, I'd contradicted all his arguments and ended by saying: "You must know Mussolini personally to talk about him this way."

"Certainly, not only do I know him very well, but I also know his wife."

"I'm glad to hear it," I remarked sarcastically, "because I am Signora Mussolini."

The young man had been struck dumb. He did not

find his tongue again until two years later when my husband had come to power.

In Rome, Benito also became acquainted with a mass of people to whom – he now discovered – he was indebted for something.

We kept each other informed of our activities during the daily telephone calls we arranged before he left for the capital.

"You know," he said, one evening, "you'd be amazed how many veterans of the last war I keep meeting. Today, for example, I had a visit from someone who helped take me to the hospital when I was wounded in 1917."

"I hope you told him how grateful you were," I said.

"Of course I did. But there's just one problem. He's the four hundredth man with the same story. When I was wounded, there must have been six or eight people carrying me."

Another day he told me that, during the afternoon, he received two visitors. The first was a man who insisted on seeing him only to mutter once he was in his office: "I wanted to see you, I wanted to see you," before fainting. The second was a sergeant of the Carabinieri who had brought a truncheon. He wanted to beg the Duce's forgiveness for having arrested him during a demonstration in Forlí and to offer him the truncheon he'd whacked him with.

"I forgave him and took the truncheon," said my husband, philosophically.

After forty days we saw each other again. My husband had come back to Milan, incognito, but the news of his arrival soon spread. We managed, however, to have one week of family life from December 16 to 22.

As we could speak more freely and at greater length than we did on the telephone, I took the chance to ask him about his new life, his job as head of government and his impressions of it all. It was then that he described his first conversation with King Victor-Emmanuel III. He told me that he found the Sovereign's bearing and edginess rather disappointing. "I got the

62

impression," he added, "that the whole Court had packed and was ready to leave at the first sign of insurrection. But I think Victor-Emmanuel relaxed as soon as I had told him what my objectives are. I think he'll trust me now and that I can rely on his support."

I digress here to say that I heard a report of the King's reactions soon after he saw my husband and that it coincided with Benito's impressions. The King had said: "There's a fellow who'll go a long way. I had imagined he'd be different before I saw him."

I gathered from Benito that, as soon as his position was secure, he'd had to contend with the demands of the more ambitious Fascists. They now came to claim their rewards and titles. For instance, one of the men chiefly responsible for the March on Rome had insisted on being made a marshal forthwith. And because of their overbearing manner, Benito had been forced to arrest some party members who ignored paying bills in restaurants and cafes.

"Victory," he commented, "has gone to their heads and they're reeling with it. They're getting arrogant and pretentious. They'll exaggerate the slightest difference of opinion into a rift. They even fight amongst themselves. If only they would realise that now we have power, we must restore the rule of law, if necessary to protect the losing side. But they won't and I seem to spend an inordinate amount of time sorting out the petty quarrels of the people who should be helping me, instead of dealing with important national and international problems."

To avoid further disturbances, he hastened to send home everyone who had taken part in the March on Rome and, later, to create several new departments in the Ministry of the Interior so that all veterans and Fascists could be assimilated into such bodies as the border police, the forest guards and the Customs officers.

Fortunately, it didn't take long to unravel their knotty points, to put all the would-be dictators in their place.

The most important task still remained – to set the

faulty mechanics of the state in motion again. To start with, my husband had put his office as Prime Minister in the building housing the Ministry of the Interior at the Viminale Palace. He then transferred it to the Chigi Palace, which was little more than a shell with no working amenities. "I've inherited a leaky vessel and a bunch of amazingly unbusiness-like civil servants, especially among the higher ranks," he confided. "They're the ones who come to work at ten in the morning. One day I was going up the stairs in the Ministry when I met someone coming down. It was just after eight. 'Is there anyone up there?' I asked. 'That madman Mussolini must be there. He's always in at eight,' he answered. Then he recognised me and was very embarrassed."

An Italian diplomat once remarked that no one outside the diplomatic corps could have the least idea of Italy's international standing, adding that, unified, Italy commanded less respect than she had divided. So as soon as he took office my husband was concerned to restore his country to what he considered her rightful place on the international scene.

I lack the authority to comment on the Lausanne and London conferences. But I do know that he was as disappointed by his trip to London as he had been delighted by his journey to Lausanne.

"It's a dreadful town," he claimed. "There's a greyish dust which gets into everything – the rooms, the clothes, even the suitcases. It's worse than desert sand. I won't be going back in a hurry. The English don't understand our problems, or don't want to. Italy's just a trifle to them. But we'll change all that, you'll see."

Some people wonder why, over the next twenty years, Mussolini only left Italy to go to Germany. I think it was because he felt uneasy abroad and his impressions of London did nothing to make the idea of travelling more attractive to him.

On a personal level, his position of power doubtless had an effect on my husband. He had left Milan with a pair of black trousers and a blue jacket. He came back boasting well-cut suits – some of them in tweed – stiff-collared shirts and dark, but lovely neckties. His new hats greatly amused the children, especially a straw hat and a bowler from which he refused to be parted. Even if it was no longer fashionable, the bowler recalled happy associations for him. "There may be only three of us in the world wearing one – Stan Laurel, Oliver Hardy and me. But this hat has protected my head from truncheons more than once."

This particular penchant for hats was responsible for an incident which caused much laughter in the family, even if our chauffeur Cirillo found it less amusing. He had stayed in Milan and was still unused to fancy hats with odd names. One day, Benito, who had just arrived from Rome, sent him to fetch his gibus, or crush hat, from the car downstairs.

Cirillo disappeared. When he failed to reappear after some fifteen minutes, Benito grew impatient. Finally, he sent me to see what was going on. I found Cirillo leaning against the car and asked him what he was doing.

"I'm waiting, Donna Rachele."

"But what are you waiting for?"

"Signor Gibus. The Prime Minister told me to go down and fetch him. Perhaps he's late."

On another occasion, Benito laughingly told me over the telephone that one of his old friends, a journalist on the *Popolo d'Italia*, had 'phoned to ask him how he should address him in the future, whether he should give him his full title of Prime Minister or carry on using the familiar second person.

"Can you imagine it?" my husband joked. "Who does he take me for? I'm still called Benito Mussolini and, as far as I know, I haven't changed. Do you think I've changed, Rachele?"

"Not since last week perhaps. But you're more stylish now. You look more 'middle-class'."

"But I have to be like this in Rome. I am the head of government after all. I have to set an example and behave correctly towards foreign visitors. And they take their deportment lessons seriously at court, I can tell you."

"I'll have to take some so that I can come to Rome."

"That's all you'd need."

"And what about me, Benito, what should I call you?"

"Idiot, you're not going to start that Forlí business again!"

And we burst out laughing.

The 'Forlí business' was well known in the family because Benito liked to tease me about it. It dated from 1910 when we had decided to live together. Benito was a qualified teacher and like everyone else in Forlí, I addressed him according to his profession. That is the usual custom in Italy, even today. When we settled down together I went on calling him "teacher" whenever I spoke to him. In fact I found it somewhat hard to use familiar speech. So that eventually he asked me if I was waiting until we had four children before I could bring myself to call him Benito.

I did not manage to do so until the night he went out on his unforgettable spree. I was so angry I overcame my shyness. But the question of how to address Benito remained, if not for me, then for others like Cirillo. In 1912 he had become "editor" of the paper, which meant he was entitled to be called a "direttore". In 1921 he was elected deputy, which meant "onorevole" and a year later he was Prime Minister or "Presidente".

"I'll call him Duce," Cirillo told me, "because he is the Duce and that's the only title which doesn't seem to change."

He was quite right, for the Socialists – amazingly enough – had christened him Duce in 1912. Admittedly he was one of the best known members of the party at the time. It happened during a banquet held to celebrate his release from prison, when Olindo Vernocchi, one of the veterans, said to him: "From today, Benito, you are not only the representative of the Romagna Socialists, you are the Duce of all revolutionary Socialists in Italy."

And so Benito Mussolini, the Fascist leader, went down in history with a title the Socialists had given him. It is true that he always remained a Socialist at heart, but I shall return to that later.

Whoever else may have regretted Mussolini's rise to power, a priest, Don Cirio Damiani, certainly did. A long-standing friend of the Mussolini family, he was also an inventor, first having perfected an ingenious draught system for domestic chimneys, and then a kind of multi-barrelled gun which, incidentally, the Russians later produced and called the "Katioushka".

In 1922, Don Cirio and my husband were exchanging letters about a new form of luminous mudguards for automobiles. On January 26, Benito wrote that in March he would personally deal with this invention because, as he wrote: "Everything new is exciting to me, and in this case I have just helped to set up a workshop for making mudguards. I have also helped a young man to perfect a new sparking plug and your scheme looks very interesting to me."

Unfortunately, when my husband left for Rome, all Don Cirio's plans seemed to dissipate.

Anything new invariably looks good, and as soon as my husband had settled in Rome, the invitations came flooding in. I was asked to be godmother to various children and to sponsor a number of organisations. I declined politely but firmly, but I could not refuse to accompany my husband at certain public appearances, particularly in our native Romagna.

It would take too long to describe all the meetings I attended or chaired, for these were quite numerous. Yet I remember distinctly my first official appearance during the summer of 1923. I took my place on the platform for the first time in the very towns where I had known poverty, in Forlí and Predappio, where I had spent my childhood and early youth. Of course, both Benito and I were proud and moved to be there. As we sat in our special compartment waiting for the train to reach Forlí, Benito said with a smile: "Do you realise, Rachele, that some of the policemen there to salute me will be the same officers who once put handcuffs on me, dragged me off to prison, insulted and beat me. What shall I do to them?"

"Give them a good kick," I answered, for I had my own ideas on the subject.

"No, I can't do that. They were only doing their duty. They'll do even better now because they'll be afraid I remember. Besides there's no point in being vindictive. I've even forbidden the castor oil treatment."

"You're wrong, you'll see how wrong you are."

Probably I should explain that the "castor oil" treatment was a form of Fascist punishment used during reprisal operations, but only on important people – men of a certain social standing. If a lawyer, for instance, had paraded his anti-Fascist opinions or helped their opponents, the Fascist squadre would go to his house and force him to swallow the oil – not sufficient to make him seriously ill, but enough to confine him to his home for several days.

Later, the Fascists were accused of inhuman practices. I don't condone what they did, but surely the lavatory is preferable to a hospital bed and wounds inflicted by the present-day chains, stones and Molotov cocktails.

One of the first measures that Mussolini took as Prime Minister was to forbid this use of castor oil, with harsh punishment for offenders. So, obviously, it was no treatment for the Forlí police.

As the train pulled into the station, an astonishing sight met my eyes – a great, surging mass of people. Never before had I experienced anything like it and found it extraordinarily impressive. All formality was swept aside and we were carried to the car. There I discovered another drawback to success – the pretty flowered hat I'd brought to wear was reduced to a handful of rags. Benito, more accustomed to these occasions, spoke to the people in Romagnol dialect as the car crept slowly forward.

During a ceremony at the prefecture, I noticed Countess Merenda who had been our landlady in 1910 when we first lived in Forlí. The moment was ripe to settle accounts with her, for I'd never forgotten her

remark about us thirteen years before when my husband was not distinguished. Visiting the building one
day, she had reached our floor when, speaking to her
manager, I overheard her say: "Can there really be such
squalid people living in my house?"

I'd repeated her words to Benito the next morning,
when he was shaving. Before I had even finished what
I was saying he'd run to find a sheet of writing paper,
his face still covered with soap. "Remember Countess,"
he wrote, "my wife is a nobler woman than you."

Nothing further was done at the time, but her comment had lingered, and now I was determined that the
"squalid people" should have their say – and in public.
At some point of the ceremony someone asked me to
speak. I accepted gladly and attacked from the start.
"When you become an important person," I began,
"everybody wants to know, to put out the red carpet for
you. But when you are poor, well . . . I have never
forgotten certain titled ladies who are, moreover, here
today . . ."

My speech was quickly interrupted. Sensing a verbal
storm, Benito made excuses, called me over to him, and
asked for the ceremony to continue. Since then, I must
admit, Countess Merenda has been extremely kind to
me. Her friendliness has compensated for her aberration
in 1910.

Unfortunately, not every year was a happy one, nor
for that matter, every month.

After the initial shock, the political rivals attacked
Benito more fiercely than before he came to power.
There were the violent inter-party quarrels, and the
assassination of the Socialist deputy, Giacomo Matteotti, shook Fascism to its very roots. Even Benito could
not escape stricture, for it was proved that some Fascists
had taken a hand in the crime. I think it was one of the
few occasions when I saw my husband disgusted,
offended and demoralised all at once. He did all he
could to trace the criminals, and once apprehended
harsh sentences were pronounced for all – Fascist
members or not. But the Duce went further. He per-

sonally ensured that the Matteotti family were provided for and even took a close interest in the children's education.

Benito had come to realise that danger lurked even in friends, that he could no longer trust anybody. He said so more than once. He observed: "I don't believe I could trust even my mother if she came back to life."

He didn't mean it, for Benito Mussolini's trustfulness bordered on naïveté, as the future was to prove.

I felt that the previous ten years had taught me all there was to know about life. I had experienced anxiety about duels, arrests and war, uncertainty about the future, the thrill of success and – I had discovered another Mussolini.

I shall not catalogue all the attempts on Benito's life. There were not many. But together with the murder of Matteotti, they went far towards establishing the dictatorship. The parliamentary opposition tipped the scales by withdrawing to their ivory tower on the Aventine. Benito explained that he was assuming supreme power for a single purpose – to prevent freedom of action to both friend and foe.

Two attempts on his life affected me deeply. Not that I was insensible to the others, for no woman could ignore the risk of her husband returning home dead or badly wounded. But these two incidents I could never forget.

The first – in April 1926 – was in fact the second bid to destroy him, occurring the day he presided over a medical congress at the Capital in Rome. As he was leaving, an English woman, named Violet Gibson, fired five shots at him with a revolver. Yet in that instant, as if by a miracle, Benito turned his head, looking up towards a balcony, so that only one bullet found its mark and that in the nose. He is reputed to have said at the time: "And it was really a woman!"

When he told me about it, he made it sound almost funny. "You know, Rachele," he explained, "It wasn't the English woman who nearly killed me, but the doctors. I was unlucky. It was a medical congress and a score of them jumped on me, all of them hoping for the honour of saving Mussolini. I was afraid I'd never survive in the crush and had to fight my way out with fists."

On October 31 of that year, when I myself witnessed an attempt to kill him, I realised that my husband had not exaggerated the Gibson episode. That was the time we attended the opening of a new sports complex in Bologna. There were thirteen women at table, and Benito exclaimed: "It's a bad omen."

In the afternoon, while I was waiting for my husband at the station, the Marquis Paulucci arrived. He looked dreadful and it was all he could do to say: "Be brave, Excellency, be brave." Momentarily I felt numb, but before I could panic Benito came from behind him in a surge of the crowd. He told me that, while he was still in his car, a young man had fired on him and missed. In that moment Benito had caught a glimpse of his pale tormented face, but before the police could intervene, the crowd had summarily lynched him.

"It's insane to make such a young boy the instrument of a crime," said Benito, more shaken by the fate of his would-be murderer than by thoughts of what might have been his own gruesome end. His escape from death had been slender. Not until we were travelling home did he notice the scorch marks on his jacket, and at the Villa Carpena I noticed blood on both vest and shirt. A bullet, grazing the skin above his heart, had been deflected by a notebook.

Some minutes after our arrival, while the rest of us were still recovering from shock, Benito was alone in his room playing his violin. He stopped only to say: "It's sickening to do such a thing, to give a weapon to a lad like that. He may have a mother waiting for him this evening."

CHAPTER 7

Mussolini and women

There was a man who liked his women plump. He didn't mind if they were blonde, brunette or red-head, just so long as they wore no perfume. And that man was Benito Mussolini.

My husband's liaisons with women and his alliance with Hitler were, at one time, among the favourite topics of the world's Press. But, putting everything into its true perspective, I can say that Mussolini's tally was no greater than that of any attractive Italian male. There is no desire – out of spite – to make it sound trifling, but brief thought should be enough to expose the truth.

My husband always slept at home, save when he was travelling. He left at eight in the morning, came home at one, left again at four and returned at about eight in the evening. Every time he left the Palazzo Venezia, a telephone call to the Villa Torlonia, where we were living, informed me that the Duce was on his way home. If he went elsewhere, I was given the precise location.

Therefore, when and where did he have his affairs? I suppose I know where: at his office, where he'd furnished a little room, not with a bed, but with a couch to rest on. And when? In his spare moments.

That was Mussolini's great love life. Many men must have done as much. Indeed, some men have greater scope. They can go to a hotel, tell their wives they intend to have a drink with friends or invent that late meeting at the office. One other thing is certain. At no time did Mussolini pursue a woman. Women were drawn to him on physical grounds, because they hoped to profit by the relationship, or just to shock their friends by saying: "I'm the Duce's mistress."

Two anecdotes bear this out. One day a young widow came to the Duce's office in the Palazzo Venezia. Her husband, an airman, had met a hero's death in combat. Benito was extolling her husband's virtues and intending to console her when suddenly he realised that the widow was regarding him with sensuous eyes unmarked by tears. He put an end to the interview as soon as he could.

When he told me about it that evening, he was so obviously disturbed that I never had a moment's suspicion.

On the other occasion, he showed me a letter which, written by a princess, contained some particularly offensive remarks because he'd spurned her. Seeing that I couldn't conceal a trace of suspicion, Benito pulled up his sleeve and said: "Look, Rachele. I have goose flesh just thinking about it. If I was lost in a forest with that woman and a monkey, I'd take the monkey. Not that I don't like women, but I don't want her. So she's taking what revenge she can."

After Benito's death, I met this woman's husband and revealed to him my opinion of his wife and why; moreover, that I considered her attitude scandalous – an assertion he has never denied.

And yet my husband was no saint. I knew practically all there was to know. I didn't make a fuss when I heard that Magda Fontanges braggingly claimed to be Benito's mistress. It so happened that her tantrums so annoyed Benito that he wouldn't let her return to Italy. That was why she shot and wounded de Chambrun, the French ambassador who had the responsibility of telling her. I also kept calm when Cecile Sorel was seen leaving my husband's office, flushed, untidy and radiant.

I knew my husband better than anyone. I'd known him since his adolescence, when he took money from his sister's purse to buy ice cream for his girl friends and take them dancing. After that, ironically she'd to comfort them when they cried on her shoulder because he'd left them. Before I met him he'd left a trail of broken hearts in Predappio and Forlí, then in Tolmezzo, Onaglia, Galtieri, in Switzerland – in fact, wherever he went. He never denied that he liked women, but with one reservation. As he said to me one day: "After you, I'll never look at another pretty woman. Beauty is not to be trusted, it makes you lose your reason."

I don't think he ever lost his. If a woman found him attractive – or vice-versa – the relationship would be passionate, reckless, but short. Mussolini couldn't be bothered with the women he'd seduced. I think women were drawn primarily by the way Benito looked at them, with those eyes that subdued me as a child. Moreover, he carried himself well and had a deep, melodious, almost spell-binding voice. Once he had won them, it was his roughness that kept them. Like all Italian men, he thought that a woman's place in society was in the home. Accordingly, he tended to treat his mistresses like objects and never became deeply attached.

Even so, there were three women who hurt me: Ida Dalser, Margherita Sarfatti and Clara Petacci. I summoned all my strength to fight each one of them. It was an anonymous letter which I received which first made me anxious. My husband, it revealed, was involved in an affair which was potentially troublesome. I decided to meddle in his affairs a little, but before I could do so, I was overtaken by events.

Benito had gone to Genoa to borrow money from a friend, Captain Giuletti, who was in charge of the seamen's union, when a strange woman came to the house. She was no beauty and despite her garish make-up looked older than me. Curiously she declined to give her name but brazenly asked for details about our private life. She even asked Edda if Daddy loved Mummy. This visit greatly disturbed me and on Benito's return I told him about it.

"That's the Austrian woman, Ida Dalser", he said.

He confessed to their relationship, of which I had been completely ignorant till then. He had first met her in Trent and then again in Milan, and since then she'd been pursuing him – even to the office where everyone knew that if she called Mussolini was "out".

"She's dangerous," he said. "She's a fanatic."

When she told him she had borne him a son, he immediately recognised the child, whom she called Benito Albino. We thought that things would rest there. But one day in December 1915, when I was out shopping, the police came to our house telling my mother they'd a warrant to take the furniture. My mother was too bewildered to protest. I was equally puzzled, for only recently I'd received a letter from Benito – then at the front – saying that all was going well.

I soon found out what it was about, for later that day the police came back to arrest me and take me to the station.

"Are you or are you not Signora Mussolini?" they demanded.

"Yes, I am," I answered.

"Then that's it, you're the guilty woman."

I was very taken aback. I asked what I had done, what I was guilty of. With heavy sarcasm, the officer "reminded" me that I had set fire to a hotel room in Milan.

"But I've never been to that hotel," I protested. "I've only left the house to go shopping. How could I have set fire to a hotel? Why should I want to?"

Surprised by my idignation, the superintendent asked for further identification – my name and forenames, date and place of birth, parents and so on. He then realised that they were seeking another "Signora Mussolini". He checked what I had told him against his information about the mysterious woman and we discovered that she was none other than Ida Dalser.

I was then told that my husband had paratyphoid and was in hospital in Cividale. I went there, in a cattle truck, and told him about my adventures.

"There's only one way to stop Ida Dalser spreading the story that she's Signora Mussolini," he said. "We shall have to get married."

"I'll think about it," I replied, deliberately casual to punish him for my troubles. "But I warn you, I am quite capable of saying 'no' at the last minute."

"The awful thing is that you would," he sighed, taking my hand.

Benito was right to suppose that Ida Dalser would use our unofficial union to her own advantage. In 1910 revolutionary doctrine recommended common-law marriage. I remember Benito getting very angry after he had registered Edda's birth at the Town Hall in Forlí in 1910. He'd asked that the certificate should read, – "Edda, daughter of Benito Mussolini and another". The registrar had spread the story that we were legally married to hurt his reputation. Benito had gone to see him and squared the record with two sharp blows.

Naturally I agreed to a civil wedding and the ceremony took place some time later in the hospital at Treviglio. Benito was in bed with jaundice and looked very apprehensive under his woollen cap. When the time came he pronounced the formal "yes" in a clear and joyful voice. But I said nothing. I pretended not to have heard though I was watching Benito out of the corner of my eye. When the official asked me a second time, I was as silent as before. Benito looked at me, wild-eyed, wringing his hands with fear. Finally, at the third request, I said "yes". Benito sighed deeply, falling back onto his pillows as if the strain had over-powered him.

"Were you afraid?" I asked. He just glared at me.

I thought the Dalser episode was dead and buried, but I was wrong. In 1917, Benito was seriously injured when a shell exploded during exercises, giving him 43 shrapnel wounds. There was even talk of amputation, though it did not prove necessary, and after several weeks of intense pain he was moved to the military hospital in Milan.

One morning, on my way to visit him, I noticed a

dark-haired disagreeable-looking woman. I didn't recognise the Austrian fire-raiser, Ida Dalser, but she remembered me. When we reached my husband's ward she jumped on me, hurling insults and crying: "I am Mussolini's wife. I am the only one who has the right to be with him."

The other patients found this highly amusing. I was furious. I lashed out with fists and feet and even began to squeeze my hands about her neck. Benito was so trussed up in bandages that he could hardly move, and in trying to stop us he fell to the floor. Luckily the hospital staff intervened or I would have strangled her. She fled and I burst into tears.

Then Ida brought an action against Benito, and the court ordered him to pay a monthly allowance of 200 lire for the child, followed by 100,000 lire when he was 21. Ida Dalser came to a sad end. She died in San Clemente, a mental hospital in Venice, in December 1937. Her son was studying radio-telegraphy in La Spezia, but he too died in July 25, 1942, in Milan.

When Margherita Sarfatti came on the scene, I determined to stop the affair from getting out of hand. But I had to be tougher and more cunning because she was more dangerous and a more intelligent woman.

She worked as a journalist, covering the literary and artistic columns of *L'Avanti* and then of the *Popolo d'Italia*. I had known about the relationship for some time, but whenever I mentioned it Benito told me that she was too intellectual, too cultured for him to get involved with. But after my experiences with Ida Dalser I kept my ears open, for I'd realised that in Benito's case the danger came not from him but from the women; they didn't want to leave him.

As far as I know, the affair didn't start until 1918, but after that I began to hear more detailed information which made me apprehensive.

In 1921, while he was recovering from his aeroplane accident with Radaelli, she came to see him at home for professional reasons. I pretended to be quite ignorant of the affair, while she behaved impeccably. Yet the mere fact that she'd dared to come angered me. So, as I settled Benito back into bed after she'd gone, I let slip, quite casually: "Some people have the most incredible cheek. All you can do with them is throw them out of the window." Benito must have felt a pang of guilt, since he merely remarked – in an unconvincing voice – that I must be imagining things.

In fact, from 1922 to 1926, my husband continued his affair with Margherita Sarfatti in Rome. The more persistent the rumours became the more I determined to fight back. So when, therefore, I heard in 1925 that Benito was ill with a stomach ulcer, I decided to visit him in Rome. Rather surprisingly, I was turned back at the station by none other than the questor of police himself. I listened to the rigmarole about how my presence at my husband's bedside might be misinterpreted as a sign that his illness was worse, which would lead to all sorts of political speculation. In the national interest, therefore, I ought to stay in Milan. I finally agreed, though I was not at all convinced. In my mind I'd merely postponed a confrontation with Margherita Sarfatti.

In 1926, the children and I spent Christmas in Rome. Benito could not have been more charming or attentive. The children have glorious memories of that visit. I myself was particularly happy because he had sworn that his affair with the journalist had ended. And he did break off all links with her, even dismissing her from the paper with a pension. Indeed, I thought that peace had returned at last, especially after my husband burnt all the woman's letters before my eyes at the Villa Torlonia.

However, one day in 1931 I opened the *Popolo d'Italia* and was astounded to see Margherita Sarfatti's name at the bottom of an article on an inside page. My blood ran cold and I thought: "So *she's* back. Well, we shall see what we shall see."

I could not ask Benito for an explanation in person as I was in Ferano. I had gone there for eczema treatment and to conduct some discreet enquiries into Austrian sympathies among the authorities. But I could send a telegram.

Seeing me grab my coat and handbag and dash out of the room, Carolina Ciano, my son-in-law's mother, realised I proposed to create a fuss. She followed me, already fearing the worst because she knew my fits of temper.

At the Post Office I took a telegram form and wrote in detail – regardless of the expense. The counter-clerk openly shuddered when she saw my message and, more than that, the name and address of the man I was sending it to. Carolina Ciano, who'd been reading over my shoulder, was deathly pale. She exclaimed: "Rachele, you're not going to send it."

"And why not?"

The post mistress was both horrified and highly indignant. "I can't send a telegram like this. I refuse to take it."

After all these years I cannot remember the message any longer. But every woman will know what one says to one's husband at such times. "You will kindly take it and send it immediately," I replied emphatically. "If you want any more details, then you may as well know that my name is Rachele Mussolini and the gentleman I am writing to is my husband."

When she refused again I took another form and filled it in like the first, addressing it to Arnaldo, the editor of the *Popolo d'Italia*.

That very evening Benito 'phoned me. "What is all this?" he asked, half angry and half worried. "I don't know which article of Margherita Sarfatti's you're talking about. All I do know is that I have nothing more to do with her and I don't want to hear her mentioned again."

I recognised the ring of truth in his voice but this did not make me any less angry. I determined to strike while the iron was hot.

"All right," I said, "but I am telling you once and for all and you can pass the message on to Arnaldo. If I see the name Sarfatti in the paper just once more I shall go to Milan, get hold of a bomb and blow up the *Popolo d'Italia*. And you ought to know, Benito, that I'm quite capable of it. What's more, it'd be a public service. Nobody likes the *Popolo d'Italia* any longer. It's getting tedious."

My threats must have left their mark because Margherita's name never appeared in the paper again. Not that she suffered unduly. She later sold Benito's letters for 70 million lire. If I had done the same with all the letters he received from women, asking improbable favours, I'd be rolling in money now, especially as some of them were signed by well-known figures – "society women" as they say.

The third and last of Benito's affairs – which possibly caused me most suffering – was with Clara Petacci. I should also say that, since my husband's death, whenever I pray for the rest of his soul I also think of Clara Petacci, for I believe one should have the magnanimity to forgive, – more so from the other side of the grave. Of all the women who were infatuated by my husband, only she paid for the affair with her life, when she could have fled abroad and benefited from Mussolini's generosity – as Margherita Sarfatti did. For that reason, I do not feel resentful as I tell her story – merely sad and immensely compassionate.

For a long time I knew nothing of the relationship between my husband and Clara Petacci. Everyone else knew – my children, the staff and so on. There was a conspiracy of silence about it – more to spare me pain than to protect the relationship – and the few times I was near to discovering something through my private police network, I came up against this barrier. It worked so well that I remained in complete ignorance until I read the newspaper reports on July 26, 1943, after my husband's arrest. Whenever an idol has been toppled from power, everything becomes public knowledge, and that included Clara Petacci.

Irma, our maid, still remembers how furious I was when I read these "revelations". And my concern for Benito's life did nothing to improve matters.

I believe my husband met Clara Petacci in about 1936. She came from a very good family, her father being the doctor to Pope Pius XI. There has been such a glut of stories about this affair, but I am sure that it ripened at the time our enemies were looking for material for a propaganda campaign against Mussolini. Besides, everything I subsequently discovered about her, after 1942, leads me to believe that Benito did not regard her any more highly than any of the women he had known.

However, they made some costly mistakes, for the Mussolini-Petacci affair provided an ideal target for the enemy Press. It was through this medium that I found out – and Irma later confirmed – that my husband had installed a direct line between the Villa Torlonia and the apartment where she was living with her family. He never realised that all their conversations actually went through the switchboard and were recorded.

As I have already mentioned, Benito always slept at home – even throughout this affair. He never formally presented Clara to other people or appeared in public with her. They were forced to meet for brief moments, usually in a little apartment he had furnished – as I later found out – in the Palazzo Venezia.

I made no move to interfere until 1944, and even then it was one of the most difficult situations I have ever had to deal with. At that time Benito, the children and I were staying at the Villa Petrinelli in Gargnano on Lake Garda. Clara had also come to live in the area – in a villa a few miles away.

It had also come to my knowledge that certain people intended to use her presence at Gargnano to reflect discredit on my husband, and I knew too, that certain Fascists considered the situation distasteful and disturbing enough to exploit it for their own ends. So I decided to see her myself and warn her of her possible fate.

Before leaving for the villa where she was staying, I 'phoned Benito, telling him of my intention and arranging for two friends to accompany me and the chauffeur. I wanted Guido Buffarini, the Minister of the Interior for the Salo Republic, to come with me as well, and therefore stopped at the Ministry on the way. I had no love for Buffarini, since I knew that he was a schemer and was in contact with Clara. Consequently, I wanted him to be present at our meeting.

When his secretary announced my arrival, he came rushing out in his shirt sleeves anxious to know why I was there.

"Finish dressing and come with me," I said.

"Where are we going?"

"I'll tell you when I consider it necessary. Come along – quickly!"

We drove off and in due course drew up at the main gate of Clara Petacci's villa where I rang the bell. Buffarini wanted my friends to leave, but they refused. It was pouring with rain at the time and our excited little group at the gate must have looked rather sinister.

I had to ring several times before a German officer appeared, informing us, through the gate, that we could not enter. Furthermore, he added, it was pointless to insist. I spent over an hour trying to find some way through the railings, but it was no use. Finally, my friends had to threaten Buffarini with violence before he signalled – sweating with fear – to someone at the window to let us in.

Seeing my fierce expression, he asked: "Are you armed?"

"I never take a weapon when I go visiting," I answered.

I was shown into a small room. Buffarini, the German officer, and another soldier stood nearby while I sat vainly trying to regain some composure. After some minutes I glimpsed a wraith-like figure descending the stairs. It was Clara Petacci. For some reason her frailty, her hesitant, almost awkward walk and the way she was clutching at a handkerchief completely disarmed me. I managed to hide my anger by avoiding her eyes, for I knew she would be able to read my feelings in them, and asked quite calmly: "Signora or Signorina?"

"Signora," she replied, in a low and slightly harsh voice

which belied her apparent physical weakness.

"Signora," I said, "I shall endeavour to remain calm. I have not come here as the jealous wife to insult you, much less to threaten you. Our personal feelings have nothing to do with the crisis affecting our country. I am therefore asking you to make a sacrifice. My husband must have a quiet mind so that he can work. But more than that, I am determined to put an end to the scandal arising from your presence here so close to our house. Love should be capable of sacrifice. As Benito's wife I would be quite prepared to go away, to live alone far away from him, in a castle or on the top of a mountain, if my leaving would help to save him. You say you love him. Well then, stop seeing him. Let him live in peace. I'm not asking you for my sake so that I can have him to myself, but for his."

Clara sat curled in an armchair, listening in silence. I went on: "You must know, too, that my husband adores his children and that since Bruno died, there are only the four of them. So for their sake, as well, I am asking you to go, to stop upsetting the family. Leave Lake Garda."

I wished she would fight back, refuse to go, defend herself. But instead she broke into convulsive sobs, shaking her head as if she could not bear to hear more. Exasperated by her weakness, I told her exactly what I was feeling: that I couldn't tolerate women who thought tears solved everything; that I thought it quite appalling of her to have deposited photocopies of my husband's more compromising letters in Switzerland and Germany; that she should never have agreed to a direct line between her villa and ours when recordings of all conversations were sent to Berlin; and, finally, that she was obviously incapable of caution, seeing that she had even formed contacts with unreliable people.

Still she said nothing. I caught hold of her arm and shook her till she spoke. "The Duce loves you, Signora. I have never said an unkind word about you. He would not have tolerated it, because he loves and respects you."

I could not help pitying her. Out of her depth in such

a situation, she'd only her unrequited love for Benito to urge her on. All anger left me, and now I remembered her courage when Benito was arrested on July 25. Badoglio, now our common enemy, had even imprisoned her in Novara. So I begged her: "If that's how it is Signora, why don't we both try, together, to do something to help my husband at such a difficult time.

She got up, went upstairs and returned some moments later with a bundle of letters. Handing them to me, she explained: "Here are 32 letters your husband sent me." I could see in a glance that they were only typed copies. Then I completely lost my temper. I shouted at her. I told her just how seriously she was compromising Mussolini by talking to him while the Germans listened in to their conversations, how the partisans and Allied spies were using her for their own gain.

Clara's sole reaction was to fall from one fainting fit into another while Buffarini bustled about with a bottle of cognac. She had only the strength to whisper that my husband could not live without her.

"That's not true," I protested. "My husband knows I'm here. Call him and ask."

She took up the challenge and heard him say: "Yes, I know my wife's there, but she's right. We must end it."

I got up, my eyes blazing, and fired my parting shot: "You will come to a bad end, Signora. They'll put you on the Piazza Loreto."

It was there, in Milan, that the Germans had executed Italian hostages as an act of reprisal, and there that the partisans had threatened to put us.

Outside in the darkness my friends were waiting in the rain. I went back to the Villa Petrinelli. My husband was still in his office at the Villa Orsolina. I sent word that I had returned home, having done no injury to Clara. Then I locked myself in my room and, for the first time in my life, I wanted to die.

Later I found out that Benito had 'phoned several

times. Finally, he wrote me a little note asking if I would agree to see him.

He spent hours trying to appease me, holding my hand, kissing me tenderly, begging me to forgive him. I'd won my husband back yet again, but I was sure he knew how close we'd been to disaster.

CHAPTER 8

Mussolini and money

Some time ago, I read in a newspaper that Mussolini's wife had collected jewelry and furs. I found this highly amusing since I've only ever owned a bracelet in my life. Even that we'd to sell in 1931 to pay back a loan from the bank. In any case, the very fact that I owned it was unusual, for we never made a habit of giving presents in the family. For special celebrations, Benito might receive a tie from the children and bring me a signed photograph of himself. Once, however, my brother-in-law Arnaldo bought his wife a bracelet and Benito felt obliged to give me something.

As for fur coats, I never possessed one. Whenever I attended social functions, I borrowed a coat from Edda. Hers were a little long for me, but I managed.

After the war there were endless anecdotes about the Mussolini fortune. If we'd cached money anywhere we would never have experienced such financial straits after Benito's death. When I returned to Rocca delle Caminate, I realised how deeply the myth had taken root, for the walls were in ruins, the gardens dug up and the wainscoting torn down.

Anyone who once thought, or still thinks, that Mussolini hid a fortune somewhere need search no longer. There is no Mussolini treasure to be tracked down either at the bottom of Lake Garda or anywhere else.

During its two years under the Duce, even the Salo Republic had its own economic structure and banking houses and functioned like any other State. The

Ministers didn't walk about with their pockets bulging with notes any more than my husband lugged the crown jewels about with him.

Once and for all, I can declare that Mussolini never received one scrap of his salary as Prime Minister during the 20-odd years he held office. He even refused his parliamentary pay – to the advantage of the Chamber of Deputies and their expense fund.

None of this was meant as an ostentatious sacrifice, nor did we have to live on thin air. My husband owned a successful newspaper, the *Popolo d'Italia*. He wrote articles for the foreign Press – more especially the American Press – and was highly paid. He also received handsome royalties for his books, some of which were even translated into Chinese.

This meant that we'd enough on which to live comfortably, more so when we resided in Rome. Despite Benito's protests, Prince Torlonia insisted that we occupied his villa for a paltry annual rent of one lira. The government provided our cars – apart from those the children, my husband and I had bought for our personal use.

We even accumulated some savings, with which we bought plots of ground in Romagna and Ostia and a villa at Riccione. Altogether my husband was offered several houses, including one in Naples, the Villa Roseberry (the gift of an English family and now the summer residence of the President of the Republic), another in Rome, the Villa Chiara (today a public park), and Rocca delle Caminate. Benito donated all these to the State, except Rocca delle Caminate because it was donated by the people of Ravenna and Forlí, each person had subscribed one lira towards the cost.

Any gifts or legacies which came his way were automatically assigned to charitable organisations or religious orders. In 1924, he decided that all the large sums which people paid to acquire an aristocratic title should also be made over to charity. Until then, such underhand dealings had lined individual pockets; now they had become official. Mussolini presented each case for the King's assent, since only the Crown could confer a title.

All this seemed so extraordinary that, after the Second World War, several commissions looked into Benito Mussolini's administration of public money. Giulio Andreotti, the recent Prime Minister, announced their findings in an interview published by the Leftist weekly *l'Espresso*, stating that Mussolini was innocent of any fraud in this area during his term of office.

My husband's disinterestedness arose simply from his belief that money was no more than a means of coping with one's needs. Over and above that it was a useless burden.

I must admit that this attitude created friction between us, for I rigidly hold the view that anyone who works deserves a wage. Therefore, I could not accept my husband's refusing his. But I could not change his basic nature. He'd always shown the same lack of self-interest, even as a young man.

When, for instance, he was looking for work in Switzerland in 1901, he was completely broke. Remembering that he'd kept one coin for a "rainy day", he went into a baker's took a loaf and held out his coin. The baker took the money but immediately pushed it away, muttering that he couldn't be fooled that way. Benito Mussolini's "coin" was no more than a nickel medallion of Karl Marx. "I didn't eat for another two days," laughed my husband, "until I managed to get taken on pushing stones in a wheelbarrow on a building site."

Later, in 1909, when Cesare Battisti appointed him editor of his paper in Trent, he was offered a salary of 75 lire a month. He actually replied that 50 lire would be enough to live on and the other 25 could go to the paper. He repeated this trick on me twice more after we'd set up house together. On the first occasion, when he edited the *Lotta di Classe* at Forlí, his salary was 120 lire a month but he gave 20 to the party. The second time was at *l'Avanti*, as I have already described.

When he was appointed head of government, he assumed that the office of Prime Minister was purely honorary. Guessing that he'd refused to accept his rightful salary, I took the precaution of saying: "That's all very well. You can do what you like, but I have a house to run and children to feed. Besides, some people on your paper are doing very nicely while I have to go without. I never worried while you lived in Milan but now that we are to live apart, I want a regular allowance from the paper for our expenses."

That was how I came to receive 6,000 lire a month. The newspaper also paid the rent, as well as for the car and the chauffeur's salary.

I was glad that I had this security after my first slightly disturbing trip to Rome in 1926. Benito had been living alone in the capital for four years and I in Milan with the children. When he came to see us he was very much the solid citizen and family man. But in Rome he behaved like a playboy, with his stylish clothes, his sports car and a puma on a lead to impress the ladies. When I opened the drawer of his bedside table and found 12,000 lire, I lost my temper. After a terrible scene, he explained that on receiving money, he just put it there for want of anywhere else. Previously he had given it to me. This incident served a purpose and was probably the origin of Arnaldo's attempt to persuade his brother to lead a more orderly life.

Once the family settled in Rome, Benito resumed his former practice of giving me a monthly sum for the housekeeping – about 15,000 lire, and anything else I might ask for. Like a true Latin, however, he never told me exactly what he earned.

Concerning the kind of life we led in Rome, I remember that on the day after the Duce was arrested – on July 26, 1943 – an officer approached the Villa Torlonia where I was still living. As I came in from the garden with my apron full of eggs and vegetables, he mistook me for the maid.

"I would like to visit the Mussolini house," he explained. "Will that be all right?"

"Of course," I replied, "I'll come with you."

I put down the eggs and vegetables and, as I showed him the way, asked him for news about the situation. He told me that Mussolini's wife had been arrested on the Duomo Square in Milan with a suitcase full of bank notes and jewelry. I pretended not to be interested and we continued on our way. In one of the rooms the officer noticed a photograph of my son Bruno and smiled.

"What a marvellous boy he was," he said. "Very simple and kind. We went to school together."

"Yes," I sighed. "He was a marvellous boy."

Perhaps the tone of my voice gave me away, for the officer stopped, looked me closely in the face and said: "But who are you? Are you one of the family?"

"Yes, I'm Bruno's mother, Signora Mussolini."

He grasped my hands, kissed them, and asked me to forgive him for what he'd said about my arrest in Milan. "I never thought I'd meet the Duce's wife with an apron round her waist. If anyone had told me, I wouldn't have believed them," he kept saying. "And I was sure Mussolini's house was a palace full of magnificent furniture. There's nothing luxurious here. It's like anyone else's house."

He seemed almost disappointed, but perhaps he was also glad to discover the truth; for when he left he was obviously affected by his visit and asked if he might kiss me.

There were hundreds of other examples of this kind. But we couldn't arrange conducted tours of our house, open cupboards and drawers and say to the world: "You can see how simply we live. We're not *nouveaux riches*, you know." As far as we were concerned, our life was quite ordinary – the way we had lived it since we were young.

Incredibly enough, one of Benito Mussolini's greatest delights on becoming head of government was to be able to change his sheets every two or three days. One morning he said to Irma, the maid: "And yet it would be wonderful to be able to change them every day."

G

The exterior of the Villa Torlonia was attractive, if a bit solid. Standing in the residential part of the via Nomentana, the grounds were vast, with a great variety of plants which grew so thick and fast that it was like a forest. There were also large greenhouses and a charming little antique theatre.

I was disappointed by the house's interior. Admittedly, it was large, but there was so much wasted space, so many nooks and crannies, so many useless little rooms. Every time I entered a room I collided with a pillar. The furniture was dark and heavy and, quite frankly, in Benito's room it was black and ugly. But my husband would not interfere because it was not our property; by no means was Prince Torlonia to be annoyed. Gradually, I managed to change things, starting with the chairs. I disliked to see them broken by Germano, one of my nephews, who damaged them every time he came to see us.

Commandeering the help of relatives and friends from Romagna, over a period of months we modified the whole building – from the plumbing to the decorations – until the villa was cosy and pleasant to live in.

On the ground floor, there was a large reception room where we watched films in the evening. It was a lovely, high-ceilinged room, with two wide staircases leading up each side to a pillared gallery on the first floor. The children found the design particularly useful when I chased them to scold them for some naughtiness, for they had two escape routes to choose from.

On the same floor were smaller reception rooms – each dotted about with candelabra – and the rooms the children made their work area. Vittorio produced his first newspaper there. A delightful feature was that the rooms opened onto the grounds through large bays and French windows.

The first floor contained the oval dining-room and our bedrooms – my husband's in the right wing, with a bathroom and study; mine in the left wing, but communicating with his through a dressing room.

On the top floor the children's rooms occupied the left wing, while the linen room and the staff quarters were in the right.

Our way of life had changed since the days in Milan. Vittorio and Bruno were growing fast and Edda was by now a young lady, whose boy friends already gave us trouble. After a romance with a young Jew, whose life and whose father's life she saved during the war, she was almost engaged to a young man from Forlí, called Orsi Magelli. But the betrothal collapsed after a private talk with my husband.

"Duce," he said, "I'd like to speak to you about the dowry."

"What dowry?"

"Your daughter's dowry, Duce."

"But she hasn't got one, any more than her mother had."

Edda never saw him again and on April 24, 1930, she married Galeazzo Ciano, whose father Constanzo, an admiral with a distinguished record, was one of my husband's closest friends and his only official successor.

I had a larger house to run and while I could elude public life in Milan, in Rome I had to remember that I was the wife of the head of government. I had less freedom of movement, though I managed to create my own little Romagna in the grounds – with hen-houses, rabbit hutches and even some pigs.

My husband's pattern of life had also changed. After 1929, he became a family man again and stopped the minor eccentricities of his years alone in Rome. On Sundays, the family would drive out to Ostia or into the mountains. During the week, we sometimes went to the theatre or the opera. But, unlike the children, we were not free to go to the cinema. First, we had to contend with the security police, who followed us everywhere, and then with the frenzy which greeted Benito's public appearances. Early on he'd enjoyed it, but eventually it began to pall.

I remember several stories to confirm this. Once on the way to his office in the Palazzo Venezia, he stopped his car at the top of the via Nazionale. His escort of three policemen in the car behind had no time to intervene before he was on the pavement, calmly walking down the street and enjoying his sense of freedom. His "guardian angels" were helpless, not daring to press too close to get him back into his car. He continued on his way as if it was the most normal thing in the world.

After a while the passers-by began to wonder if they were seeing things or, more daringly, to call his name and move to shake him by the hand. Benito was forced to stop. Suddenly there was a crush of people reaching to touch him, cheer him, kiss him. When he told me about it I could see that he'd been really frightened, not of an attempt on his life but of the surging torrent of people. There is no knowing what would have happened to him if the police had not interfered. He never repeated the experiment.

Twice during the holidays, we tried to evade our security guard. One day in 1933 we went, just the two of us, to la Fratta – a small town between Forlimpopoli and Bertimoro – to see the thermal baths. At about 1.30 in the afternoon, we parked the car to continue our way on foot – still without our guard. While waiting for Professor Collitti, the Spa's director, we chatted quietly with the manager of the Godoli restaurant. I remember Benito was expressing his dislike of the theatre's frontage (which he thought badly built), when the police descended on us, starting pandemonium which had previously not existed.

"So, they've found us," my husband sighed. "Come on, Rachele, our walk is over."

Some days later, at Riccione, I suggested going for a romantic stroll on the pier. We'd only gone a couple of yards when we heard the plodding footsteps of the police behind. "You see," Benito said, "there's no point in trying. They'll always be on our tail. I can't relax knowing that some fellow's keeping me under his eye. I wonder if they're here to protect me or spy on me."

"To spy on you, you can be sure," I declared.

We found ourselves increasingly turning inwards

during our leisure time. Benito only really relaxed and became himself at home. And he built an impenetrable barrier between his private and public life.

In the fourteen years we spent at the Villa Torlonia, we invited no one whom the family didn't know intimately for a meal, whether they were Ministers, friends of my husband or important foreign visitors. The only people we usually entertained were friends of my sons. Even journalists and photographers were barred from the house. On the rare occasions when the villa's interior was filmed, Benito agreed only to the presence of the cameramen – because they were American – and even then he resented it. He once said: "When I go home and hang up my hat I become Signor Mussolini and nothing else. The Duce, the head of government, stays at the Palazzo Venezia."

I remember someone – Galeazzo Ciano, I think – asking him why he did not entertain at the Villa Torlonia. My husband replied: "Everyone already thinks I am Duce twenty-four hours a day. If I start believing it, too, I'll go mad. I must have a minimum of rest and quiet to clear my head and keep my identity. I'm not a robot and I'm not wedded to Italy. Hitler may have said he was married to Germany when I asked him why he didn't make one of his gorgeous lady admirers his wife. But I'm a normal man who wants respect for his privacy as well. Basically the English are right not to want strangers in their bedroom. It's a symbol of their private life. They're right and I'm like them."

CHAPTER 9

The minor mysteries of a dictator

My husband's day began about 6.30, when Irma woke him by drawing the curtains. He didn't loiter in bed, and while she was laying out his clothes he shaved and drank a glass of orange or grape juice. All this took no more than ten minutes or quarter of an hour. Then he went down into one of the reception rooms for a quick bout of gymnastics before going into the grounds to join Camillo Ridolfi, his fencing master since the duelling days and now riding master, as well as close intimate – a sort of confidential friend. Every morning Ridolfi came to the Villa Torlonia with three or four horses and depending on his mood, Benito would jump a series of fences or take a ride in the grounds. This never lasted more than half an hour at the most.

At about 7.30 he went up to his bathroom, took a shower, rubbed himself down with eau de cologne, put on the clothes Irma had laid out for him and went to the dining room to gulp down his breakfast – a meagre diet of wholemeal bread, milk with a dash of coffee and fruit. Often he would send Irma to ask if I wished to eat with him. But I usually answered that I couldn't because, already busy with the housework, I lacked the time.

I remember one day, after I had answered him in this way, how Irma came back to me, quite overwhelmed. Benito had confided to her: "You know, Irma, my wife is like that. But under her rough exterior she's a wonderful woman, a book telling a marvellous story. The trouble is that it won't open, so that you can't read what's written there."

When she passed on this comment I just grunted, but deep down I was very moved because he may have been right. And to be quite honest I think that, although he gave me a difficult time, I wasn't very easy to live with either.

I feel I ought to pass on a few anecdotes and some personal details about my husband's clothes and habits, if I am going to observe the rules of the game and really tell the truth about Mussolini.

I shall begin with his clothes. My husband never paid heed to whatever he wore. It was Irma who had charge of this side of his life. Every evening Benito's personal secretary gave her a list of his appointments and public appearances for the next day, together with the uniform, decorations and civilian suits he ought to wear for the occasion. If Irma had ever made a mistake he might quite easily have gone to a military ceremony in a dark suit or received an important foreign visitor in uniform, which would certainly have caused a sensation. But both Benito and I had complete confidence in her and we never had cause to regret it. I still recall how panic stricken she grew when she'd to make a choice from among the fifty uniforms and formal suits in my husband's wardrobe.

The only items of dress in which he took a keen interest were shoes and gloves and, in the early days, hats. Benito was noted for the original headwear he sported and which often bore no relation to anything else he happened to be wearing. It was his personal touch, his reaction against convention. So, he might choose to dress in a bowler hat and a riding habit or a Basque beret and a dark suit with a stiff collar. But as the years passed, he began to pay more regard to established rules, keeping the hats – which amused the children so much – for holidays at Rocca delle Caminate.

The white spats which he was so fond of also disappeared. These, incidentally, had a story of their own. In

January 1922, when my husband went to Cannes to cover an international conference as editor of the *Popolo d'Italia*, he also called on Aristide Briand, whom he greatly admired. However, just before his interview with the French statesman, he noticed that his shoes were somewhat dirty. Resourcefully he resolved the problem by resorting to fashion, hurriedly buying a pair of spats to conceal most of his shoes. Appreciating their practical use, he started to wear them quite a lot – so much so that it was hard convincing him that in certain cir- cumstances he should leave them off.

Benito used to wear his shoes without laces "so as to save time when I put them on", and to ensure comfort, always one size larger than he needed. Later he began to wear zip-sided boots because an old wound in his right leg, dating from the First World War, caused him pain. One of these boots is above his tomb. The par- tisans opened the sole to see if anything was hidden there.

Being very practical, when he liked a pair of shoes he would refuse to throw them away. In 1930, I think, I had to have one pair resoled four times simply because he felt good in them.

He also had a weakness for gloves. He had quite a collection of them, given by Italian tradesmen par- ticularly in Milan and Rome. But his favourite were the doeskin and soft leather ones. The others made of pec- cary, wool and so on stayed in his drawers for years.

There have been many unlikely tales about Mus- solini, one of which would have one believe that he used to pour pints of eau de cologne into his bath. To start with, he seldom took baths, but almost always showers. And then, he would never have indulged in this kind of eccentricity because he was far more down to earth than he was made out to be.

On the other hand, he did take particular care of his body, as much for hygienic reasons as for dandyism, though that is not strictly the word I am looking for. He went regularly to the dentist and every Thursday he received a manicure and pedicure. He always said that he couldn't tolerate a man whose hands were uncared for, and an ingrowing toenail made regular chiropody essential. And as I have already explained every morning he rubbed himself down with eau de cologne. When I teased him about it, he replied that if he didn't keep his body in perfect condition women would not like him any longer and a man who was no longer attractive to women was worthless. This scarcely tended to put me in a good humour for the rest of the day.

Because they have become legendary, I would like to set the record straight on two small points relating to the Duce's physical appearance and enormous vigour. Comment has been rife about my husband's Roman-style head and about the mischievous pleasure he derived from rushing up stairs four steps at a time, leaving a whole procession of generals and other dignitaries puffing in his wake.

The fact is that my husband shaved his head because he was losing his hair. According to him, after he wore a helmet during the First World War his hair began to drop out. For a while he convinced himself that, by using various lotions, he could prevent this deterioration or even, perhaps, grow more hair. Each morning he cast a critical eye to see what effects, if any, these lotions were yielding. When, after some weeks, there were no positive results, he finally decided on a drastic course: he shaved his head completely. Thus was born the Duce's image in the manner of a Roman emperor. I must admit that it suited him well enough, but the ones who got the greatest pleasure from it were our children and later our grandchildren, for they discovered their favourite pastime – playing with my husband's wart.

The origin of the staircase sprints dates from the day Benito found himself stuck in a lift. After this mishap, he had reservations about such contrivances and preferred to walk up stairs. And, so did all who were with him for they dared not do otherwise. I must confess that he enjoyed watching them puff and blow, for it was his desire that the whole nation should engage in some kind of sporting activities.

To return to his routine, each morning Benito left the Villa Torlonia at about eight o'clock with two or three security officers in a second car. His chauffeur, for a long time Ercole Borratto – about whom I shall have more to say – reached the Palazzo Venezia within minutes, for the traffic police changed all the lights to green immediately they saw my husband's car.

When he arrived at the Palazzo Venezia, awaiting on his desk were all the reports from the Carabiniere, the police, the prefects and the party. Reading them quickly, it was his practice to make annotations with a large red or blue pencil which he used right down to the stub. If he needed to make other notes, he would frequently use the envelopes of letters he'd received, unsticking them to write on the back.

Next came his daily talks with the Ministers of the Interior and Foreign Affairs, the director-general of the police and, during the war, the army's chief of staff. In theory mornings were set apart for important inter- views, such as the reception of foreign governmental visitors or ambassadors; the afternoons, to less impor- tant visitors, parties, students, distinguished tourists or people from the provinces.

Thursday and Monday were the only days when my husband was not the first in the office: it was then, at ten o'clock, that he went to the Quirinal. About two he returned to the Villa Torlonia. As he left the Palazzo Venezia there would be a telephone call to our care- taker who, on seeing the car approach, would signal the house by ringing a bell. What followed was like a chain reaction. The cook would put the pasta in boiling water, a duty policeman (standing in an antechamber by the entrance) would descend the steps to open the front door and take the brief case which my husband always carried. It was still with him when he was executed on April 28, 1945.

Except on Thursdays and Saturdays, when we took lunch together, the children and I had always finished our meal by the time my husband arrived. We didn't leave him on his own, however, but kept him company during his meal.

Before sitting down at table, Benito glanced through the newspapers for some minutes in his study. He had a good command of French, English, German and Spanish which he had tried to teach. This review of the Press was always accomplished at the same speed as when he was in Forlí. With the customary red and blue pencils (which nobody was allowed to touch at home "because they are State property"), he ringed or underlined the passages which interested him. He kept the papers he had marked and threw the others down to the right of his chair – an indication that he didn't want them any longer; we could now destroy them.

Finding it beneficial to his health, my husband fasted on one day a week, maintaining this practice for several years. But when he did eat, it didn't take long – a few minutes at the very most.

An ulcer caused him pain from time to time. Due to that and the treatment his doctors prescribed, Benito drank only mineral water and milk. He didn't eat dishes with sauce or much meat, and his diet was composed of pasta, sometimes eggs, a lot of vegetables and fruit. Preferring his vegetables raw, he would eat them in a rather unusual way, mixing large quantities of all kinds in an enormous salad bowl. Near him stood a salt dish in which to dunk the salad before eating it.

When Benito had to attend an official dinner, he would come and "pick" from our plates before he left, so that he would be less hungry when later he sat down to eat. He would say: "I can't eat with some fellow standing behind me, watching my every move and taking away my plate before I've finished. It makes me lose my appetite."

Once, after tucking his napkin into his collar, he brought a horror-struck silence to the King's table. "When I eat," he told me, "I like to be comfortable. With all their fuss and bother, they make a real sweat of those few minutes. And then, how tedious it all is!"

I can still recall the smouldering expression on his

face when he first caught sight of the butler we had hired at home. The man had stood there, spotless in white jacket, waiting to serve us. "I'll end up eating a sandwich in my room," he grumbled glancing ominously at this imposing figure. Happily, he soon got used to it, and for over ten years we possessed our own butler.

Benito relaxed at home with the family until four o'clock. When the weather was bad, the children dragged their father off to play billiards or maybe he and I went into his study for a chat. From experience, I found it the ideal time to get his acceptance to a costly bill, to plead a cause or wring some agreement out of him. There were the children's problems to talk about, too. The youngest boy, Romano, had his work cut out trying to explain why he didn't always do well at school. His brothers also had their difficulties, particularly when they came home with low marks for mathematics, because Benito was emphatic about the importance of that subject. But we always settled everything in the end, even the time when Romano, rather than show his report card, hit on the idea of forging his father's signature. At his first attempt he made a mess of the "M" in Mussolini and crossed it out to start again alongside.
"Do you suppose the Duce makes mistakes when he signs his own name?" his teacher scoffed, for he wasn't deceived.

If the weather was fine, my husband liked to walk in the garden. He would put a mint leaf behind his ear and stroll down the paths. In the vegetable garden he picked peas, beans and radishes and wiped them before eating them just as they were. Or he would visit our menagerie, for quite often we were given wild animals which we housed there. Fortunately, we didn't have to find accommodation for all of them at once, and usually they stayed with us only a matter of weeks – two or three months at the most – before going to zoos in Rome or Milan. The only animals which we kept permanently were dogs and cats.

Apart from Pitini, a dog which Vittorio brought back from Abyssinia, we owned Charlie, a marvellous mongrel which stayed with us for seventeen years, I think, and which had the intelligence not to bark because it disturbed my husband. Charlie had been a family celebrity since the day when, while we were still in Milan, Vittorio and Bruno had invented a pedigree for him after a neighbour asked what species of dog he was.

"He's a spangled dog," Bruno replied.

"Ah, I know," exclaimed the man, "that's a great breed, the spangled."

We never knew which one was taking a rise out of the other.

There was also Brock, a Canadian dog, and some cats, one of them given to my husband by a female admirer, the wife of a distinguished and elderly aristocrat.

When it came to wild beasts, we had, in succession, a couple of lions, "Ras" and "Italia", which were particularly affectionate towards the Duce and delighted us by producing three adorable cubs; then a jaguar, a lovely royal eagle, the monkey "Coco" (who remained for some time), a stag, two gazelles, a falcon, some parrots, a few canaries and two adorable ponies which had come straight from England.

Sometimes, however, I did not appreciate these leisure hours at all. This was during the "football period" when Vittorio, Bruno, and their father used to play with a ball after lunch. From the moment I saw my husband take off his jacket I trembled for the windows. And with good reason, for Benito came in quite regularly looking rather sheepish and having heralded his arrival with the noise of breaking glass. "You know, Rachele," he would say, "I didn't do it on purpose. I was aiming at Bruno and the shot went crooked. But don't worry, the glazier will come. We've already told him."

Then to try and wring a smile out of me, he would add: "The glazier likes us. He's working with us. Besides we have to stimulate the national economy. Glaziers must work like anyone else."

"One day I'll come and break the panes of your Palazzo Venezia, you'll see."

"All right. But be careful of the windows on the right, they're mine."

I was happier when they gave up lunchtime football for tennis. Even so, soccer still remained one of the family's favourite sports; so much so that Vittorio organised inter-class matches in an arena, with his school friends. These taxed the over-worked security forces, even more, but my husband would not budge an inch; my sons' friends, he ordered, could come to our house even if it was the Duce's residence.

One must not imagine that the Mussolini family spent all their leisure hours in sport, sport and still more sport. My husband and I also had our moments of privacy during the day – after lunch, to be precise. Then, like two school children, we would slip away quietly to the terrace steps. Because Benito always felt the cold keenly, we stayed in the sunshine, under an old fig tree which listened to our secrets. If that tree had the power of speech, I'm sure it would have plenty to say. There we settled our small marital problems. Benito also told me his news, both good and bad, and I in turn revealed any disturbing rumours about the activities of various Fascists, Ministers or not. For it was common knowledge in the family that I was the secret agent, the arch sleuth.

One day, hearing us laughing, the children asked to know the reason for our amusement, but we refused to tell them for fear they told their friends that Benito Mussolini had just entertained me for some minutes with his impressions of a Japanese Minister who was then in Rome with a delegation. He had called on my husband that very morning and Benito had regaled me with details of the interview. "Think of it," he said, "for nearly half an hour I had to strain myself to avoid laughing. Several times I was startled during his speech, when the Minister shouted in a shrill voice: Kokode!

Kokode! or something of the sort. And somehow I got it into my head when I heard this cry that he was going to lay an egg. It's stupid, but the more I reasoned with myself, the more I felt like giggling."

On another day he described the chaos the American child prodigy Jackie Coogan, the famous "Kid" of the Charlie Chaplin films, caused at the Palazzo Venezia. "At the end of his visit," he explained, "he asked me for a signed photograph, and so I took one and wrote on it: 'Benito Mussolini – to the greatest of the little men.' He promised to send me one of himself for the children."

It was beneath that fig tree that my husband broke the sad news of my inevitable separation from the children during the Abyssinian war, and then from Bruno in the Spanish Civil War. It was also there that we assessed the chances of our daughter Anna–Maria when she was gravely ill in 1935; there, too, that Benito told me of his anxieties before the Second World War.

Not long after, Benito went back to the Palazzo Venezia about four o'clock. Irma had some milk taken to him, for it was his habit to drink it in the afternoons. As I have already mentioned, at this time of the day his schedule was less tight and, while he ate some fruit he liked to watch the traffic from behind the windows of his office. What fascinated him was the policeman in white gloves who marshalled the hundreds of cars on the Piazza Venezia with his gestures. "If you only knew, Rachele," he once said enthusiastically, "it's really wonderful. Sometimes he makes grand sweeps over his head like a robot, and at particular moments he creates a kind of unspoken sympathy between himself and the drivers. He uses a discreet little gesture behind his back to signal them to go forward, to pass, to wait. On this level it becomes an art."

Having learnt that the Duce took an occasional interest in the traffic on the Piazza Venezia, the police authorities hastened to assign officers who were particularly proficient and brought a military bearing to the duties. Everybody benefited from it: the traffic, the

Morning ride at Villa Torlonia (Radio Times Hulton Picture Library), Mussolini with his violin, (Radio Times Hulton Picture Library), Mussolini's office at the Palazzo Venezia. (Keystone).

(above) *Mussolini and Rachele rowing* (Keystone), *(left)* *Donna Rachele in the 30's* *(right)* *Mussolini on his motorcycle in 1932* (Syndication International).

drivers, the tourists who used to gaze in wonder at the sight – and my husband.

At nine in the evening he came home to the Villa Torlonia. Eating his dinner as quickly as his lunch, Benito would have vegetable soup, sometimes a little meat or some eggs, vegetables and fruit. In the evening our practice was to remain at the table chatting for a few minutes while the film projector was set up in the great drawing room. In fourteen years at the Villa Torlonia, this routine only changed a dozen times or so; then there had to be a worthwhile reason – like Edda's marriage, for instance. After that celebration I decided that any similar functions must be held elsewhere but not at home. It created such turmoil and the house felt even emptier after all the excitement and the departure of a child. Sometimes the routine was varied for an eminent visitor like Gandhi, Chamberlain, Hitler and Laval, or finally, because of the War.

Other than that, the routine was inflexible. After dinner we would watch a film in the great drawing room where everyone gathered, including the staff. There would be no question of protocol: indeed, my husband used to sit in an armchair at the back of the room chatting quite naturally with all and sundry. I remember we had two relations who disliked each other intensely. One day Benito mischievously called both of them over to him and deliberately put one next to the other. He then awaited results. Now and again during the film he gave me a sly nudge, drawing my attention to the way they were taking furtive glances at each other and scowling. Quite sensibly, they patched up their quarrel in the end.

The programme started with news reels. My husband was intrigued by the foreign ones and for this reason he arranged for the projectionist to show documentaries about the Soviet army and the occupation of Poland which he'd secured from Vittorio or other people. I believe it was while he was watching these films in 1940 that he came closer to deciding finally about Italy's pro-German entry into the war in June 1940.

He also interested himself in Italian documentaries produced for foreign markets, wishing to make certain that his country was given the correct image. On his instructions several were shelved.

Finally came a feature film, the choice of which didn't concern him. If it was a comedy or based on history I was sure he'd stay till the end; or, indeed, if Greta Garbo was the star. He would then be attentive and quick to show his appreciation. But if the film lacked appeal, he never threw his shoes at the screen or blamed the projectionist from the Luce Institute; instead he would get up and tiptoe out.

While Irma was tidying his clothes, he invariably drank a glass of milk or camomile tea, then went to bed and fell asleep in a matter of minutes. Nothing would wake him until morning – not even the air raids, as I later saw for myself at Gargarno. To complete the whole picture, I can even state that Mussolini never snored.

CHAPTER 10

Never 13 at table

Like anyone else, Benito Mussolini had his petty obsessions. He could not bear illness, for example, either in himself or in others.

One day a maid began to cough. I saw him frown and it was not long before he said: "Let her go and rest. I don't want to hear her coughing in the house."

It required a great deal of effort on my part to convince him that it was not serious, and the poor woman avoided him for several days because every time he saw her he glared at her.

It was the same with the children if he himself had a cold. He would then barricade himself in his room and expressly forbid them to go in. "I don't want to see you," he would cry. "If you have something to tell me you can say it through the door."

On the other hand, if his illness was not contagious, he ordered them to keep him company and read the newspapers to him. And woe betide the one who stumbled over a name.

The only person who was exempt from this treatment was myself. So that I should not be left alone when I was ill, he had a table put in my room and ate all his meals with me, whether or not there was any risk of contagion.

Dictator though he was, my husband was obedience itself in the hands of his doctors. However much he might curse them and their medicines, whenever they were in his presence he accepted everything without grumbling and even agreed to replace the night shirt he usually wore with a fine pair of pyjamas.

As well as the authority of the medical profession, he also respected the influence of the "jettatore" or people with the evil eye. For like every Mediterranean, Benito Mussolini was superstitious.

He would never sit down at table if the total number of guests – including himself – was thirteen. On Sundays, at home, he made certain of checking the numbers himself. And quite often one of the children – usually Romano or Anna-Maria – would be banished to eat in the kitchen when there were guests. In the same way he would never start on anything important on a Friday and it was quite usual for him to put his right hand over a specific part of his body, even in public, to ward off bad luck.

As I have just said, he was particularly scared of people with the "evil eye". One of his colleagues at the *Popolo d'Italia* had this reputation. Benito liked him well enough but in the end he politely made it quite clear to him that he would rather not see him too often.

I teased him but I must admit that, by some disturbing coincidence, on several occasions when this man had come to the house there were small mishaps, lamps shattering, a coffee pot exploding, plates breaking without anyone having touched them. Then my husband would exclaim: "You see. I told you so. He has the evil eye."

There were a number of distinguished people whom he agreed to meet only because there was no alternative. On one occasion, for example, he had to visit the King of Spain, Alfonso XIII, who was in Rome. But this monarch was also reputed to be a "jettatore". Everywhere he went, so they said, disaster followed: bridges collapsed, chandeliers fell down, and so on.

On the way home, Benito warned his chauffeur to be especially careful and did not stop worrying until the following day when he thought the effects of Alfonso's evil eye must have worn off.

The boys laughed at all this until the day when

110

Romano, the most superstitious member of the family, found a piece of gilded porcelain in the shape of a crescent. He got it into his head that it was a lucky charm and every time he played cards with Vittorio or Bruno he held it in his hand. Despite this, he consistently lost the game. He therefore gave it to one of his friends who, when he had found it equally useless, in turn gave it to another school friend. After going all round the class, the charm came back to Romano. One day he suggested to his brothers that they should try an experiment. During a game of cards they took it in turns to hold the piece of porcelain and, to their astonishment whoever was holding it always lost. They had to agree that there was something odd about it.

As well as being superstitious, my husband also believed in ghosts. And so did I. In fact I still do believe in them, just as I am sure that one sometimes has premonitions. I've had them and they've always come true.

My children used to laugh at me when I told them that as a child I had seen ghosts at Salto one evening. I explained how my sisters and I had heard singing and got up. Pressing our noses to the window panes we had seen men with long beards, in white shirts, staring at us in the dark. We weren't afraid because they didn't look harmful and for a while we heard strange music coming from the yard. I'm still convinced that they were ghosts.

Benito nodded his agreement whenever I said that there really were ghosts. Sometimes he and I attended spiritualist seances, both in Romagna and in Rome. One evening a table walked round the room, over-turning everything in its path, and another time, at the Villa Torlonia, we witnessed something quite extraordinary. Prince Giovanni Torlonia had summoned up the spirit of his mother, which said: "As soon as I disappear, Giovanni, violets will flower on the table." And immediately afterwards a scent of violets pervaded the table in front of us.

In Romagna there are a great many houses which are said to be haunted. One of them, which stands on the road from Forlí to Predappio, was inhabited for a long time. Each resident left after hearing a mysterious musician playing the violin in the night.

Rocca delle Caminate also had this reputation and Benito was very impressed that I wasn't afraid to sleep there alone. "How do you do it?" he said. "Aren't you afraid? I couldn't."

"But the spirits are friendly," the caretaker replied. "I often hear music in the night myself. So I sit myself down on the stairs and listen. They've never bothered me."

Spirits were once the cause of a fine rumpus at Rocca delle Caminate. It happened in 1927 during the course of additions to the house. The Admiralty were installing a beacon on the top of the tower which would be lit every night, and the work had been assigned to a group of soldiers led by an officer.

Unfortunately, they, too had heard stories about the ghosts. Moreover, they'd been told that a house a few hundred yards away was also haunted. So they sent for a peasant woman who informed them that to get rid of the ghosts they would have to heat a cauldron of water and plunge a black cat into it. Then they had to throw the water round about the house.

Acting on her advice, they took a cauldron, filled it with water and boiled it. When everything was ready, they thrust in the black cat they had caught. Needless to say, it was not the cat's idea of a joke. With a tremendous leap into the air, it dashed away shrieking – literally like a scalded cat.

The soldiers also ran, certain that the ghosts would take their revenge. Some days later a fresh contingent arrived, presumably less superstitious, for they stayed until the work was finished.

There was another aspect of Mussolini's character which might seem surprising. He was convinced that anything which got off to a bad start could not be put right. That is why he was very shaken when, on June 18, 1940, scarcely a week after Italy had entered the war, the plane carrying Italo Balbo was mistakenly shot down by a burst of anti-aircraft fire from the Italian ship *Sangiorgio*. He was convinced that it was a bad omen and used to reflect on it from time to time.

Much later, just before July 25, 1943, when Vittorio, Romano and I were urging him to take some action against his enemies and, at the end, on April 28, 1945, to take refuge somewhere, he invariably replied with a disenchanted smile: "There's nothing more to be done. I must follow my destiny to the very end."

CHAPTER 11

Mussolini and Gandhi

Perhaps my husband's idea of governing the country was a trifle unorthodox, but it was certainly extremely effective. As far as he was concerned, the only things that mattered were action and results. He didn't care if the means were out of the ordinary. His tools of the trade were the telephone, the aeroplane, direct contact with the public and his presence at the grass roots, even if it meant spending hours in the harvest fields, bare-chested among the peasants.

His practical approach came into conflict with various eminent archeologists in Rome, but he paid no attention to them.

On one occasion, for example, he drove them to despair over the construction of the first subway line in Rome. My husband had given instructions for the work to push forward fairly quickly because he wanted to build a new city, the EUR, on the fringe of the capital. His aim was to organise a huge exhibition there in 1942 to commemorate twenty years of Fascism in Italy. At one point, however, the workers were held back by the discovery of some ruins and from then onwards the whole project came to a halt. There followed a succession of meetings between the engineers and the archeologists to decide what ought to be done.

Finally my husband intervened, instructing that the ruins should be ignored and the work resumed. To the horrified archeologists, he observed that respect for the

115

past was undeniably commendable – but a country's progress imposed certain sacrifices.

"They accuse me of disliking museums," he said. "It's not true, but I'd be happier if they contained more standards captured from the enemy than antique statues. We always want to live off our past. Why shouldn't we ourselves build for future generations? Whether we're capable of it or not, we'll only know by trying."

Even on the personal level, it was this same practical approach which guided him. I remember once, when he was already head of government and I myself still lived in Milan, he tried to convince me that women in Rome were currently wearing their hair tomboy style, or cut very short. I had little enthusiasm for it and stubbornly continued to brush my hair into a chignon or wear plaits at the side. One day as I was passing the barber's saloon where Benito was being shaved, he called me. On going in, he asked me to come closer ostensibly to whisper in my ear. I leaned forward, quite unsuspectingly, and suddenly, while he was murmuring some trifle, he cut off one of my plaits with one clip of the scissors. I had no alternative but to do the same with the other. I was furious, but he had got what he wanted.

One morning in the Palazzo Venezia, he received a report that the milk supplied to schools, hospitals and nurseries by a particular co-operative was watered down. He ordered an inquiry at once to find out the people responsible. Because proceedings were still dragging on to no effect, he made a decision which astounded everybody – that is, all except myself because I knew his temperament. Since no-one was prepared to confess, he sacked the co-operative's entire staff, from the porter to the director.

Already I have mentioned several times I was compelled to have the same pair of shoes resoled because he felt comfortable in them. His attitude to dress generally was very much in keeping. If his clothes were still in good condition but no longer fitted him, he saw no reason why they shouldn't be made into suits for the children. Therefore Irma, a skilful dressmaker, cut clothes for the boys out of their father's suits for some years.

My husband's ideas about his tailor were also in character. Galeazzo Ciano once suggested that, as head of the government, he should now go to a well-known tailor. Benito answered scornfully that his present man gave satisfaction and he didn't see why he ought to change. "When I go out, I don't walk about with a board on my back saying where I buy my clothes," he added.

For him the most practical answer won the day. Furthermore, he realised that his presence was an incentive to production. Therefore if he had to go into the field, he went.

One notable instance was in 1933 – the year of the famous "wheat war". Italy had always imported an excess of grain and produced a surplus of rice, which the inhabitants of some areas refused to eat. He therefore decided to step up the production of corn and absorb the excess rice.

Having introduced his plan in the previous year, he sometimes spent several hours daily in the fields reclaimed from the Pontine Marshes, working bare-chested among the peasants. In the evening he collected his wages like the others – three lire, I think. Surprisingly enough, he was really happy when he came home with his few lire. As an incentive, he instituted special honours and competitions and danced with the peasant women who were good workers.

This behaviour may seem childish now, but it was effective at the time. And by the end of 1933, the struggle for grain had been won. That year 179,805 hundredweight of cereals were imported as against 1,091,866 the year before. I found these figures in the newspapers.

He then had to absorb the surplus rice and persuade the Italians to eat it. His strategy hinged on an official Press campaign, with the alliance of the medical profession: he knew that people would listen to the advice of a doctor. Referring to the successful technique of an earlier campaign at a Fascist medical congress held in Rome in 1932 for the consumption of grapes, he explained that rice was not – as was thought – an exclusively poor people's diet, but an energy-giving form of nourishment which had sustained Italian soldiers in the First World War. He asked the doctors to carry this message into Italian homes, as well as explaining to Italian women that pregnancy would not make them ugly – as they might fear – but the very reverse.

Parallel with this, he organised a vast national campaign to demonstrate the different ways in which rice could be eaten. He equipped thirty coaches as mobile kitchens, carrying young women to the various centres to cook rice in public and offer it for free tasting. He himself declared that if every family ate a small amount the surplus would soon be absorbed. And that is what happened. In a few weeks, it had all gone. Ironically, the areas which were resistant to rice, consume the most even to this day.

On the other hand, his schemes of a practical nature didn't always achieve what they set out to do; for instance when he tried to start a one-way system for pedestrians on the pavements. From his window in the Palazzo Venezia he had gazed on the jostling crowds in the streets at rush hours. To him the endless pushings and shovings were pointless, and so he decided to create a one-way system for the pavements to enable the human stream to flow faster. But the outcome was disastrous, and one day I told him about the public reaction as it had reached my ears. People were saying: "Now he wants us to walk in a queue like geese."

He was no more successful when, keen to focus importance on family life and to create an atmosphere conducive for its expansion, he officially ensured harsh punishments for men who beat their wives. During activities as a "secret agent" in Predappio, I heard the objections that were being raised. "That lunatic in the government wants to deprive us of all our rights," was the usual comment. "If we're not allowed to beat our wives any longer, what have we left?" Benito burst out laughing when I reported these comments.

In all fairness, it was he who created virtually all the motor-racing competitions which are still run in Italy. He never hesitated to make a tour of the circuit behind the wheel of a racing car. Indeed, he found it an enjoyable combination of the useful and the pleasurable – like the day when in 1930, he opened the first autorail between Rome and Riccione to boost the railways. The previous day he'd said to me: "I've not forgotten that I promised you a long time ago that we should have a honeymoon one day. Well, this is it, we'll go tomorrow." And seeing my amazement he added: "You'll come with me on the first autorail and we'll go to Riccione. Not only will it be free, but you'll have your own special driver – your husband."

The next day, just as he had said, he made everybody get off the train, ordered the proper driver to sit on another seat, put on a cap and remained at the controls all the way to Riccione. I don't think many heads of government can boast of having driven an autorail. My husband did, and to great effect.

I could write a whole book of anecdotes of this kind, but I am sure that to relate them in quantity would become tedious. I would, however, like to say that the winter sports resorts in Italy, the beaches on the Adriatic coast (particularly at Riccione) and at Ostia, and the Italian spas were either promoted or developed by my husband.

At Terminile, a ski resort, which my husband and I literally discovered, we had some fantastic times. No matter the effort, Mussolini was determined to promote skiing and promote it he did. He devoted the same attention to Ostia, but this time popularised it by appearing more often in person, for people would rush to see the Duce bathing. In this respect, it was the same at Riccione, where we went for family holidays. The children and I always knew when Benito entered the water from the shouts we could hear. Eventually my husband had to arrange for part of the beach to be private so that, in theory, he could get some peace. And once he was in the water, he swam as far as possible from the beach so that at least he left the non-swimmers behind. Even so, this didn't stop him coming home with lipstick marks on his arms and neck. It may seem implausible, but anyone who saw these frenzied scenes knows how Mussolini's presence could give a boost to some venture.

I remember another of his unconventional, but very logical and essentially practical decisions. It concerned the ancient rivalry between two parishes in Romagna – Castrocaro and Terra del Sole. Visitors had long since ceased to patronise Castrocaro's thermal baths and unfortunately for the people both the economy and the administration were controlled at Terra del Sole. This curious situation had fanned friction for over three centuries, ending only after my husband visited the area himself. Sending for surveyors to work out the precise half-way point between the two communities, he then marked the spot and announced that a new municipality embracing both towns was to rise there. The cemetery and the church would remain on Terra del Sole land, next door to the town hall and exactly opposite the registry office, which would be on Castrocaro land. "That way," he decreed, "you'll be married here and when you're dead you'll go there." And that is how it has been ever since.

Whenever my husband told me what he had been doing to promote a campaign or a town, he always said the same thing: "And now I must find something else."

Before ending this chapter, there are two interesting episodes I would like to describe. One of them is of a private nature and shows clearly how indifferent he was to souvenirs and presents, the other gives an idea of his way of helping people. In the second case the Duce's practical approach was overshadowed by the common-sense of a nun, the Mother Superior of a convent.

The first episode occurred in 1931. Some time before, my husband and I had visited the homes of the peasants who worked on the land we had bought after moving into Rocca delle Caminate. Their living conditions made a deep impression on Benito and he told me that something had to be done to improve them. So he asked Camillo Ridolfi to secure a bank loan so that the houses could be repaired and made a little more comfortable. He got the loan without any difficulty, a total of 300,000 lire – quite an appreciable sum in those days.

Benito promptly forgot all about the final settlement date and when the time came he hadn't enough money to pay it off. He could have earned it by writing for the foreign Press, especially the Americans who paid well. But either he didn't think of it or he hadn't the time. Moreover, in his dual position as Prime Minister and editor of a leading daily paper (which printed six or seven weekly publications as well), he could have raised this sum in one way or another. But there it was. My husband considered it a private matter to be settled privately.

One day, after thinking it over for hours, we decided to sell some of the many presents we'd received and which were now hoarded in a huge room – christened by Benito the "Chamber of Horrors" at Rocca delle Caminate. There was something of everything there: vases, carpets, knick-knacks, trays, pottery, pictures and so on. We were convinced that among that lot we would find more than enough to raise 300,000 lire.

The same evening a jeweller arrived from Forlí and we retired to the "Chamber of Horrors". It must have been an extraordinary scene, for there we were – the Duce, his wife and a jeweller, haggling like carpet sellers, judging the weight of things and evaluating every article from the smallest coffee spoon to the tiniest piece of Saxe porcelain. But it was no good, we couldn't accumulate 300,000 lire. Even a magnificent tray – the gift of the town of Genoa – which we'd been told was gold, turned out to be plate. "More junk," said Benito laughing. "Do you realise, Rachele, from all this we can't even raise 300,000 lire. When I think of all the time that must have been wasted in discussion before giving me these presents! And what do we find? That it's tinplate!"

Each discovery really amused him, but for my part I couldn't see the funny side of it at all. But we had to find a solution.

"Tell me, Benito," I said, "supposing you were to sell your decorations?"

"No, absolutely not. Never. Can you imagine what the Shah of Persia would say if he ever found out that Mussolini had sold the Order he sent him?"

"Wait, I've an idea. There's the bracelet you gave me."

Benito looked at me, hurt. "That's the only present I've ever given you."

"Well, you'll give me others. In any case, I'm not very fond of it and Augusta has one exactly the same."

"All right, go ahead."

So together with the sum raised from the glories of the "Chamber of Horrors", we now had enough to repay the loan.

The second incident took place in 1935, in a Franciscan convent. Perhaps I should start by explaining that when my husband visited the working-class areas of Romagna, he used to tell me – if I was going with him – to hand out discreetly a few notes to the needy. His commonsense told him that a gesture of this kind was more useful than fine words. And when I wasn't there, his secretary or the police commissioner escorting him fulfilled this mission. On this occasion Benito and I had gone to a little town near Rimini, accompanied by the Prefect of the province, to inspect some irrigation works.

While Benito was talking to the engineers, I went to a Franciscan convent which befriended destitute children. I had never forgotten the poverty of my childhood and was trying in my turn to lighten the burden of others. If every rich person could remember, even if only occasionally, the times of personal suffering – and everybody has had some unhappy experiences – I am sure there would be no more misery in the world.

When I was about to leave the convent, the Mother Superior took me by the arm and said: "Excellency,

Mussolini bathing at Riccione, June 1935.
(Keystone.)

(*above*) *Mussolini's birthplace in Pre-dappio,* (*right*) *Bruno with Gina Roberti at the announcement of their engagement,* (*below*) *the family together at the Villa Torlonia.* (Syndication International.)

couldn't you ask the Duce to come and see us before he leaves the town?"

"But Reverend Mother, he can't," I replied. "Your order forbids you to receive men in the convent."

"Come now, what's forbidden to others doesn't apply to the Duce. Ask him to come, we'll be happy to see him."

She was so emphatic that I had no choice but to agree and when I rejoined my husband I passed on the invitation.

"You're joking, Rachele," he said. "You know very well that a man may not enter a Franciscan convent. Do you want me to get into trouble with the Vatican, when everything's going so well. I'd like to come if only to please them because they make a real effort for the children, but I'll go no further than the door."

On reaching the outside of the convent we saw that the door was wide open and the Mother Superior was waiting for us. Benito and the Prefect were very surprised. What was more, in the courtyard refreshments were laid out.

At the end of his visit the Duce asked the Mother Superior if she needed financial help. When she answered in the affirmative, he turned to the Prefect, instructing him to arrange for a donation to be sent to the convent. At this juncture there was an even greater surprise. The Mother Superior murmured to the Duce that it would suit her much better to receive the donation there and then.

"But Reverend Mother," he replied, "we don't have that sort of money on us."

"Couldn't you give me a cheque then?"

"I haven't a cheque on me either."

"And what about his honour the Prefect?"

Astounded, my husband turned to the Prefect, who put his hand in his pocket and brought out a cheque book. The Duce told him the amount, the Prefect signed the cheque and gave it to the Mother Superior. "Now, will you please tell me why you've been so insistent on having it straight away when you can't do anything with it?" my husband asked, slightly angry.

"To start with, Duce, don't you worry about our cashing the cheque. We'll get round that somehow. As to why I insisted, that's simple. With you, we can be sure of getting the money, but with the government one never knows."

"And who'd think these holy women have no contact with daily life and know nothing about the workings of government," my husband commented in amusement, glancing at the Prefect who was still clasping his cheque book.

Through personal publicity and by promoting new ventures himself – in a way, incidentally, that nobody could ignore even if they didn't always agree – my husband was achieving the aims he'd pursued since 1922 when, returning from his first and only trip to London, he said: "If people want to see me now, well they have only to come to Rome."

He must have succeeded in this, for the other day I made some calculations. During his twenty years in power, he received 229,000 people, shook them by the hand, and talked to them individually or in groups. That comes to about 40 people a day.

It is all very well to say that Mussolini was a madman, a dictator, a good-for-nothing. I'd agree. But in that case he was not the only one. Forty to fifty per cent of those 229,000 were like him since they were not Italians and can't have hoped to gain by singing his praises after they had met him.

I can't recall all the names, but among them many foreign tourists came to visit Mussolini as they might the Coliseum or St. Peter's, and near public figures like Roosevelt's son and the Count of Paris, of whom my husband said later: "He doesn't seem very intelligent, but he has marvellous eyes." There were artists in every medium – painters, film-makers, writers, novelists; Walt Disney, for example, who brought a life-sized Mickey Mouse which could walk for Anna-Maria. When it came to political visitors, I need only say that the chief of them were all the Prime Ministers and heads of State of the day, not to mention the Ministers. They included Haile Sellassie, the Emperor of Ethiopia, to whom the Duce had given an aeroplane and even planned – as I can now reveal – to keep him on his throne after the Italian conquest. "I'll put a governor alongside him," he said.

Then, when the Emperor left his country, he added: "The English have urged him to run, for world-wide propaganda purposes. They're afraid we'll interfere with their Empire in Africa. It's not Ethiopia they're interested in, but the countries surrounding it."

There was also Mahatma Gandhi, who came to Rome in 1931 to attend a concert. As very seldom happened, my husband organised a reception in his honour, in the same huge room where we had our film shows. I can remember this visit quite clearly, not only because Gandhi was an unforgettable figure, but also because he was one of the men who made the biggest impression on the Duce – perhaps more than Hitler himself.

I can still see the faces of the society people who had also been invited. When Gandhi came into the room with his little goat on a lead, there was utter silence. Everyone was struck dumb, first by the few clothes the Mahatma was wearing and then by the goat. During the few days he spent in Italy, Gandhi and his goat were headline news.

At home, too, all conversation revolved around them, especially among the children. There were Gandhi's adventures (at the Coliseum, where the goat nearly dragged him away); the problems of protocol involved in keeping a watchful eye on the goat to protect the carpets (actually it was extremely well-trained); and people's astonishment on being confronted by a small half-naked gentleman with a little goat. They found it all very amusing and laughed so heartily that their father sharply rebuked them. "I want you to stop your jokes," he ordered them. "Don't you realise that the little man and his goat, whom you find so funny, are undermining the British Empire between them. Gandhi is a saint, a genius who is using a political weapon unheard of till now. And that is goodness."

Gandhi, on his part, was quick to pay tribute to Mussolini. Eventually, after hearing Mussolini's praises sung so often, I wondered how he managed to bewitch all these people – Italians or not. To discover his secret I even went to the length of hiding behind a half-open door at Rocca delle Caminate and listening to his conversation with a visitor.

This is what happened. This is how my husband's psychological tactics worked. His visitors would be left waiting in a reception room. When they were shown in Benito used to get up and stay behind his desk or walk forward to welcome them, depending on the circumstances. During these few seconds he would not take his eyes off the visitor, who, faced with this searching scrutiny, immediately became embarrassed and unnerved. Then Benito began to speak. He usually started with a few words of greeting, but soon came to the point of the interview and let the visitor have his say.

While he was speaking, Benito showed no sign of impatience. He never fiddled with his pencil or paperknife, never pulled at his shirt collar. Very relaxed, with his forearms resting on the desk, he used to listen, leaning his head a little to the left, frowning slightly and never taking his eyes off his visitor.

When he spoke my husband could be persuasive, mollifying or harsh as the occasion demanded, but his voice was always smooth, very warm, rather low and even a little shy.

And when the interview came to an end, he would administer the final blow in the shape of a warm clasp of the hands, a smile and a last spell-binding look.

All the commentaries I have been able to read, written after having met him, give the same impression that people surrendered to his charm. Even Churchill recognised that Mussolini could inspire sympathy and respect. In one of his volumes on the Second World War, he wrote: "On the two occasions in 1927 when I met Mussolini, our personal relations had been intimate and easy."

Hitler was not of the same opinion. He thought that

strength should be more in evidence than charm. He once said: "What a shame the Duce loses all the strength he generates during public speeches as soon as he has a private conversation. Then he turns into a charming man."

In public my husband was quite different. His low, well-modulated voice became harsh and clipped. I must admit that, for anyone who knew him well, he was more pleasant to listen to in private than in public.

Stories have been circulated about Mussolini practising before a mirror, as Hitler did, before he made a speech. This is absolutely untrue, for the simple reason that he began speaking in public when he was just sixteen. By the time he became head of government, he knew all the ropes. He could sense the mood of the crowd and when he wished, he could touch off the cheers, the shouts and the frenzy.

He knew exactly when to stop, throw his head back, thrust out his chin, put his hands on his hips or cross his arms. I believe it was a talent, and that there was a sort of invisible link between him and the crowd.

I became even more aware of it when, on September 18, 1943, he addressed the Italian people on the Radio Munich waveband, from a studio set up in the ground floor of the Karls Palst Hotel. I was quite close to him, I remember, and was trying to catch his eye as he spoke into the microphone. For I knew that having to speak into a vacuum without any contact with his audience, made him inarticulate. It was only while I was staring at him that he could think of me as a listener and regain his confidence.

There has been much criticism of Mussolini's delivery, of the grand ceremonial of the demonstrations, the tone he gave his régime. Agreed, but one has only to look at television, at the official demonstrations in democratic countries – in the United States, France, England and even in the USSR – and note the impressive public appearances their leaders make to realise that Mussolini's showy style was no great matter, all things considered.

Perhaps Mussolini may have been one of the first men to start a public relations programme. To this extent I would like to add, just for the record, that Mussolini's success had unexpected consequences. His books were translated into Chinese, at the orders of Chiang Kai-Shek, and he was nominated President of the League against Blasphemy and Honorary President of the Mark Twain Society of Kirkwood, as were André Maurois, Jan Masaryk and others.

CHAPTER 12

The story behind the Lateran Treaty

Benito Mussolini once said of the kingdom of Italy: "It is a marriage bed for two." He would have done better to say "for three", since after February 11, 1929, when the Lateran Treaty was signed between the Holy See and Italy, there was also the Vatican.

For me, on a personal and family level, this important phase in the history of my country began on December 29, 1925, when Benito and I had a religious wedding. Our three children, Edda, Vittorio and Bruno, had already received Holy Communion in 1924 from Cardinal Vannutelli in an old Franciscan monastery at Camaldoli, a little place in the Appenines where we were spending our holidays at the time.

Then one day in Milan, while I was in the kitchen cooking tagliatelle, Cina, our maid, came in. "The Prime Minister has come," she said, "with the editor [Arnaldo], a priest and Marquis Paolucci. The Prime Minister would like you to join them in the drawing room straight away."

I answered that I was busy and would go in a minute. After a while Benito himself came in. "Off we go, Rachele. That's enough now. Don't make me insist."

And as I pretended not to hear, he undid my apron himself and pushed me towards the sink to wash my hands. Then he swept me off into the drawing room. And there, in that very room which had become a chapel for the occasion, Monseigneur Magnaghi, rector of the church of San Pietro de Sala, celebrated our religious marriage, with my brother-in-law, Arnaldo, and Paolucci di Calboli as witnesses.

When the ceremony was over and Benito had kissed my hand, I remember saying to him with some sarcasm: "And now I hope we've finished getting married."

And I had good reason. This was the third instance of the kind in our relationship. I wasn't particularly excited by the idea of a religious wedding; indeed, every time Benito had spoken about it I had evaded the issue. But for him this ceremony was of consequence, both in view of his plans to reach an agreement with the Holy See and because he wanted to put our marriage on a regular footing.

In fact, since 1921, when he was still only a deputy, my husband had made his attitude towards the Vatican plain. In one of his first speeches to the Chamber, he'd attracted notice by the friendly terms in which he spoke of the Holy See and the necessity of reaching an agreement.

On February 5, 1922, the day before the election of Pius XI, he went to St Peter's Square with Constanzo Ciano and Acerbo in the hope of seeing the white smoke which was to announce the decision of the Conclave. It was then, eight months before becoming Prime Minister, that he said: "It is incredible that the liberal governments should have been so blind to the fact that the universal nature of the Pope is the heritage of the universal nature of the Roman Empire and represents the greatest glory in the history and tradition of Italy."

Consequently, as soon as he came to power, he strove to make a comprehensive plan of conciliation between Church and State succeed.

I do not think he was motivated by, say, clericalism. My husband always remained basically irreligious until the later years of his life. But such a venture appealed to that aspect of him which wanted to put everything to rights and to his commonsense. I should perhaps explain. For some years Mussolini was a revolutionary. Then, faced with the pressure from the Reds, the civil disorders in Italy and the weakness of the government, he became a defender of law and order, in that he thought a social revolution could only be brought about through legal means.

Once he had become head of government, he undertook to put Italy back on its feet. He started social reforms, put the functions of the authorities on a solid base and brought stability to his own family life. It remained to settle the position of the Church by bridging the gap which had existed between herself and the State since 1870.

Then, too, there were practical considerations. The Vatican was the centre of attraction for Roman Catholics throughout the world. So why not use this interest to his advantage, make the situation official and ensure that Rome could profit by this universal appeal? This would not be an innovation, but a return to the ancient Rome which had inspired the Duce in his building of the Fascist régime.

These were the underlying ideas. The time had come to put them into effect, to erect a bridge between the two shores of half a century of separation. And it was there that the human and personal factors, which were to be determinant, came in.

First there were the personalities. Pius XI and Mussolini were both of humble, peasant origin, and therefore had more mutual understanding than others. I remember Benito saying of the Pope: "Basically, what helps things along is that both of us have the mentality of the peasant."

Then there were the middlemen: Arnaldo, who played an enormous part, the lawyer Francesco Pacelli, the brother of the future Pius XII, and Cardinal Pietro Gasparri, Secretary of State to Pius XI, who signed the Lateran Treaty with my husband. I almost forgot Professor Barone, a Councillor of State, who set the machinery of the negotiations in motion.

According to Benito, the negotiations were not always easy, for there were people on both sides who were opposed to the venture. My husband had to reckon with the old Republican tradition which he had once personified. There was also the King who was not very keen, various Fascists who were no more enthusiastic, and the other creeds, not to mention the Freemasons and the Popular Party of the time – now the Christian Democrat Party – which was led by the famous Don Sturzo, whom my husband described in 1919 as "a little long-nosed Sicilian priest who might talk well of Paradise but would achieve nothing on earth." Others at the hub of the Vatican were not in favour of the plan. Finally, certain foreign governments would have preferred to see the Treaty remain unfeasible.

After 1922, then, the slow haul to a normalisation of relations began. My husband took the first steps by restoring the crucifix to schools and law courts and strengthening the laws against blasphemy. Later, religious instruction was given in the primary schools and equal treatment accorded to both State schools and private confessional schools. In 1924 and 1925, the government voted a subsidy of 6,500,000 lire for the Catholic churches in the new Italian provinces, like Trentino and the African regions. Then the Catholic University of Milan was officially recognised and the authorities took part in religious ceremonies. Better still, chaplains were appointed to the forces and the clergy was exempted from military service. In 1925, a law was passed giving an allowance to priests – to the benefit of 30,000 members of the clergy.

In 1925, another momentous law declared Freemasonry illegal. Mussolini had to suffer the consequences of this much later, for through this law he lost the support of a secret society which had numerous branches and numbered the King and Marshal Badoglio among its members.

Then we had our religious wedding and there was the Plenary Indulgence. Everyone did well out of that. Coming from many parts of the world, millions of tourists brought foreign currency and were able to learn about the new Italian régime because the government lent every support.

The Church benefited from these considerations on

the part of the State seeing that they encouraged Catholics to come in greater numbers, and Pius XI made his satisfaction plain in a speech to the Consistory.

The atmosphere was right. All that remained now was to surmount the last hurdle. Today this belongs to history, but I can add a footnote by pointing out that most of the negotiations never took place – as might be thought – in formal surroundings, under gilded ceilings and sparkling chandeliers, but quite simply in my husband's apartment in the via Rasella in Rome. To guarantee more privacy, Pacelli came around nine in the evening and left at about one in the morning. Some hours later, he would inform the Pope of the latest stage in the negotiations, and this went on for months. Cardinal Gasparri also met Benito in a monastery on the outskirts of Rome. The *Popolo d'Italia*, on Mussolini's behalf, and the *Osservatore Romano*, for the Pope, sustained public interest and enlivened the atmosphere whenever necessary.

Finally, the great day arrived on February 11, 1929. My husband and Cardinal Gasparri, the one for Italy and the other for the Holy See, signed the bilateral Treaty at the Lateran Palace. The Duce delivered a speech lasting forty-five minutes during which, as he later told me, Cardinal Gasparri nodded his approval several times. times.

That evening, when Father Facchinetti arrived, I was busy with the children at home. An old friend of the family, my husband had first delighted this Franciscan monk by making Francis of Assisi Patron Saint of Italy in 1925. But on that February day, Father Facchinetti was radiant with happiness.

"What's happened to you, Father?" I asked, "Have you found a fortune for your poor people?"

"It's even better than that, Donna Rachele."

As he spoke he produced two bottles of champagne from his soutane and set them, religiously in the middle of the table.

"Where did you get that, Father?" I asked.

133

He didn't answer straight away, and I carried on feeding soup to Romano who, at fifteen months old, kicked up a fuss every time I stopped. Then, looking up, I saw Father Facchinetti kissing everybody – the children, Cina and Pia, the two maids.

"But what's happened, then?"

"That is it," he exclaimed with a tremor in his voice. "The government and the Vatican have signed the agreement. The Duce has succeeded where men like Cavour and saints like Bosco failed. He can be proud, Donna Rachele. Can't we 'phone him? I'd like so much to congratulate him."

I wanted to make him happy, but I was afraid of disturbing my husband. Even I never called him, except in emergencies; instead he usually called me. It had always been like that even during his official travels. And the same rule applied to everybody, to me and to his Ministers.

At that moment the telephone rang. It was Benito outlining the news. "Rachele, the golden age of Fascism began today," he proclaimed. Then he told me what had happened and was full of praise for Pius XI – "so sympathetic, so simple and sincere in his ways and so intelligent!"

Now that I am reflecting on all this I must say that the men who invented the sordid story that Mussolini assassinated Pius XI didn't know my husband at all. They should have conjured up something else, for he would never have endangered the life of someone who had given him so much joy.

I congratulated my husband and because Father Facchinetti was gesticulating in front of me, making signs that he wanted to speak to Benito, I handed him the receiver. I couldn't see Benito's expression, though I knew he didn't like long telephone conversations. But I sympathised with the Father's elation and dared not ask him to hang up. Marvellous Father Facchinetti! He was the very picture of a lovable priest – lively, cultured, good, capable of giving those on earth a glimpse of the Paradise beyond.

However, I prefer not to dwell on it, for it would remind me of those twelve years my husband lay without a Christian burial after he had done so much for the Church, and I would spoil Father Facchinetti's happiness.

There has been much comment about the Lateran Treaty, with discrediting remarks that Mussolini was the only one to profit from them. That is untrue, for several people benefited. My husband certainly did, though he'd to overcome some hostility among his friends. Indeed, eventually he had to be emphatic and say: "I am only happy when I do something useful for Italy." Other beneficiaries were the King, who was finally recognised by the Pope as sovereign and, most of all, the Vatican.

If I wished to be malicious, I might say that the Pope would never have signed the agreements if he had seen no personal gain. Certainly he was officially renouncing Rome, which the Church now accepted as the capital of the Italian State – something which the Vatican had always rejected since 1870. But he was not losing his authority.

I am no expert; far from it. But neither am I the "cabbage" I was made out to be, for the simple reason that I had eyes to see, ears to hear and a mind to reason.

Let me quote one example. In theory, one of the vital missions of the Church is preaching the Gospel, or so it seems to me. Thus one has only to think of all the Churches which opened their doors wherever Italian influence spread. When the Italian forces went on campaign, the priests followed: in Africa, in the Dodecanese, even in Russia when our troops fought in the Ukraine alongside the Germans who had no love for priests.

Added to that there was the financial support which the Vatican received; it was not merely a matter of exchanging smiles. Finally, from 1929 onwards, the Holy See figured increasingly in the excercise of power in Italy. I don't mean that a cardinal or a bishop sat at the table each time a treaty was made. But after the

Lateran Treaty had afforded official means of reaching the country's farthest corners, the Vatican became a weapon – a spiritual and a temporal force – which could sway Italian politics one way or another, influencing the course of events as it chose. For these reasons, I suggest that after 1929 the government of Italy changed from a marriage bed for two – shared by the King and Mussolini – into a bed for three.

I will restrict myself to giving just one more example of the Vatican's strength. After 1937 – 1938, when Mussolini drew closer to Hitler, the Pope dissociated himself from Fascism, not hesitating to put it in the same category as the Nazis whenever he condemned them.

Until then the Treaty had been strictly adhered to. The Church remained the defender of ideals, of international morality and of respect for the liberty of the peoples. But then, for some reason the Vatican released information about Italy to the Americans, with whom we were officially at war.

The Holy See performed a humanitarian rôle, I agree. But to interfere in favour of a country – which perhaps it considered more deserving – and against the man who had hoisted the Papal flag higher than ever, was going too far.

Of course, there is always the rejoinder that I have no proof, that it is a slander or, at least, an accusation of intent rather than action. But these are logical arguments. Meanwhile, I would be glad to know what President Roosevelt's special envoy, Myron Taylor, came to do during his week in the Vatican. For if I am not mistaken he landed in Rome on September 20, 1942, and left again on September 28. Although few people are conscious of it, during the last world war, certain enemy countries still kept an ambassador in the Vatican. But, as the Holy See had no airport, these people travelled to and left from Rome, which meant that they could, with impunity, move across the capital of a country in conflict with their own.

And the Vatican stayed where it had always been – in its 480,000 square metres in the very heart of Rome. The Pope, with more than 30,000 priests scattered throughout the country, was the most well-informed person in Italy.

At this point I should make myself clear. I'm not saying that these priests were spies in enemy pay. Absolutely not. But, within the precincts of the Holy See, it must have been difficult not to let some information filter through.

However harmless these facts appear to be, they were valuable to those people who made it their business to draw conclusions which were not apparent to ordinary mortals. That is what dear Myron Taylor did. On his return to the United States, he assured President Roosevelt that the Italians were growing weary of the war; by intensifying the pressure the Allies could bring them to their knees. That is what actually happened. Anyone who doubts it has only to recall the period when Allied air attacks on Italy escalated – after September 1942.

From our own information services, my husband quickly learnt of Myron Taylor's activities in Italy. He was extremely angry and to Galeazzo Ciano, the Foreign Affairs Minister, he declared: "This joker, Taylor, has told the Americans that the Italians have had enough of the war and that stepping up the treatment will break their resistance. You can tell them in the Vatican that, Concordat or no Concordat, if Myron Taylor sets foot in Italy again I'll lock him up."

Needless to say, Taylor never returned to Italy – at least not while my husband was in power.

I have often been asked why the Duce allowed the ambassadors of enemy powers to travel freely round Rome. Firstly, they did not have access to the entire capital but only to the Vatican. All the same, the opportunities open to them were endless and, even if they couldn't quit the Holy See, people could visit them, Though aware of this, my husband tolerated it because, to a certain extent he had no alternative. Otherwise there would have been dramas. Besides, he knew that the Vatican gave sanctuary to Jews and others escaping from the Germans. He preferred that they should be there rather than in Italian territory, for that would have strained relations with Germany which were already tense enough because of my husband's reluctance to embark on racial persecutions.

There was a third reason why he couldn't prevent enemy ambassadors from crossing Rome: after February 11, 1929, the Lateran Treaty guaranteed the Vatican the status of an independent State in relation to Italy. Even if the Holy See was geographically inside Italy, the Vatican was free to keep up diplomatic relations with any country it chose. The Italian government itself had its ambassador in the Holy See. In fact, the first was a member of the Quadrumvirate – Cesare de Vecchi – whom the Duce appointed to signify the importance of the relations between the two States. Consequently there was no question of forbidding these diplomats from entering a State where they represented their country.

These explanations may seem puerile and useless to the experts, but many people lack knowledge of the special situation existing between the Italian government and the Vatican. The one was obliged not to interfere in the spiritual rôle of the Church, while the other's self-imposed duty was to grow offshoots, as indeed it did, all over the country, precisely because of that spiritual rôle which the Duce's government could not oppose since he himself had ensured that the Catholic religion was the State religion of Italy.

I must also stress that Mussolini never communicated with enemy nations through their ambassadors in the Holy See. He was opposed to asking the Vatican to fulfil anything other than a humanitarian function.

It was only in this sense that he agreed to negotiate with the National Liberation Committee in April 1945, through the arbitration of Cardinal Schuster, Archbishop of Milan, with a view to surrendering to the Italian Socialist Party the power invested in the Salo Republic. A first scheme for such a step had been rejected by Sandro Pertini, the recent President of the Chamber of Deputies, who was then a member of the National Liberation Committee.

For my husband it was a question of saving human lives, now that the war was virtually over, and of finding a legal solution. He was not doing it to save his own life, for he would never have agreed to fall into Allied hands alive. "I'll never go to the Tower of London or Madison Square Gardens, where the English and Americans would put me on show like a freak after they've caught me," he said. "I couldn't, never!"

But to return to the talks with Cardinal Schuster. The facts of this meeting are well known. In one of the reception rooms of the Archbishop's residence in Milan, Cardinal Schuster and my husband sat down on a couch facing, on one side, the representatives of the National Liberation Committee – including Cadorna, the son of the First World War generalissimo who had given him his total support when Mussolini formed his first government – and Marazza. On the other side were the Fascist delegates accompanying the Duce, including General Graziani, the Minister of Defence of the Salo Republic.

The talks had begun and General Graziani was explaining why the military surrender demanded by the National Liberation Committee could not be signed, when Ugo Bassi, the Prefect of Milan, who had just entered, whispered in his ear and Bassi, it transpired, had heard from Father Bichierai, the Cardinal's secretary, that the Germans, having negotiated their surrender for two months were waiting in another room for General Wolff to sign it.

My husband immediately put an end to the meeting, declaring that he had been betrayed both by the Germans and by Cardinal Schuster. "It's July 25 all over again, only much more serious," he shouted. "The Germans are paying us back for September 8, 1943, in our own coin."

He was sincerely accepting the responsibility for the signing of the armistice between the Allies and

Badoglio. Even if he had had him arrested, Badoglio was the legal head of the Italian Government in his eyes. Three weeks earlier, the same Cardinal Schuster had said to Vittorio, my son: "Your father has almost always had poor backing, but his name will be written deep in the history of Italy. With the Conciliation, not only did he bridge the gap between Italy and the Papacy, but he also found a definitive solution for the problem of the temporal sovereignty of the Church in Rome which has been with us since 754. With the Lateran Treaty," Schuster went on, "the Papacy has regained the freedom to rise higher in the people's minds. Nobody can take this exceptional achievement away from Benito Mussolini."

If he felt like that, why didn't he tell my husband about the German surrender, seeing that everything was over? He could have done so, if only out of gratitude for what the Duce had done for the Church, and it wouldn't have changed the situation at all.

I suspect that, leaving his humanitarian duties apart, Cardinal Schuster had chosen which side he proposed to support. Since the Allies and the partisans were winning, he intended to join them and deliver Mussolini to them. The Duce had declined to admit this. He was therefore all the more offended that Cardinal Schuster could have listened so coolly to Graziani's speech without consulting the Germans. He actually thought that nobody knew about it.

A few years ago I said to a French lawyer – Jacques Isorni – whom I greatly respected, that the Devil must have gobbled Cardinal Schuster when he died. I added that if ever I heard that he'd been canonised, I'd go and throw a bomb at the Vatican myself. I'm too old to do it now and I've finally found peace of mind. But I can't help feeling a little bitter when I think that my husband, who had given so much to the Church – and I'm quite prepared to repeat myself – lay for twelve years in a box, and I mean a box, without a Christian burial. Since he was buried near his family in the San Cassiano cemetery in Predappio, several priests, to my knowledge, have refused to say a mass for his soul. Admittedly, they were once chaplains to the Partisans.

Neither can I help feeling profoundly sad when I think about two episodes in my life, separated from each other by about thirty years.

The setting of the first, which arose due to a river in spate, was a monastery in Predappio at the time the Duce was at the very peak of his glory. Sitting on the back of a motor-cycle driven by one of my security officers, I arrived at this monastery to ask the Abbot if he would take in peasants of the Rabbi valley; their homes had been devastated by the floods. I had myself donated money for the restoration and expansion of this monastery, but it was soon obvious that the Abbot didn't remember me. He ran out in front of the motor-cycle, shouting: "Go away, go away this minute! Women are not allowed to come in here."

Even when we tried to explain who I was and the purpose of my visit, he stubbornly refused to listen. To get rid of me, he said at last: "Write to the Pope then. He'll give you his permission to use this monastery."

I was fuming and left him with the retort: "That's a good idea. I'll do that and then we'll see!"

Driving to the main Post Office in Forlì, I 'phoned the Duce in Rome, describing to him the details of the situation. He answered that he would do what was necessary straight away. Two hours later, the astonished Abbot was opening his monastery to the homeless peasants.

The second incident happened in 1959 or the following year. I wanted to go to the Vatican and meet Pope John XXIII. It so happened that I knew his brothers. They had explained what a good person he was, but by all accounts he was very unhappy as Pope. No longer could he drink the good wine he loved, nor have the freedom to go about; in fact he felt like a prisoner. An image formed in my mind of a priest unlike the rest, to whom I could bare my soul and perhaps make my confession also. I had no desire to go as Mussolini's widow, but as a woman who had important secrets to disclose. Furthermore, I could do so only to a Pope, since besides being head of the Church he was also a statesman who could understand the significance of various messages and certain secret information.

My confidence that I would be given an audience was backed by the fact that I had sent regular telegrams to the Holy See since my husband's death on the anniversary of the Lateran Treaty. For the audience I proposed to wear a lovely black dress and a black mantilla – a gift during a trip to Spain and in which I wish to be buried. One day, however, a bishop arrived at my home. Very embarrassed he explained that the Holy Father could in no sense see me because "politically it was not feasible."

I was overwhelmed. I had never used my husband's name nor his authority to my own advantage except to do good. In the circumstances I was unable to appreciate how the Pope could possibly imagine that, fifteen years after his death, his widow would use an audience at the Vatican, with political and other reasons in mind, as an excuse for self-glorification. I had always been assured that the Holy See was not involved in politics, and now I knew to the contrary. There had been a time when the Vatican's doors opened at the mere ring of a telephone; now they were hermetically sealed.

CHAPTER 13

Mussolini and Hitler

As soon as the tide of the Second World War had turned, there was immediate criticism of Mussolini – both in Italy and elsewhere – for his alliance with Hitler. He made a convenient scapegoat. If we turn back to April 28, 1945, one might ask why all the false patriots (who sang hymns to victory as soon as they were out of danger) and the foreign military and political leaders did not give Mussolini the public trial that was planned for Hitler.

Because the partisans had arrested him, Mussolini was essentially in Allied hands. There was no longer any doubt as to how the war would end, and, by trying my husband, they could have put a spectacular end to Fascism. Instead they contrived a hasty execution for him. By carrying it out in total secrecy, they scratched away his chance to put up a defence, and publish the documents in his possession which might have compromised a number of his Italian opponents and foreign enemies.

The victors might have found it embarrassing to realise that, for as long as Mussolini's friendship with Hitler was to their advantage, several nations made use of my husband – including France, England and America. Churchill, along with many others, might have found it annoying to see the leader of Fascism expose the letters they'd written to each other – even after the beginning of the war, when they were supposed to be enemies.

It was more convenient to silence him, then blame him for his alliance with Hitler; indeed, to stop him explaining why he'd agreed to this alliance. It might have spoilt the happy atmosphere of the Yalta agreement, when Roosevelt, Churchill and Stalin divided the world between them like fellow thieves dividing their spoils.

In fact, Mussolini was never obsessed with Hitler, as Allied propaganda would have had one believe. From the beginning, my husband greatly admired Germany – not the land of the Third Reich, perhaps, but the country that had given the world Beethoven and Wagner, Kant and Nietzsche, Frederick II and Bismark, Goethe and Schiller, Luther and Marx. It was they who had been his spiritual masters and shaped his pattern of thought.

In my husband's mind, then, Germany was the nation of nations. Europe could only gain from an alliance with her, as far as the construction of a Western dam against the tide of Bolshevism was concerned.

But Germany was also the country Mussolini had encouraged the Italians to fight, the country he had himself fought in the First World War.

Such was my husband's attitude when he first met Adolf Hitler in Venice on June 11, 1934. For Benito, there was no question of love at first sight. When he returned to Rome, he said: "He is a violent man with no self-control, and nothing positive came out of our talks."

A fortnight later, Benito came home with a bundle of newspapers under his arm. Throwing them on to his desk and underlining the headlines in thick red pencil strokes, he indignantly exclaimed: "Look at this. That person makes me think of Attila the Hun. Those men he killed were his closest supporters, who raised him to power. It's as if I were to kill Federzoni, Grandi, Bottai and the others with my own hands."

Taking one of the papers, I read that Röhm and other politicians had been executed by Hitler. Compared to the Führer, Mussolini was never a real dictator. He never had that kind of blood on his hands.

If the English and French had shown greater vision in the two months after Hitler and Mussolini first met, the Second World War might never have broken out. For, after his initial impressions of the Führer, Benito would have missed no chances to make war on Germany, especially after the assassination of Dollfuss, the Austrian Chancellor. For the Duce, this was not only an appalling crime but a personal affront in view of Hitler's assurance in Venice that he would drop the Anschluss. Moreover, Dollfuss had been an intimate friend.

We learnt of his death on July 26, 1934. Frau Dollfuss and their two children had already been residing for several days in Riccione, where we'd rented a villa for them. Her husband was to have joined them on the 25th – the very day he was assassinated in his office while preparing to leave.

When the news reached Benito the following afternoon – while he was visiting some public building works near Forlí – he hurried back to Riccione, pale and shaken. "They've murdered Dollfuss," he shouted from the doorway. "Come with me. We must tell his wife and see if we can help her."

We went straight to the villa and found her resting while the children played on the beach. Benito didn't inform her straight away of her husband's death, but the poor woman became distraught when he told her gently that Dollfuss, now lying seriously wounded, needed her. I held her hand and tried to comfort her but, as always at such times, I felt awkward, especially as I knew the truth.

That same evening, on the Duce's orders, a special plane took Frau Dollfuss back to Vienna. It was then, during the flight, that she learnt in an odious manner the bitter truth of her husband's terrible death. The children's governess, who in reality was a Nazi spy, callously told the children of their father's tragedy and they, in turn, had the sad privilege of informing their mother.

On our way home, Benito gave me further details. Dollfuss, he revealed, might have lived had he not been left bleeding in his office. That evening, he telephoned orders from Riccione, launching a hostile Press campaign and concentrating troops and aircraft on the Austrian border. Temporarily at least, these precautions sufficed to stop Hitler.

But the Duce had discovered that he could not rely on the other great powers, notably France and England. He said at the time, and again when Germany annexed Austria: "I have been disappointed by the friendly Western nations. I had expected a more energetic response. Less apathy on their part and things might have been different. As soon as Hitler realised I meant business he disowned the murderers of Dollfuss, but I'm still wary of him. He wants Austria and he'll have it, especially if I'm the only one to march on the Brenner. The other powers ought to show some interest in Austria and the Danube basin."

Shortly afterwards, Frau Dollfuss brought to Rome the keys of Venice which Austrian forces had taken to Vienna after the conquest of Venetia. And with her came the toys that her husband had intended for our children, and his letter asking Benito to protect his family if tragedy befell him. The Duce honoured this last request. When the Nazis raped Austria, he arranged sanctuary for Frau Dollfuss and the children in the United States.

The Allies had missed their chance to nip Nazism in the bud. Even later, when the situation changed, the French and English governments were too obtuse or biased to grasp whatever opportunities presented themselves. Perhaps too, the English thought – as did the French – that Mussolini's Italy would alone wage war on Germany and that both countries would exhaust themselves in the process.

After these events, three years elapsed before Mussolini and Hitler met again. Their second encounter occurred in Germany. By now Hitler fully understood the true meaning of Mussolini and Fascism. When, after the Abyssinian campaign, the League of Nations imposed sanctions on Italy, Hitler alone offered economic and political aid and was the first to recognise the Empire. The Führer had made a profitable investment; he would gain in political capital when Italy came to decide about the German alliance. For the Duce remembered this support when Hitler made overtures for an alliance. It was a determining factor, plus the vision of what such an alliance could achieve against Bolshevism – already graphically seen in the Italian-German intervention in the Spanish War.

The wind seemed set fair for Benito's visit to Germany. He left Rome on September 23, 1937, expecting a cordial welcome; he returned overwhelmed. In those five days, Hitler was his constant companion, attending to his slightest needs. He ensured that Benito had the hard pillows he liked to sleep on and personally supervised the sleeping arrangements every night. He made sure my husband had warmth because Benito was susceptible to cold. Indeed, Hitler showered the head of protocol with endless questions. Were Benito's curtains too dark, and had the picture which his guest might not like been removed?

Nothing was overlooked – right down to the flowers in the Duce's room and the train stops to allow adequate rest.

From the first evening, when Benito 'phoned me as usual, he expressed his amazement at the tumultuous welcome he'd received. He was particularly impressed by the parade on the Königsplatz in Munich.

The visit reached a climax in Berlin with one vast demonstration after another. My husband made a speech in German and called me immediately afterwards to ask if I'd heard it, and what I thought, ending by saying: "You wouldn't believe what I've seen here. It's all so well organised and the people are extraordinarily tough. With that kind of support Hitler can embark on anything."

Hitler, realising that his show of strength had impressed the Duce and anxious to strike while the iron was hot, immediately laid the foundations of an agreement which was to become the "Pact of Steel". But all that now belongs to history.

When he returned to Rome, Benito told me every detail of his trip. What surprised me most were his words about German war power. "If you only knew, Rachele," he explained, "it's unbelievable. I've never seen such a military machine with all the wheels turning so smoothly."

Obviously the man who'd welcomed the Duce had changed a great deal since the day he'd hesitantly left his plane in Venice – in his badly-fitting, putty-coloured raincoat, awkwardly clutching his grey hat. A French journalist had described him as "a little plumber holding a chamber pot [his hat] in front of his stomach." Benito had laughed on that occasion, but this time his German visit had confused him. He'd found an awe-inspiring leader backed by a whole nation – and a well-oiled military machine.

Faced with these inexorable facts, Benito realised that were Italy to oppose Hitler it must not be in isolation. The Duce had to reconsider his whole attitude. An alliance with Germany might not be attractive, but in the framework of an anti-Comintern agreement it might be a necessity. Benito told me: "We're trying to create an anti-Bolshevik front stretching across Europe from the North Sea to the Mediterranean. The Führer and I agree about Russian pressure in Spain. For the first time we are, so to speak, on the same level of defence against Bolshevism. We shall try to enlarge this defence system and strengthen it."

However, my husband added a qualification which he stood by until Italy entered the war in 1940. "For my part I see this plan from a solely defensive point of view without any immediate military objective as a non-aggression pact. If we succeed in forming a block of really powerful nations, it'll be easy to persuade Moscow to limit it's field of activity to within its own borders. Italy and

Germany represent the Latin and Teutonic worlds. Their mission is to defend European and Christian civilisation against all Bolshevik, atheist infiltration."

Perhaps they were just words, but I stress that after 1937 Mussolini looked upon Germany as a power better to ally with than oppose. From then on, he was totally preoccupied with preventing a war but equally determined that Italy should not suffer for her neutrality. When it was crystal clear that the unreasonable attitude of France and Britain prevented this, Mussolini was forced to become entangled as well.

One other thing had impressed Benito during his German visit – Hitler's sense of humour. During the Berlin parade, the officer conducting the fanfare dropped his baton, striking a soldier on the head. The man's sharp reaction startled a horse, which bolted right to the rostrum where the Führer and the Duce were standing. At first the incident embarrassed Hitler, but, seeing that Benito was appreciating the humorous aspect, he relaxed.

"I told him," said Benito, "that such incidents were not unknown in Italy either. Then Hitler whispered: 'Imagine what the fate will be of that poor soldier. Our perfect organisation will already be grinding into motion. The general will reprimand the colonel and he the commander, who will take the same disciplinary measures against the captain. The captain will punish the lieutenant who will punish the adjutant. The adjutant will certainly reprimand the sergeant who will then take it out on the corporal. The corporal . . . that poor soldier.' "

Eight years later, in June 1944, Hitler revealed a similar sense of humour in more dramatic circumstances. He was showing Benito and Vittorio the damage caused by the bomb which had almost killed him. "You realise my trousers were torn to pieces," he said. "Luckily there were no women around or they would have been treated to an unusual sight."

I saw Hitler for the first time in May 1938 – from some distance, admittedly, as I was standing on the first floor of the Palazzo Venezia. But that was close enough for me. For, on the one hand, I loathed appearing in public, and, on the other, I felt no great sympathy for the Führer, though he never treated me badly. Indeed, whenever the occasion arose he was very attentive, and generous with gifts. After his visit in 1938, he sent me a bouquet so vast that it couldn't pass through the gates of the Villa Torlonia and had to be dismantled. Unthinkingly, I compared it to the King's bouquet the previous year when the Empire was proclaimed. With my usual malice, I reflected how little the Empire had cost.

Much later, in 1943, when I joined Benito in Germany after his rescue from the Gran Sasso, not a day passed without my receiving the Führer's flowers and presents of all kinds. When my husband returned to Italy before the creation of the Salo Republic, Hitler courteously put at my disposal his personal car. The SS guards at Rocca delle Caminate even thought that Hitler himself was in the car and were terribly scared. But this is digressing from the point.

On Hitler's arrival in Rome Benito told everyone including the staff at the Villa Torlonia – to go to the Palazzo Venezia. It would be a sight, he thought, that no one should miss. Without adding to the many existing accounts of the visit, I must say that the six days Hitler spent in Rome tested my husband's patience and tact to the brim. The main cause of tension was protocol which dictated that Hitler's official host must be no less than the King himself. But Hitler and Victor-Emmanuel shared a mutual dislike for each other and the Duce was caught in the crossfire of their remarks.

The trouble began the moment the Führer arrived at the Saint Paul station. On leaving the train, he was received by the King in full dress uniform, surrounded by his generals. My husband, observing protocol, stood slightly apart. Hitler was at a loss. In his view, the Italian ruler – whom he had received so magnificently in Germany – was Mussolini. He was mystified why a little King with glittering generals greeted him while his friend, the Duce, waited to one side. His bad temper towards the King began that moment, worsening outside the station. He asked for Mussolini but the Duce had left separately to satisfy protocol because he, the Führer, was to go to the Quirinal where he would stay. Hitler's exasperation merely increased. He grumbled about everything – discreetly enough not to be rude – but he grumbled all the same. He commented on the horsedrawn carriage, asking if the House of Savoy had ever heard of the automobile. He hailed the Quirinal as a museum of antiquities, and thought the Court reactionary and anti-Fascist. He even criticised the King's table, claiming that both service and dishes were rather poor.

When Benito repeated these comments, I half agreed with Hitler. But before I could utter a word, Benito cried: "Don't you start. I already have Hitler and the King on my back." For Victor-Emmanuel was equally biting in his remarks about his guest. He repeated endlessly that Hitler was a psycho-physiological degenerate and had even asked a maid to remake his bed in his presence. The Duce was in constant fear of a diplomatic flare-up.

Hitler did not regain his good humour until May 9, when he left Rome for the relaxing atmosphere of Florence with my husband. The Führer so enthused over Florentine art that he promised to return if ever he needed a rest. His admiration for whatever he saw nearly led to an accident at the outset. While driving through Rome with Benito, Hitler was so overwhelmed by the spectacular flood-lit Coliseum that he leant too far from the car and would have fallen had Benito not grabbed him.

When he returned to the Reich, Hitler was determined to cement the Italian-German rapprochement, especially after watching the impressive naval display in Naples on May 5. As the procession of submarines, cruisers and battleships passed by, Hitler remarked to the Duce that Italy could control the seas – more particularly, the Mediterranean. And he must have been right, for soon after Italy entered the war, the English hurried to sink three of Italy's finest ships in the harbour at Taranto.

Hitler's and Mussolini's personal feelings for each other surprised me. Hitler, oddly enough, considered the Duce his superior. His office in the Brown House in Munich possessed two adornments: a portrait of Frederick II and a bust of Mussolini: The Führer actually adored my husband and when speaking of him, either to his own supporters or the Duce's, the tears welled in his eyes. Ciano noticed this during a conversation. My husband noticed too, that Hitler was on the brink of weeping when he left Italy in May 1938. In 1943, on Edda's arrival in Germany, she saw the Führer shake with emotion as she told him of her father's arrest. "But why didn't he tell me?" he kept asking. "How could he have. . . ? Why did he take his life into his hands and go to the King's villa? And after I've always told him not to trust that hypocrite."

Some weeks later Vittorio, then in Germany, had a similar experience. Hitler's face was wet with tears when he learnt that the Duce had been 'rescued by Skorzeny. When Benito arrived, the Führer made no attempt to hide his feelings. While Nazi officials saluted stiffly, he shook his hands warmly, then drew back to allow Vittorio to embrace his father.

Benito's explanation for this was that, on coming to power, Hitler recognised his master in Mussolini and his ideal in the Italian regime. He therefore borrowed many of Benito's ideas, imitated many of his achievements. The theory of *lebensraum*, or living space, was originally Mussolini's. After his youthful experiences and the discovery when he came to power that numerous Italians had to emigrate to survive, it was a logical step to provide them with land on which to live and work. Hitler took this idea to the extreme, destroying the native characteristics of occupied countries, instead of adapting to them as the Italians did.

From the Fascist "Balilas" was born the Hitler Youth Movement. The Fascist salute, which Benito began for hygienic reasons, to avoid hand-shaking, became the Nazi salute. The Nazi brown shirts were the German version of the Fascist Black Shirts.

Hitler clearly idolised Mussolini, but my husband was more reserved about Hitler. He was touched by his courtesies, he respected German military strength and the single-mindedness of the people who had invested Hitler with power, but he was slightly afraid of the change in Germany. He saw his alliance with Hitler as a marriage of convenience.

Mussolini's fear centred on his dwindling influence after 1940 as Hitler began to call the tune. There were many reasons for this. Hitler was a dictator, Mussolini was not. Hitler's supporters were a belligerent people, but Mussolini had forgotten his hero's welcome after the Munich conference in September 1938 for preventing war. The German generals owed total allegiance to Hitler; their Italian counterparts to the King; they would use this as an excuse at a point of crisis. And, to be harsh, the Germans were militant to the core, some Italian leaders were only as militant as their uniforms made them.

Benito often said that had the German general staff had its way, they would have removed the Italian army from the front, dispatched the King to some backwater and sent a Nazi governor to rule Italy – as in the case of Poland, Czechoslovakia and elsewhere. Only Hitler's respect for the Duce averted this.

The German attitude manifested itself on my return from Germany to Rocca delle Caminate on November 3, 1943. Benito had preceded me. I was stunned to find that, though back in his own home, he'd retreated into a modest room, while the German officers assigned to serve and guard him ostentatiously occupied most of the house. Their well-shined boots stood sentinel-like outside the rooms they'd taken over. They had eaten virtually all the food and our poor maid was driven to distraction. I lost no time acquainting them that my house was not a hotel, even less a barracks, and that they would have to leave.

They left at once. I concluded that the highly disciplined Germans must either respect or destroy anyone who stood up to them. On that occasion they had listened to me, and I think Hitler would have done as much for Mussolini if the Duce had not shared the leadership with two partners.

Hitler was now in the habit of acting on his decision before he informed Benito and when my husband reproached Hitler for it, the Führer invariably had a stock reply: Mussolini lacked total power in his country. As Hitler trusted neither the Court nor the Italian general staff – of which Victor-Emmanuel was supreme commander – he preferred his plans to remain secret.

And yet no member of the German general staff suspected Mussolini's loyalty for a moment. There lay the paradox. My husband was governing a country and, as a leader, was negotiating with an ally who admired him greatly. Everything should have been for the best in the most ideal of all possible worlds. But, because Mussolini respected existing institutions, he had to stay his hand against the monarchy which formed the chief obstacle to better co-operation with Germany.

I must admit that Hitler's attitude was borne out by events, especially when it concerned the King's loyalty to my husband.

CHAPTER 14

Mussolini and the King of Italy

In a sense, Victor-Emmanuel III and Mussolini were almost old acquaintances when they met on October 30, 1922, at the Quirinal Palace.

They had already met twice before this historic encounter; the first time, in the Cividale Hospital during the First World War. My husband, who was then in the army, was being treated for paratyphoid when the King came to inspect the hospital. They didn't say anything to each other on that occasion, but six months later, in Ronchi Hospital, they chatted for some moments.

My husband was confined to bed, hovering between life and death and ravaged by fever. The doctors had recently removed the forty-three shell splinters I have already mentioned.

Victor-Emmanuel asked to see Sergeant Mussolini, and for a specific reason. He was undoubtedly well aware that in civilian life Mussolini edited a newspaper of weighty influence and that, until then, he had always himself been fiercely anti-royalist. But now Mussolini was no longer attached to a political party and there was no knowing which path he would take next. The King may have been mulling over these ideas as he walked towards the bed where Benito Mussolini lay, pale and with his eyes protruding from his cheeks.

"You must be in pain, Mussolini," said the King.

"It's agony, your Majesty, but one must keep going."

"Do you remember, I saw you six months ago at

Cividale Hospital? General M. told me many good things about you."

"Thank you, Your Majesty, but I've only done my duty like all the other soldiers."

"I know, I know. That's fine, Mussolini."

And there, the conversation ended, however significant it may later have become. Five years hence, on October 30, 1922, the King and my husband were to meet again, this time at the Royal Palace of the Quirinal.

One was the conqueror; the other, having lately sustained what amounted to a defeat, had summoned Mussolini only because of the pressure of events and was afraid of losing his throne. Victor-Emmanuel had no option but to give assurances of friendship and loyalty. Mussolini wanted to rule the country, to make Italy a great power and to put the machinery of State back on the rails. With or without the King, it didn't make much difference to him. But since the sovereign was there, and was willing to co-operate, there was no reason why he might not become a nucleus for the unification of the country, together with a head of government rather than a party leader, in the shape of Mussolini.

The King would not suffer by it, since Mussolini constituted an effective barrier against the advance of the Bolsheviks – the Communists of the time – who, if they had gained the upper hand, would doubtless have swept away the House of Savoy in the same ruthless manner they had deposed Tsar Nicholas the Second. Besides, Victor-Emmanuel was killing two birds with one stone; he was also disposing of the whole array of politicians who were a force that he'd had to reckon with as a constitutional monarch and who were of no further use to him now.

My husband also profited from the arrangement: he had avoided a violent revolution and had taken power in accordance with democratic procedures, while remaining the victor. Later he made this comment on the event: "The House of Savoy has been towed into

Rome for the second time. First in the wake of Garibaldi and now of Fascism."

The first few minutes of the meeting on October 30 set the tone for future dealings. The King wore uniform, thereby signifying his intention to remain at the head of the armed forces. In contrast, my husband had discarded his Fascist black shirt, favouring instead a white shirt with stiff collar and a hired frock coat, the correct dress for the occasion. This subtly indicated that he was willing to recognise the existing authority.

In this way, the two men shared the leadership of the country. The King reigned and retained command of the army and the head of the administration governed.

Mussolini's seat of government was in the Palazzo Chigi and then, after 1929, in the Palazzo Venezia. Every Thursday and Monday, right up until the war, my husband donned his frock coat and top hat and went to the Quirinal to obtain the King's signature for decrees and the nominations of Ministers or military leaders. The King would study them closely, muttering to himself before he signed. But sign he always did.

In the main, the King and my husband managed to establish a fairly honest partnership. It had its ups and downs, for the King was basically suspicious, but the Prime Minister had no mental reservations. To be perfectly honest, I think the Duce always regretted that the King was not tall and well-built, like the Scandinavian monarchs. When he was angry with him, he even went so far as to say: "He's much too small a fellow for an Italy on the path to greatness."

And it was precisely this question of stature which gave rise to the real quarrels between them. My husband wished to make Italy into a great, powerful and respected country. And because he was moving towards a goal on the political, social and diplomatic levels, the King left him alone to do as he wanted in those areas.

Indeed, whatever comments he made stemmed from friendly concern, as when he criticised the Duce for travelling by air too much. "If he carries on trying to stop me doing what I want, I shall turn Republican again," my husband grumbled.

But that was more of a whim than anything else. At the time of the Matteotti affair, Victor-Emmanuel played fair, refusing to act on the counsels of various politicians that he should get rid of Mussolini. Soon afterwards, on February 7, 1929, Mussolini made him a gift of the Conciliation between the House of Savoy and the Throne of Saint Peter. I should point out, in this context, that my husband was given special dispensation from kissing the Pope's ring during his audience with Pius XI.

The serious quarrels began when the Duce wanted to alter one of the main elements in the expansion of Italy, namely, the army. Although my husband merely wanted to improve the armed forces, the hackles of Victor-Emmanuel rose at once; everything of a military nature was the jealously guarded province of the Crown and therefore protected game.

On one occasion, for example, Benito had designs to introduce a new uniform. Until then the Italian soldiers had worn battle jackets with tightly buttoned collars which they opened as soon as they could, thus looking untidy. With his practical approach, my husband concluded that a change of collar would stop the soldiers from doing this.

The result was a terrible fuss, involving months of explanations, surveys and committee meetings before the King would finally agree.

In another instance, my husband was keen to abolish the wearing of puttees dating from the First World War. He had worn them himself and condemned them for reasons of time and health. Several minutes were wasted, he argued, while the soldiers unrolled them before putting them on, while health – a matter of primary importance to Benito – was endangered; the puttees affected circulation and were a source of infection in themselves. Thus there were further tensions, further meetings and explanations. But the King agreed again and the Italian army began to wear boots.

The first really big crisis between Victor-Emmanuel and Mussolini flared up in 1928 after the vote on the electoral law which made the Fascist Grand Council, chaired by my husband, a constitutional organ. Under the new measures, the Grand Council became the chief machinery of the State, since its opinion had to be sought in regard to all constitutional questions. These embraced such matters as the succession to the throne and the prerogatives of the Crown. To take an example, the King could no longer dismiss his Prime Minister without first consulting the Grand Council. Fifteen years later Victor-Emmanuel applied this law to dispense with my husband, but at that time he did not value it at all.

Furiously he declared that the Fascists had no right to interfere in the affairs of the Crown. According to him, the question of the succession was settled under the constitution and if a party meddled in the succession then that was the end of the monarchy.

That was as far as he went. In fact, from what my husband said, Victor-Emmanuel feared that after his death the Fascists might give the throne to the Duke of Aosta, his nephew, whose Fascist sympathies were well known. He had, in fact, taken part in the Black Shirt procession before the Quirinal in October 1922. Since his presence on the balcony was essential, behind his uncle, he'd ascended by a private staircase, holding jacket collar tightly closed so that the King wouldn't notice the shirt.

From 1928 to 1938, there were virtually no problems. Every Monday and Thursday "Mister President", as protocol demanded the King should call him, met "His Majesty" at the Quirinal. Their relations on a personal level even seemed to grow cordial.

Benito once went to Victor-Emmanuel's bedside when he was ill, only to be asked point-blank: "Tell me, my dear Mussolini, how do you manage to have lovely apples at your table? The ones they bring me are so small you wouldn't believe it. I don't understand it at all."

Making discreet enquiries, the Duce discovered that the King, believing the Palace bills to be excessive, had decided on a fixed sum to cover all expenses. But he'd omitted to allow for the fluctuations in prices and in the quantities and kinds of products. Consequently the staff were sometimes obliged to pick cheaper goods so that they could pay for everything else.

When Benito told me about this, I found it easy enough to believe, for I'd already heard rumours about the King's stinginess. Besides, I didn't find him very likeable, and on several occasions Benito had to interrupt me when I began to explain that the King of Italy needed a ladder to mount his horse.

At the same time, I had great respect for the Queen and was fond of the Queen Mother, Margherita of Savoy. I met her in 1926 in Milan, where I was still living, during a concert at the Palace of Sports, to which Margherita had also gone.

I was quietly pointing her out to Edda, Vittorio and Bruno, when an aide-de-camp approached me and said: "Her Majesty the Queen Mother asks if you would kindly join her in her box. She would like to meet you and the children."

At first I refused. "I'm not used to being in the presence of Queens," I answered. "Would you kindly convey my excuses to Her Majesty, but I cannot and will not disturb her."

The aide-de-camp, however, was so insistent that in the end I accepted the invitation and, pushing my children before me, I went to the royal box. The Queen Mother was extremely friendly and I can still remember how she greeted me. "I wanted," she said, "to meet the Duce's wife to tell her that the House of Savoy should always be grateful to her husband for all he has done and continues to do for our country."

When she died a few months later, I learnt that she had made my husband an executor of her will. She had also bequeathed to me a small medallion of Saint Anthony, which Benito always wore until he died. It was then stolen together with everything else he had with him.

In the Spring of 1930, during the period of peaceful relations between the King and the Duce, I got to know Victor-Emmanuel III and Queen Helen, his wife. When we first met, at a reception in the Quirinal, I was dutifully whiling away the time among the ladies of the bedchamber – who incidentally were not very forthcoming – when the King came towards me. Pointing to a chattering group of elderly ladies, he said jokingly: "You'd think we were in a hen-house."

That was the only noteworthy remark I heard him make and I found it amiably down to earth.

A few weeks later, Queen Helen invited me to a performance given in honour of her daughter, Princess Maria, the Queen emphatically asking Benito to make certain that I accepted. I therefore went, but in a terrible state because I had to feed Anna-Maria, my youngest child, who was only a few months old, and I was afraid I'd forget to keep an eye on the time.

In fact it was the Queen herself who put my mind at rest. Every now and again she looked at her watch and when the time came she gave me leave to go, after presenting me with a lovely rose. I was very touched by such great kindness and simplicity. Later the Queen offered the Duce the use of an apartment in the hunting lodge at Castelporziano on the outskirts of Rome, so that he could relax there whenever he so desired.

Everything seemed to be for the best in the best of all possible worlds. Between 1937 and 1938, however, there were two incidents, of which one, the second, amounted to a serious crisis between Mussolini and the King, who never forgot it.

The first quarrel was of the puttee and battle jacket type. This time it concerned the parade step. My husband had always been outraged by the way the Italian soldiers marched past. "With their rifles at the end of their arm, they look as if they're carrying a suitcase and are going to catch a train," he grumbled. He added that the Italian army was the only one which didn't have a parade step. When he went to Germany in 1937, he came back full of enthusiasm for the military carriage of the German soldiers. Their way of marching had also impressed him and he decided to introduce a "passo romano",·which was a sort of less rigid "goose step" in our army. He thought this would give the troops more military bearing, but for the King it was another encroachment on the prerogatives of the Crown, which included those of Supreme Commander of the Armed Forces and therefore the right to dictate how the Italian forces marched.

However much my husband explained that every army in the world had a parade step, Victor-Emmanuel III and his general staff didn't wish to know. The step may have been an impressive one, but it remained the "German step".

That was one of the rare occasions when Benito lost his usual reserve with me and made an acid comment about the King. "It's not my fault if the King is pint size," he exclaimed. "Naturally he won't be able to do the parade step without making himself ridiculous. But the height of the King is no reason for stunting the army of a great nation as he has done."

Finally the storm blew over once more and the King agreed to sign the new measures. But what mountains he made out of molehills!

The Duce's concern did not stop, however, at puttees and battle jackets, but he had a much more gruelling time when he wanted to reorganise the Italian army completely, changing both its weaponry and its outlook.

March 1938 saw the eruption of the final crisis between him and the King, but it did not reach its last chapter until July 1943. On March 30, Benito made a speech in the Chamber praising the army. When he had finished Costanzo Ciano, President of the Chamber, proposed the creation of a new rank of "Marshal of the Empire" to be conferred on the King and the Duce simultaneously. The law was passed by acclamation and the Senate approved it on the same day.

The drama broke when my husband went to the

Quirinal to ask the King to ratify the law. He found an extraordinarily irritated man. "This law is another mortal blow at my sovereign prerogatives," he protested. "I could have given you any other rank as a sign of my admiration, but to place me on the same footing as you puts me in an impossible situation. If it were not for the imminent international crisis, I would rather have abdicated than submit to such an insult."

My husband didn't want to aggravate the situation either. But he said to Ciano: "I've had enough of this. I do the work and he does the signing."

The title meant little to Benito although it must have pleased him if only because he was now – in one detail at least – on the same level as the King. But Victor-Emmanuel found it especially offensive because he was afraid that this law would indirectly enable the Duce to establish a Fascist control of the army, for which Fascist veterans had yearned for some time. However, in order not to offend the King, the Duce avoided wearing the uniform of Marshal of the Empire in his presence as much as he could.

Some time later, after Hitler's visit to Italy in 1938, Victor-Emmanuel told my husband that he would be glad to visit Rocca delle Caminate. Crown Prince Umberto had already been there in 1936. The whole atmosphere had been very warm and Umberto had spent a while meditating by the graves of the Duce's parents during a visit to the house where he was born.

Despite his old revolutionary ideas, Benito was very flattered by the King's suggestion, especially as he was to come to our home, in our region. This made it different in Benito's mind from an official visit to places owned by the State.

I was responsible for my husband's first bout of nerves. A few days before, he had said: "We must provide something special. Don't forget it's the King who's coming to the house."

On June 8, he asked me, "Well, Rachele, is everything ready? Have you organised everything properly? Have you thought about the drinks?"

Because his fretting was beginning to exasperate me, I became edgy too. "Of course, I've thought of the drinks," I said. "I've thought of everything. I've ordered orangeade and sandwiches from the buffet at Forlí station. Is that good enough for you?"

He was stunned, poor man. "But is that all? Nothing else? We are talking about the King after all, Rachele." "King or no King, that doesn't cut any ice with me. As far as I'm concerned, whether it's the King or Minghini [a peasant friend of the family] it's all the same."

While this conversation was taking place, the King was paying a traditional visit to Predappio, with speeches from the Baccanelli "podestà", flags in the streets and a cheering crowd of local people. I must say that the view from Rocca delle Caminate, in the lovely June sunshine, was rather beautiful with the country-side all green, flags along the winding roads and the Romagnols dressed in their Sunday best.

Finally the King dispelled all my husband's fears when he and his retinue reached the main door of Rocca delle Caminate. He was carrying a big bouquet of roses which he held out to me, saying: "I'm bringing these from the Queen, but I'm very afraid they've wilted a little in the sunshine of Romagna."

I took the roses with a few conventional words of thanks and then something funny happened which would certainly have worried my husband slightly more if he had been aware of it. I gave the roses to my nephew, Germano, to take care of. He didn't want to miss one second of the visit and handed them on to Armando, the caretaker. But Armando also wanted to watch everything. So he ran off and put them in a basin used for the laundry and forgot all about them.

The King walked round the house, complimenting me on the way Rocca delle Caminate was laid out, on the hall of the Grand Council – which was indeed rather attractive – and more particularly on the portrait of myself which had been painted when I was thirty. Very courteously, Victor-Emmanuel III remarked that I hadn't changed at all. These gallant words moved me very deeply, as they would any woman who is forty-five and is told that she only looks thirty.

After taking a rest and drinking a glass of orangeade from the station buffet, the King took his leave, but not before he had told my husband how pleased he was by the heartfelt welcome of the people of Romagna. He informed us that no other monarch had received such a greeting in Romagna and he was all the more moved because he had once been whistled at by the crowd when passing through our region. This had made him so cautious that, during subsequent travels, he'd preferred to make a detour to avoid us.

Once the King had gone, Benito wanted the flowers he had given me to take to his parents' grave. Armando went to fetch them and we heard shouts of "What a calamity. My God, what a calamity!"

I thought there had been an accident or something serious. We rushed in to find Armando weeping over the basin. When he had put the roses in there was soap in the water which had made the blue of the ribbon run, had taken the yellow out of the petals and withered the leaves. It was not a pretty sight and my husband was very upset.

"You can at least get a plaque put on the front of the house with the date and time of his visit," he said.

"You can rely on me," I answered. But I didn't put anything up.

This story may only be of incidental interest, and may possibly show aspects of the past which most people are unaware of since they only come across the official and the formal versions. But for my husband the royal visit to Rocca delle Caminate was very important. It was a test.

Victor-Emmanuel had suggested coming to Rocca delle Caminate of his own accord, not at my husband's invitation. And however royal it was, the visit was still a private one, for Rocca delle Caminate was our home. For Benito this meant that his personal relations with the King were back to set-fair and that the monarch had forgotten the two crises arising from the assignment of constitutional powers to the Fascist Grand Council and, above all, from the creation of the title of "Marshal of the Empire".

In fact the situation was very different. But we didn't find out until five years later that the King of Italy bore an inexorable grudge against him. And even when he had all the evidence before him, Benito Mussolini could not bring himself to believe that Victor-Emmanuel III was capable of sanctioning a conspiracy against his Prime Minister, let alone playing an active part in it. Not until he was arrested – in contempt of the laws of hospitality – and abducted by men in the King's pay, could he admit that all the warnings were not the product of a wild imagination.

CHAPTER 15

The second world war could have been avoided

I have often been asked why Mussolini wanted war in 1940. I have always replied, and still maintain, that he never wanted it. On the contrary, he did all he could to avoid it.

Intimately involved in his life at the time, I saw how distressed he was by the thought of another European war, how disheartened by his discovery that the Italian-German alliance, which he'd signed as an anti-Bolshevik, might now make him the enemy of Italy's historic allies.

And after the assassination of Dollfuss and the Anschluss, he was afraid he'd see Italy invaded and sacked if he sided with those weaklings who had neither caught on nor reacted in time, France and England.

He had seen Germany's military strength for himself. Neither French nor English statesmen had even begun to envisage what Hitler had shown him in the vast Krupp factories – now working round the clock to produce every imaginable instrument of war. He knew that, if a conflict erupted, boundaries would be swept aside like straw and that all Europe would be one enormous blaze.

That was why he did everything possible to avert the Sudeten crisis before it sparked a world war – because he knew that Hitler would stop at nothing.

Everything began on September 28, 1938. That was the day my husband saved the peace by making a telephone call. He'd spent the entire day at the Palazzo

Venezia – not even coming home for lunch. I waited for him all evening. When he returned late, he looked gloomy. Anxiously I asked him what stage the crisis had reached.

"There's some hope," he told me, "but it's as slender as a thread. I've tried everything today but I don't know if the other powers will agree to peace talks. I'm even wondering if there's still time for a conference. Oh, Rachele, how blind the French and English leaders are. They still haven't grasped that Hitler wants Sudetenland. And to get it he's prepared to go to war. He was to have opened hostilities tomorrow. By some miracle, I managed to persuade him to wait and agree to a conference. That's the last hope."

My husband then told me about his race against time.

"At about ten o'clock this morning," he said, "Ciano came rushing into the Palazzo Venezia. The British ambassador had asked, on Chamberlain's behalf, for me to mediate with Hitler. At eleven, I 'phoned Attolico (the Italian ambassador in Berlin), telling him to meet Hitler at all costs and urge him to postpone the Czech invasion, for 24 hours. Attolico dashed to the Chancellery where, as he later reported, everything was in great confusion. Although the Führer was locked in his office with the French ambassador, Attolico made the devil of a fuss – eventually managing to get an officer to inform Hitler of my urgent message. The Führer saw Attolico at once on hearing how the British had asked me to act as middle man. Hitler thought for a few moments, then answered: 'Tell the Duce that I accept his proposal.'

"Within minutes of receiving Hitler's reply, I heard of Chamberlain's willingness to go to Berlin at once to discuss the Sudeten problem with us, the French, the Germans and the Czechs. Again I 'phoned Attolico asking him to tell Hitler that I hoped he would approve of Chamberlain's proposal which had my support. I didn't mention the Czechs because Hitler would not have agreed."

As my husband spoke, I could not help wondering how long our home, and the tens of millions of homes throughout Europe, would continue to enjoy peace.

"Attolico," Benito went on, "reached the Chancellery just when Neville Henderson, the British ambassador, was seeing Hitler. Again the Führer left his office and before he even listened to Henderson's message, told Attolico that he agreed to the proposal and asked me to take part in the talks. He even added that it was up to me to choose where – at Frankfurt or Munich. Attolico 'phoned me again. I chose Munich and sent him back to tell Hitler. This afternoon the official invitations went out to London, Paris and Rome. The next three days will be crucial. But peace is hanging by a thread, Rachele, just a thread. The slightest incident could touch everything off because the German army is ready to march."

I didn't sleep a wink that night. I feared that Galeazzo Ciano, the Foreign Minister, might 'phone, telling my husband of some serious development – a change of heart on Hitler's part, or on the part of one of the other two powers involved. Happily nothing happened.

Benito had managed to sleep. He woke rested and with a less pessimistic view of the future. He left very early for the Palazzo Venezia, dispensing with his usual ride, then 'phoned me during the morning.

"I've done it, Rachele," he cried. "I've finally managed to arrange a meeting between Hitler, Chamberlain and Daladier." He was obviously excited. "I'm leaving for Munich straight away. Pack a bag for me. I shall be with you in a few minutes."

I was delighted to pack his bag, even more than on the day he left for Rome in October 1922.

When Benito arrived at the Villa Torlonia, he was radiant. All the staff knew what was at stake at Munich and wanted to say goodbye. Only Romano – whose birthday fell on September 26 – reproved his father, as he kissed him, for having forgotten the occasion.

"If all goes well," promised Benito, embracing him, "I

shall be bringing back a marvellous present for you. You know what? A peaceful world for children to grow up happily in."

"Bah! Io preferisco un treno elettrico (I'd rather have an electric train)," replied Romano, disappointed. He had no experience then of the bitterness of war.

My husband called me briefly from Munich to tell me, "The danger has been averted. There will be no war."

I need not describe the ecstatic scenes on his return, though I can say that Benito felt they were inappropriate, for knowing Hitler and knowing that he would only respect a show of strength, he was afraid that the celebrations would undermine the Führer's opinion of Italy.

At home I bombarded him with questions, naturally enough. He simply gave me a summary of the atmosphere of the talks. "I hadn't dared to hope for so much," he said. "And yet, when Chamberlain arrived, he was sceptical about what might emerge from the meeting. He was most suspicious of our good intentions and I had to talk to him for some time to convince him. Once he was convinced, his whole attitude changed; he was co-operative right to the end. As for Hitler, he was proud that England and France were waiting on his decision – not that it made him any less open-minded. Daladier was co-operative. France is obviously not ready for war. When he realised that a peaceful solution was near, he was overjoyed. It showed on his face – though I think he was the only one. As interpreter, I tried to round the edges because Hitler only speaks German, Chamberlain English and French and Daladier a little Italian."

That is how four men saved the peace in 1938. My husband had promised it as a birthday present for Romano, but he hadn't told me how fragile this toy was. It didn't last long. We'd scarcely a year of happiness, but in that time Benito derived one pleasure: an official visit to Rome in January 1939 from Chamberlain, the British Prime Minister, and Halifax, his

(*above*) *Donna Rachele today at home in Predappio, (below) an admirer kissing her hand at the anniversary of her husband's burial* (Syndication International).

(above) With the Commanding General of the Fascist Militia, and (below) Mussolini's body just after his execution, 1945. (Syndication International).

Minister for Foreign Affairs. This visit endorsed the British Government's recognition of the Italian Empire. The British representative in Rome now presented fresh credentials addressed to the "King-Emperor" and not merely the King of Italy.

During this visit, Halifax gave Benito even greater proof that the English sought Italy's friendship. He asked Lord Perth, the British ambassador in Rome, to show my husband the text of a speech on Anglo-Italian relations which he was to make before Parliament. From what Benito told me, this gesture was a specially significant sign of friendship since it was outside normal diplomatic procedure. I doubt if one government has ever communicated to another the text of a speech before it was read to Parliament. Yet Halifax did so unofficially. The archives must, I suppose, contain some record of this.

I have emphasised this point to show how glad the Duce was to receive the two British statesmen in Rome. I believe this was the high point of his career in international politics and the last public show of peace before the Second World War. The climax of the visit was an evening at the opera, attended by my husband, Chamberlain and Halifax. On this occasion Benito wore evening dress, which he had not done for some time.

Afterwards he told me that he was pleased with the outcome of this visit since he wished to maintain friendly relations with England, even if there was some conflict of interests.

"The only thing I regret slightly," he added, "is that the Roman people didn't give them a really warm welcome. They've long memories and they haven't forgotten the sanctions during the Abyssinian war. Chamberlain realised this, but it didn't make our relations strained."

Every important occasion, however well organised always has its share of "incident". Chamberlain's visit was no exception. It was no serious matter, though it caused a flutter among the police; for the British Prime Minister's umbrella disappeared.

I already knew that Chamberlain had an umbrella, just as I knew that he had a bowler hat, and that these were the distinctive badges of every self-respecting Briton. Besides, when my husband first mentioned the visit, he jokingly said: "On January 11, Chamberlain and his umbrella are coming to Rome."

Whenever he spoke to me about the Prime Minister during his stay he always managed to include the expression "Chamberlain and his umbrella". Then, on the day of the reception, Benito called me from the Capitol.

"Rachele," he said in a solemn voice, "it has finally happened."

"What? Is it serious?"

"Of course. Chamberlain has lost his umbrella. Someone has stolen it from the Capitol and the police are at their wits' end."

Then he hung up. Several hours later he called again, this time he was laughing. "I know you must be worried about Chamberlain's umbrella. Well, you needn't worry any longer. It's been found. It wasn't stolen, but someone had put it with the ones put aside for bad weather."

To return to more serious topics, I remember that my husband always had the greatest respect for Chamberlain, as he had for almost all the heads of State of his time. The only one he never liked was Roosevelt. He thought him a mistaken idealist who was fanning the flames of war and that, like all Americans, he hadn't the slightest notion of European problems.

He said to a journalist one day: "You'll see. Once the Americans have set foot in Europe it will not be easy to shift them."

He greatly respected Churchill, whom he considered a worthy adversary. "He's a real John Bull . . . a good friend and a good enemy. One of the great living Europeans who understands Europe's needs for the future, even though, as an Englishman, he cannot meet them."

Benito more than once assured his sister, Edwige, that

if she ever needed help or refuge she'd only to contact Churchill who had been forewarned.

I know – because he said so on several occasions – that the Duce kept up a secret correspondence with Churchill during the war. Indeed, I remember one day – in 1943, I believe – he told me that if the Allies won, he wouldn't try to escape but wait resolutely for them. "I have enough documentary evidence," he assured, "to prove to Stalin and Churchill that they drove me to war and that even after the war began I tried to restore peace. I have it in black and white."

He was carrying all these documents in a portfolio when he was arrested at Dongo. Needless to say, they disappeared when he was killed. There have been endless speculations about his hastily contrived execution. I myself have always wondered whether his executioners had specific orders from Moscow or from London, to prevent him from falling into American hands and to remove Communism's chief enemy.

Similarly, I have always found it odd that after my husband's death Churchill should have come to Northern Italy for a fortnight's holiday. Officially he "came to paint". I know that Churchill was resourceful enough to receive his colleagues in his bath with a cigar in one hand and a glass of whisky in the other, or to paint pictures in the middle of a war. But why did he choose the shores of Lake Garda? And why then? Surely the intelligence agents who accompanied him weren't there to hold his brushes.

I suspect that his object was to recover any documents concerning himself, since they would have embarrassed him if his Allies had seen them.

The documents are officially missing. If they have not been destroyed, they must be sitting somewhere. The Duce has been dead for 28 years and can't return from the grave. Why not, then, publish the documents which concern him? If he really was the hateful betrayer of his Allies – which his enemies claim him to be – why not add weight to this view by disclosing proof of his faults?

My husband naïvely believed that a country which

has made war and kept a code of honour, whose rulers respected international law and humanitarian principles, could not possibly be trampled on once it was beaten. The former enemies of the two world wars could not be closer now. Mussolini thought that Europe would emerge united from its harsh experiences and avoid its present turmoil. Unfortunately he was wrong.

On the other hand, he was right in his reply to Vittorio's question just before the outbreak of the war. Why, having saved the peace at Munich by discussion, our son had asked, had he not tried to arrange another meeting?

"Then what? What will that achieve?" Benito questioned. "Hitler will give us a two-hour speech full of hazy ideas from *Mein Kampf*; Roosevelt will pass for a saintly defender of the peace while he's really pressing for war; Stalin will tell us that only the people's will can triumph, as if he hasn't crushed his people already; and Churchill will listen to it all without doing anything – because he can't do anything. No, Vittorio, a meeting like that hasn't a chance of succeeding – this time. America doesn't understand Europe at all and doesn't want to anyway. Russia's only aim is to export Communism. As for us Europeans, our only chance of keeping out the Americans and the Communists would have been to build a United States of Europe. But we didn't and it'll be an expensive mistake."

Benito paused for a few moments, then wrinkling his eyes into a smile, he added: "And to be less serious, I'd have thought that Stalin, Churchill, Roosevelt, Hitler and Mussolini haven't a chance of getting on. Hitler doesn't drink or smoke, neither do I; Stalin and Churchill smoke like chimneys and drink like fish; Roosevelt smokes but only drinks tea or coffee –"

And since I'm passing on the Duce's opinions of the war's main figures, I should perhaps mention that the military leaders he most ardently admired were Eisenhower, on the American side, von Runstedt on the German and, towards the end, Kesselring because he held down the Allies for 600 days. Finally, there was

Mannerheim, the distinguished marshal, for his heroic struggle against the Russians.

CHAPTER 16

Why Mussolini became Hitler's ally

On realising that he could do nothing else to stop the war, my husband tried to keep Italy out of it for as long as possible. But, from another point of view, he felt trapped by former agreements, because he was still determined to do the right thing, even if it meant – as it once had – selling gifts to repay a debt and respect former commitments.

I realised something was in the wind when, in June 1939, at the Villa Torlonia, a chance phrase caught my attention. That day, while walking through an antechamber, Benito stopped in front of a painting given to him by a Hungarian artist. At the bottom of the picture ran the words: "Treaties are not eternal." Benito read this softly aloud several times, then remarked: "The time for juggling is over. For the first time in history Italy will have to respect her commitments."

That was his sole comment, but it was not long before I understood its significance. As the days passed, the news became increasingly alarming. Both Attolico, our ambassador in Berlin, and Ciano, the Foreign Minister, sent reports which left little doubt that Hitler was determined on war. And his excuse would be Poland's refusal to cede Danzig to the Reich. My husband was certain that Poland would be only the initial step.

First, Benito tried using the "Pact of Steel" to curb the Führer's aggression, but it soon became obvious he was labouring in vain. Then he tried to keep Italy aloof from the conflict. He told Hitler, through Attolico, that his weakened military strength and the fact that the wars in Ethiopia and Spain had sapped Italy's raw materials prevented him giving the Nazis adequate backing.

"I only hope," he said, "that honesty will be enough to restrain the Führer. Italy isn't ready for another conflict, and this time I don't think it will be localised. To tell you the truth, Rachele, I don't know where it will lead. Wars are like avalanches; no one can tell in advance how long they will last or where they will lead. There have even been wars lasting a hundred years, Rachele, but I shall do everything I can to stop this one from spreading."

Benito believed that the non-aggression pact between Germany and Russia had finally killed all hopes of peace. The Duce was surprised – not because the pact had been signed (since he had always maintained to the Führer that some kind of working agreement between Western Europe and Russia was essential), but that Hitler should have given his signature at that particular time without telling Italy beforehand.

He had said to Ciano: "I'm sure this agreement is merely a precautionary measure on Hitler's part to avoid Russian retaliation. That means he's intending to take action in Poland."

From that day, diplomatic activity between Rome and Berlin grew in intensity. Once again, the other powers appealed to my husband to arrange another Munich. And I know that he almost succeeded in doing so, although he no longer believed it would help. Yet again, the English and the French were too blind to profit from the situation. Unwittingly they gave Hitler the go-ahead, and drove Italy into Germany's arms.

Between August 25 and the night of August 31, peace hung in the balance. By the 25th it was clear that Germany was ravenous for war. Ribbentrop had distinctly said so to Ciano during a journey to Salzburg some days earlier. Just before dinner, Ciano asked: "Well, Ribbentrop, what do you want? The Danzig Corridor?"

"No, we want more than that. We want war."

During the 25th, Hitler sent a lengthy message to my husband through von Mackensen, the German ambassador in Rome, explaining how he viewed the situation in the light of his agreement with Russia. My husband brought all his papers home to have them readily to hand, and I saw that Hitler ended his letter by appealing to Italy for aid – in accordance with the "Pact of Steel" – and to my husband for his understanding.

This one word was all the Duce had to cling to in his attempt to delay the day of reckoning and to keep Italy out of the war if he could find no other peaceful solution.

His immediate reply to the Führer took the form of a "delaying tactic", advising Hitler that if he expected Italy to be on Germany's side he would need to send armaments and raw materials. Benito's message went in the afternoon. At about six o'clock Attolico gave it to Hitler who waited anxiously to know Italy's position.

On reading the message, Hitler acted swiftly as he had done over Munich. According to Attolico, as soon as he left Hitler, General Keitel entered his office only to emerge quickly, shouting to his aide-de-camp: "The order to mobilize must be delayed."

It was ten in the evening when my husband received Attolico's final message at the Villa Torlonia. Once again he had postponed the day of reckoning, but for how long? During the war Benito often talked to me about that last chance of the Allies, for Hitler was afraid of losing Italy at the last moment. But for the German general staff, the Duce might have achieved even more by playing on the Führer's friendship for him.

Proof of this came the following morning when another message from Hitler arrived at the Palazzo Venezia, asking Mussolini what quantities of armaments and raw materials he needed to prepare Italy for war.

"This may go on for days, for weeks, or for months," said my husband. "We shall have to see."

Benito aimed to remain neutral until 1942, by which time he thought that Italy would be ready to enter the war. Otherwise, he would not have continued work on EUR, the new town under construction just outside Rome where he intended staging a vast demonstration to celebrate twenty years of Fascism.

So he sent another message to Hitler, deliberately exaggerating the quantities so that the Führer could not possibly provide them. During August 28, Hitler replied, as the Duce had hoped, that he could not send Italy all she asked for, but that he would agree to her remaining neutral on three conditions which were to remain secret. (I stress the word "secret" because it had a weighty effect on subsequent events.) These conditions were that Italy was not to reveal her neutrality until hostilities opened, so that the French and British would deploy forces to blockade her; she was to indicate that she was building military might for the same reason; and the Italian Government was to mobilize a labour force for Germany to replace men leaving for the front.

On the same day, my husband communicated with Hitler agreeing with these conditions and by the evening the fate of Italy appeared to be sealed; she was to remain neutral in the inevitable war. As on every occasion when he had made a momentous decision, the Duce was unusually calm when he came home.

As I watched him at dinner, I realised that I was close to regretting the good old days of the Forlí demonstrations. This time world peace hung grimly in the balance. The nagging thought that this solitary man, who sat eating before me, held the lives of millions of Italians in his hands was painful to the mind. Only a woman in a like predicament could assess my feelings.

On August 29, Ciano came in person to acquaint Benito of Hitler's attempt to reach a deal with the British Government in London. In return for British neutrality, the Führer guaranteed safety for the British Empire. On hearing of this offer, Ciano had confirmed it in a telephone conversation with Halifax, the British Minister for Foreign Affairs. The Duce was vexed because he had not been kept abreast of affairs. But rather than risk ruining whatever chance there might be, he kept his ill-humour to himself. He was still sceptical about Hitler's true desire for peace, and thought that the Führer would only be deterred by a power block composing of France, England and Italy. Yet the idea of open discussions with Britain were quite absurd while Italy officially continued with her military build-up. This last feeling was justified as events followed in swift succession after August 30.

On that day Hitler received Britain's answer to his terms. Briefly, it amounted to a refusal. Moreover, there had been a decree of general mobilization in Warsaw. The fuse to the powder keg had been lit.

When Attolico wired at nine in the morning of August 31 that the crisis was desperate, my husband tried one last effort. He was prepared, he told Halifax, to mediate with the Führer if Britain would agree to cede Danzig to Germany, but Halifax replied that annexation was out of the question. My husband tried yet another tack: in the afternoon, he invited Britain and France to reconsider the Treaty of Versailles at a conference on September 5. If they agreed, the Duce might be able to restrain the Führer yet again.

But that very evening, at 8.30, while the Italian Government still awaited a reply from London and Paris, Ciano learned that telephonic communications between Italy and Britain had been severed. The strategy Hitler and Mussolini had worked out to give the impression that Italy was preparing for war had succeeded beyond the Führer's wildest dreams. So convinced were the British that he was deceiving them that they lost all confidence in my husband. So, as evidence of our good faith, Ciano revealed to Percy Lorraine, the British ambassador in Rome, that Italy was to remain neutral. My husband went further: he ordered that the lights of Rome should be lit.

As a result, on August 31, in a desire to help Britain and France – who had not recognised the situation for what it was – Italy actually dishonoured a secret agreement concluded with Germany. After taking up a dubious position in relation to the Allies to please Hitler, Mussolini now found himself in the same position with regard to the Reich. He had risked an attack from Britain and France and now ran the danger of German aggression – as Hitler did not fail to point out quite bluntly some months later.

Ciano's gesture of friendship to the Allies on August 31 was one of the reasons for the Führer's persecution of him. In 1943, when, through an error of judgment, my son-in-law fled to German territory, Hitler permitted him to leave on one condition: that he flew to Italy, where he was arrested on landing. Edda, my daughter, tried to plead her husband's cause with Hitler himself, but in vain. The Duce forgave him, the Führer did not.

Even in this predicament, my husband obstinately strove for peace. Before making new proposals, however, he was anxious to consolidate his position. So, early in the morning of September 1, he asked Attolico to arrange for Hitler to send him a telegram freeing him from the obligations of their alliance. This arrived quickly, to be followed by a second telegram, again from Hitler, informing the Duce that he would make no more concessions and was going ahead – into war.

Even at this late hour, my husband raised a last flutter of hope; on September 2 he hinted at fresh negotiations. Contrary to all expectations, Hitler agreed. In the afternoon, in the presence of André François Poncet and Percy Lorraine, the French and British ambassadors in Rome, Ciano 'phoned Halifax and Bonnet, the French Foreign Minister, telling them of the Duce's proposal.

At seven in the evening Halifax called back, declaring that the British would not agree unless the Nazis evacuated their troops from the Polish territory they had begun to occupy the day before.

Ribbentrop did not even reply to Ciano's message about the British decision. And, as if some comic relief were called for in such high drama, on the night of September 2-3, Georges Bonnet asked the Italian am-

182

bassador in Paris for a "symbolic" withdrawal of the German forces in Poland.

On the morning of September 3, Britain and France declared war on Germany. That evening Benito said to me: "From now on it will be impossible not to enter the war, and even more impossible and dangerous not to go in on the side of Germany."

After his hostility to Hitler, it was time for Mussolini to be cautious. In the end, there could only be a marriage of convenience – for better or for worse. The Duce had taken nine months to decide. Any of the relevant documents which might cause offence are now shrouded in secrecy. But if ever they're published, historians will be able to say who fanned the sparks of war and who tried to snuff them out.

And, as to Mussolini's scrupulous attitude to Italian-German ties – for which, incidentally, he has been criticised more than once – one queries why France and Britain should have risked declaring war on Germany, in the light of their agreements with Poland, while Mussolini was not entitled to honour those he had signed with Germany.

CHAPTER 17

Why Mussolini attacked France

To imply that Mussolini never entertained the idea of war would be false. In 1940, he felt that Italy should enter the conflict for a paramount reason: to honour his agreements with Germany because conquest fitted in with the Duce's policy for Italy's political greatness and a place in the sun. It should be remembered that Germany and Italy considered themselves poor countries when set beside the great Western powers, under their "plutocratic" régimes. So my husband looked coldly on the war as a necessary evil which would enable him to finish the work of building the Italian Empire – whose birth had begun with the subjection of Abyssinia – by seizing the French protectorates or even part of France itself.

In 1939, the Duce told a meeting of the Fascist Grand Council that Italy was claiming everything this side of the Alps as Italian territory while the other side remained French. In fact, this didn't mean very much for Italy. I think that the frontier would have run somewhere near Menton-Nice. Savoy didn't figure in the Italian Government's claims, a decision which Victor-Emmanuel III deplored, for as head of the House of Savoy, he wanted it to be attached to Italy, if nothing else.

During the same meeting, the Duce had, however claimed Tunisia as an Italian protectorate, as well as Djibouti and Corsica. In the case of Corsica, he argued that although the island had had historical connections with France since the time of Napoleon, he couldn't allow French territory to remain so close to Italian shores, since it represented a strategic threat.

These claims were never made public and the Duce's proposals remained a secret. Therefore he was rather annoyed when a speech by Ciano provoked demonstration in the Chamber and frantic cries of "Tunisia, Corsica, Nice, Savoy!"

"What an intelligent way of bringing the matter to public notice and stirring the people to action," was his irritable comment as he left the Chamber. Nevertheless, in 1940 the Duce thought the moment had come to deprive France of these territories so that the Italians could have a field of action and more living space.

Apart from these territorial objectives, my husband felt he had grounds for complaint against the French as a whole, but more so against the Leftist political elements and the gamut of successive governments up to the declaration of war. At that time he cared only for three men (besides Briand, whom he greatly admired): Marshal Petain, for whom he had profound respect, General Weygand, whom he thought capable of straightening out the military situation in 1940, and Pierre Laval, for whom he had the highest regard and had met several times. I received him myself at the Villa Torlonia and was deeply impressed by his kindness, his desire for French success within the limits of the prevailing situation. Even so, I remember at their first meeting my husband's irritation when Laval prodded the statues with the tip of his cane, though obviously that hadn't marred their relations.

My husband criticised the succession of French governments because of their Leftish flavour and the fact that they had never been alive to the beginnings of Nazism. The Duce hadn't forgiven them for deserting him after the murder of Dollfuss and the Anschluss, any more than he'd forgotten the recent incidents leading up to the outbreak of the Second World War over Poland.

Finally, the attitude of the French Press, which

(*above*) *Mussolini's yacht the* Aurora (*below*) *Rachele with Romano and his new bride in* *1962* (Syndication International).

Hitler's visit to Italy 1938, and (below) Mussolini with Chamberlain and Halifax at Rome 1939 (Radio Times Hulton Picture Library).

deliberately lavished criticism on the Italian expeditionary forces in Spain, even when it was unjustified, had deeply offended him. He was certain that such adverse comments were manifestly inspired by the Government of the Popular Front which then ruled France.

And yet the obvious need to turn against France worried him, even though he assured himself there was no other course, for he'd always rather liked the country. He even gave our younger son the name Vittorio, I remember, in memory of a French victory during the First World War.

The manner in which the French despised the Italians was another source of grievance. This went back a long way to the time when Benito himself had tried to find work abroad. In 1923 he said to Rossi, who was secretary of the Fascist Party: "We have no friends in France. They're all against us. Every Frenchman thinks of us as just dirty 'Macaronis'."

I remember his delight in June 1938, on hearing that the Italian football team, which was meeting the Hungarians in the World Cup final at Marseilles, had caused a scandal by giving the Fascist salute as they entered the stadium. "At least we've shown them that the Italians aren't afraid any longer," he said. "The Macaronis will show them what they're capable of."

Above all this he objected persistently to the French Left wing parties which not only welcomed Italian political refugees but actively participated in anti-Fascist campaigns. Men like Pietro Nenni, one of Benito's fellow prisoners when they were both members of the Socialist Party, had fled to France and were not exactly idle there. For that reason few Socialists basked in my husband's admiration. Of Léon Blum, for example, he said: "He's more a great Jew than a great Socialist."

In the early part of 1940, the victory bulletins which Hitler sent impressed upon him the need to act quickly if he wanted to sit prominently at the negotiating table. But he had a problem: the Italian forces had been weakened by the campaign in Abyssinia and Spain and we were deficient in raw materials for our war industry. One evening he told me there was one solution: to delay intervention until 1942. But the snag was that the war might end sooner. He said: "If that happens we will have done nothing and be on the sidelines, while our chief ally carries off all the prizes. How can I claim part of the conquered territory if Italy is just a bystander? It's a luxury she can't afford in view of her prestige and position in the world. Also, I don't want Hitler to be the only man talking to the British and the French for their sake."

Because of all this my husband was in a state of feverish activity, urging the general staff to plunge into the fighting. But like every general staff, ours was obviously not ready. "What good is a general staff that can't make war," he protested.

It took the pressure of events themselves to get our military machine moving, the Germans who had begun their steady march from victory to victory, exerting the greatest force. Both the Allies and the Germans were intensifying their demands on the Duce, the one asking him to keep out of the war, the other pressing him to take part. Hitler, who had freed the Duce of his commitments in 1939 while the war was confined to Poland, threatened that he would not respect our frontier if Italy stayed neutral. In short, Italy was confronted with the starkness of invasion without further ado, as the Duce had always feared might happen.

This new cause for anxiety arose after Sumner Welles, Roosevelt's special envoy, arrived at the Palazzo Venezia. As soon as he set foot on Italian soil he went straight to my husband's office where they talked at great length and "very frankly", in the Duce's opinion. "He's a latter-day Colonel House," he told me. "Like him, and for the same reasons, his mission is doomed to failure."

It wasn't long before he felt the sharp repercussions of Welles' visit. As soon as it was known to Hitler, he promptly sent his special messenger, von Ribbentrop, the Foreign Secretary, whose habit of saying things without bothering about formalities, had already delighted Ciano. Without wasting words, he bluntly informed that German troops would march in and occupy Italy if she failed to abide by her Pact of Steel with Germany.

From that moment, the Duce was convinced in his mind that Italy could not remain aloof from the war much longer. In one sense, assuming that he'd the military means, he would have been glad to abandon the position he once described as "an unstable balancing act on the very edge of the flames." But he tried to be evasive for as long as he could.

In March and April, Hitler stepped up his psychological warfare, first on the Brenner where he met my husband and outlined his plans; then on April 9, when he announced that he was attacking Norway and Denmark; again on April 11, this time sending a friendly message followed by another on the 20th; and finally letters describing the victories of April 28 and May 4.

On May 10 the major blow fell. Ciano, who had dined at the German Embassy, informed the Duce that von Mackenson, the ambassador might disturb him during the night, bringing an urgent communication from Berlin. At four in the morning they both arrived at the Villa Torlonia and Irma showed them into a reception room, where the Duce soon joined them. Handing him a sealed letter from the Führer notifying him of his decision to attack Holland and Belgium, von Mackenson also asked my husband to take any measures he considered necessary for the future of Italy. He clearly meant: "Well, I'm waiting to see what you're going to do now. It's your turn to play."

"Do you realise, Rachele," said Benito, "they'll be at our gates before long."

The constant flow of messages from America, France and Britain were of little use now. On April 24, Paul Reynaud had written to my husband expressing the conviction that France and Italy ought not to fight before the leaders had met for talks. "We should have had discussions before, not now," was Benito's bitter comment, "It's not fine words we need now, but fine guns." He replied confirming his adamant decision to remain Germany's political and military ally. Therefore it would be fair to say that the French knew in April what to expect from the Italians.

Only a few days after Hitler's ultimatum, a letter was received from Churchill. I clearly remember one sentence: "I declare that I have never been an enemy of Italian greatness, nor ever, at heart, the foe of the Italian lawgiver."

"This is a good time to write that," Benito said. "If the British hadn't voted for the League of Nations' sanctions in 1935, we could have formed a European power block." And when Churchill warned the Duce about the aid Britain was bound to get from America if she herself entered the war, my husband thought it was pointless. "Britain can't withstand the German military machine. As for the Americans, they are too far away, and even if they did intervene, the Germans would have won a total victory before they had time to do anything."

Daily bulletins about the crushing advance of the forces of the Reich were reaching Rome. It was nothing less than a triumphal march and was having an impact on the Fascist Party, the Italian army, and the people. Tens of thousands of letters poured in each morning, all on the same theme: "As usual Italy is coming in last. The Germans will take everything."

One evening Benito told us: "This time the Italians aren't satisfied with snatching suitcases like the Neapolitan *scugnizzi* (street urchins) do. They want to snatch colonies, like the British."

On May 28, Belgium capitulated and as the evacuation from Dunkirk gathered impetus, Hitler again sent my husband reports of his victory.

Two days later, the tension reached its peak. It was then that President Roosevelt sent to Benito a personal message strongly urging him to stay out of the war. My husband was rather shaken by this, and in the evening he came home to the Villa Torlonia with a parcel of photos and films, which, procured by Vittorio from film associates, showed Nazi operations in Poland. After dinner we had them shown in the same room where we'd spent such pleasant hours during the years of peace. That evening all hell broke loose. We sat horrified by the tidal wave of violence, by the steel monsters bearing down and crushing everything in their path, while Stukas roared above, their strident noise piercing the ears.

To be honest, I couldn't sit right through this apocalyptic vision. I was torn between admiration for the courage of the Polish soldiers and a horror of war with its aftermath of ruin, death and tears. I fled to my room and looked from the window at the dark mass of the garden, almost expecting it to burst into flames.

The sound of the door opening made me jump. It was Benito who had come to find me. He was pale and his voice betrayed his emotion as he declared: "All those troops, all that formidable machinery, are getting closer. Soon they will be at our frontier and if they wish the Germans won't even need to cross France, we'll have a common border. Within hours they can storm Italy. But, Rachele, there's something else we can be sure of: whether we go into the war or not, the Germans will occupy Europe. If we're not there with them, they'll be able to dictate their conditions to tomorrow's Europe and that'll mean the end of Latin civilisation."

He put his hand on my shoulder, looked me intently in the eyes and said: "Rachele, we have children as well. We're going to be frightened for them. Millions of Italian mothers will be frightened, too. But I can't go back. Not only in the interest of Italy, but also to prevent her suffering the same fate as Poland, Holland and so many other countries. God is my witness that I'd have done everything to keep the peace, but I can't spend my time putting chestnuts in the fire for others to pull out."

I said nothing. Seeing tears in my eyes, Benito took my hand and said in a deliberately playful way: "Don't

191

worry, we'll try to be as quick over it as we were in Abyssinia."

That was May 30, 1940. On June 10, from the balcony of the Palazzo Venezia, Mussolini announced to the Italian people and to the world that Italy was entering the war on Germany's side. The Duce had asked Marshal Badoglio, chief of the general staff, to begin operations at once, but Badoglio objected, contending that it would take several days to muster our divisions. The rest is well known: after four days the French were seeking an armistice. What my husband had feared became reality, for the Italian forces were brought to a halt. "It's a nuisance, that," he cursed. "Couldn't the French have gone on fighting a little longer. The Italian army has hardly had time to show its paces!"

Another point had also struck the Duce: the speed with which the French line had collapsed. "How can an army which was triumphant at Verdun admit defeat so quickly?" he asked, on hearing about the French request for peace. "And that famous Maginot Line, what use was that?"

In actual fact, while he wanted victory for Germany, Italy's ally, he thought that Hitler's troops would be exhausted after the conquest of France. But not at all.

There were further surprises in store. Hitler didn't see the need for a military occupation of the whole of France and the French colonies.

"All that the Germans had to do was enter Paris and look at the Eiffel Tower and they think they've won the war," said Benito when he came back from the Munich negotiations. "With this free zone they want to maintain, they're in for some fun and games." Then, commenting on the Führer's refusal to occupy the French colonies in Africa, he added: "They're a threat as long as we lack total victory. Hitler has made a strategic error because the African colonies can serve as a storehouse of men and machinery for Frenchmen who still want to fight. Well, let's hope my fears aren't justified."

While I am on the subject, there was one error of judgment which my husband believed to be the origin of the Axis defeat; it concerned the war between Russia and Finland.

I won't go into details for the same reason why I haven't written a book on military strategy, but I am looking back to the end of 1939. At that time the valiant fight put up by Finnish troops against the Soviet army had won the admiration of the entire world. While that is well known, few people realise that the Red Army's apparent inability to engage in modern warfare inspired Hitler to embark on a rapid conquest of Russia. My husband's opinion was quite the reverse, confident that "the Russian operations against Finland were merely a trap laid for idiots. Russia," said the Duce, "could have swallowed Finland within days if Stalin had wanted it." He therefore sent Hitler a letter through the Italian ambassador in Berlin, for he already suspected that the Führer, agreeably surprised by the Red Army's ostensible weakness, envisaged ending the Soviet-German non-aggression pact. He wrote that the Russians were not to be trusted, that they were more powerful than they looked. In the circumstances, he wasn't completely taken aback when, on June 22, 1941, Hitler informed him of the invasion of Russia. But for the moment I am still talking about 1940.

I don't see the use of describing military operations; besides I'm not qualified to do so, except from the documents my husband showed me or from the comments he made.

Like every mother, I feared for the lives of my three children who had left for the front. Vittorio and Bruno were pilot officers in the Air Force and Edda served as a Red Cross nurse. It was she who caused me my first serious anxieties on the outbreak of the war.

It happened in March 1941, during the Greek campaign, which my husband considered a defeat and which cost Marshal Badoglio his post as chief of general staff.

One morning I woke after a strange and disturbing

dream in which I had a premonition about some impending disaster. I was telling Ernestine, my maid, about it when the telephone rang. It was my husband. With his customary tact when conveying bad news, he blurted out: "Edda has fallen into the sea. She was in the water for five hours, but she's safe. I'm flying off to see her."

"How did it happen?" I asked, alarmed.

"I'll tell you when I get back."

Then the line went dead. Eventually he 'phoned again, relating the incident in detail. Hit by seven bombs, the hospital ship on which Edda was serving off the Greek coast had started to sink immediately. She stood paralysed with fright as the boat capsized. Luckily a sailor running by had pushed her into the water enabling her to escape from the backwash when the vessel went down. She was rescued five hours later.

On August 7, 1941, I experienced the pangs of grief so many mothers have felt on learning that one of their children had died. I had seen Bruno for the last time at the Villa Torlonia on July 30 coming to kiss me goodbye before returning to base. More demonstrative than usual, he had even asked me to keep his wife and their little girl, Marina, with me. The following morning he came to the house again, just as he was about to leave, and I can still visualise him on my doorstep, tall and strong with that innocent look of a child who had grown up too fast.

I have lost other members of my family – for instance, a daughter whom I adored – but I've also had first-hand experience of the despair of parents who have just lost a child and can't rebel against it because their sacrifice is the dearest gift a mother can make to her country.

Even if this is not the appropriate place to say so, I would like all mothers who read these words, whatever their nationality, to know that Mussolini's wife and Mussolini himself were always deeply affected by the grief of those who lost a son in the war.

Apart from my children, many Ministers, officials and others donned the grey-green uniform, usually for only a few months – merely a break in their career. At least that was the pattern at the beginning, but later it changed, becoming tougher during the North African campaign, in Ethiopia, Russia and finally on Italian soil.

As in every country at war, daily life in Italy had its crop of difficulties. But compared to what I saw in Germany, we Italians suffered less. For example, there were football matches every Sunday until the end of the war, the cinemas were open, the concerts carried on and the people could get out and about. Obviously we had restrictions, ration cards and very little petrol.

The Mussolinis themselves were exposed to the same stringencies and I can assert most emphatically that neither my husband nor I infringed the current laws nor allowed others to do so. Once, receiving several hundredweights of coffee at the Villa Torlonia – a gift from Italians residing in Brazil – the Duce decided to distribute it to the hospitals. Yet every time we passed near the room where the coffee was temporarily stored, the exquisite odour insinuated itself making us faint with longing. To have coffee – one's national drink – within reach, and not be able to touch it, is real martyrdom.

It would be hard to imagine the severe restrictions the Duce imposed on the family right from the early days of the war. We'd to give up our pleasure trips in the car; Benito himself used his only to go from the Villa Torlonia to the Palazzo Venezia or for other official journeys. Because I had parted with mine, the children went to school by bus. Even Anna-Maria, who wore a special bodice – the result of poliomyelitis – did as everyone else.

It was my practice to take food to the children in the care of a Monte Mario institution, but in spite of the transport difficulties I refused to end these visits. Instead I went by bus – that is until Cardinal Pizzardo, learning about it from a nun, immediately lent me his personal car which enjoyed the advantages peculiar to the Vatican.

195

I remember too, that on March 11, 1942, a requiem mass was held in Rome for the Duke of Aosta, Viceroy of Ethiopia, who had died in a Nairobi clinic while a prisoner of the British. The King and Queen of Italy attended, as did the highest authorities of the State, including the holders of the Collar of the Annunziata. I had gone there in a bus with my daughter-in-law, Gina, and after the service, when everyone took leave of the royal couple, I noticed that they still remained standing while an usher looked agitatedly for my car. Something had to be done, and quickly, for because of my husband's status the next person to leave the church should have been myself; moreover, people were waiting for me. Galeazzo Ciano ran forward to suggest taking me home; he was perplexed because I hadn't come in a car. Calmly I showed him my bus ticket and went home the way I had come.

These two illustrations will convey our way of life during the Second World War. To be perfectly honest I ought to mention that, fortunately for us, I still had my chickens, rabbits and little pigs at the Villa Torlonia, which allowed me to vary our diet and add something extra to what we got from our ration books. For the record, I should add that my husband's book – as one might expect – was number one.

To return to military operations, I say quite simply that Italy's great mistake – and I haven't the faintest idea if it originated with my husband, the Italian general staff or both – was to conduct the same kind of war as the Germans. In Africa, among other instances, our general staff were mounting operations without any attempt at liaison with the Germans. Consequently a whole series of temperamental difficulties arose between the two armies. On the African front, for example, no sooner had Hitler promoted Rommel to the rank of marshal than the same honour was conferred on General Cavallero and General Bastico, chief of the general staff and commander-in-chief of the Italian forces respectively. The sole object was to avoid letting the Italian generals appear in any way inferior. I should add that the German generals made no attempt to foster good relations for they snatched every chance to flaunt their superiority over their Italian counterparts. When Italian-German arms took Tobruk and reached the gates of Alexandria, the Duce spent a month on the African front – from June 29 to July 21, 1942 – trying to iron out differences and boost morale. Under the strain of nervous tension he returned to Rome with terrible stomach pains. That summer of 1942 saw the turning point for, after success in Africa, the troop withdrawals began and in Russia the Red Army began to take the initiative.

On the subject of hostilities in Russia, I should point out that my husband had foreseen the events of 1942 and 1943 from the very moment he received a report of the German attack on the Soviet Union.

This was on June 22, 1941. We were staying at Riccione when the telephone rang at about three in the morning and because it was near my bed, I answered it. The caller, the German military attaché at the embassy in Rome, asked desperately to talk to the Duce. To avoid waking Benito, I suggested that he should 'phone back later but he refused, stressing the urgency with the remark: "I have to tell the Duce that Germany has just declared war on Russia." I ran to Benito's room and woke him, but when he came to the 'phone it was not just to listen; he spoke long and irritably in German. When he'd hung up, he said furiously: "It's madness. It's our ruin. They should never have attacked Russia. Germany may know how to make war but not politics." He did not return to his bed, but set off for Rome at once.

Hurriedly he set up an Italian expeditionary force under the command of General Messe, to whom he specifically ordered: "It must be a lightning victory. We ought to beat the Russians in a matter of months."

For this particular campaign the Fascists displayed wild enthusiasm, for this meant getting to grips with Marxism itself. That is a salient reason why the troops of the CSIR, or Italian expeditionary force in Russia, fought better than soldiers on any other front.

"You see," my husband said to me, "even there they need us. In this way we can show the whole world that it isn't only Germans who are able to win."

Soon afterwards, in October 1941, the Duce informed me that the Führer had called him in person to tell him of the capture of the town of Orel. "That's great," he cried. "Orel is at the gates of Moscow." Then he added: "They must be careful and tighten the net quickly, for winter isn't far away." And in fact the cold from the Arctic that year was terribly severe: there'd been nothing like it in Russia for twenty or thirty years.

The Duce had noticed specific aspects of the Russian front when he visited the divisions of the Italian expeditionary force in the Ukraine. Accompanied by Vittorio, he had flown in the same plane as Hitler, who had failed to conceal his fright when he saw Benito take control of the plane. The Führer, however, hadn't dared to say anything. "Do you realise," my husband later observed, "what a hit the Russians would have scored if they'd shot down our plane. In one blow they'd have killed Hitler and Mussolini!"

As the flight occurred over German-held Soviet territory in the height of summer, the Duce could see the vast stretches of corn. It clearly impressed him, but he was shocked by the attitude of various units of the army of the Reich.

"They're too harsh with the local population," he told me. "When they forage they raze everything to the ground. That's wrong because the victors should always behave humanely towards the inhabitants of conquered countries."

The few months which the Duce allotted for conquest in Russia ran out without achieving his objective. From then onwards he grew more certain that the disaster in Russia would begin the fall of the Axis.

I can now enlighten everyone that my husband devoted months trying to induce Hitler, both in writing and by word of mouth, to negotiate with the Russians.

He even established contacts with the Russians through Japan, but nothing tangible came out of them. Hitler was never interested in discussing peace with the Soviet Union.

Before ending this chapter, I would like to make one thing clear: my husband was never in doubt about the courage of the Italians. His sole complaint related to some of our army's leaders, who had obviously forgotten that one can't wage war in comfort or by creating impenetrable barriers between the ranks. He'd seen signs of this particularly on the African front, and had made a point of telling those responsible quite openly. When he went to Russia he was impressed by the close relationship between officers and men. Hitler and he even lunched with the ratings and received the same menu.

The foreign Press has commented freely about Italian soldiers surrendering without a fight or deserting during the Second World War. This is completely untrue. For one thing, there were never so few deserters as during that war. For another, the soldiers who laid down their arms did so at the command of their leaders, as happened at Pantelleria and Augusta, two important naval bases. If they'd behaved differently the net result would probably have been much the same, for the Allied forces were much stronger, though the Italian army would have ended the fight with more honour to their name. The Italians who remained in the German ranks after September 8, 1943, and the men fighting with the partisans, were magnificent in combat.

CHAPTER 18

I was the Duce's secret agent

"Can you explain how you manage to know some things at least several weeks before I do?" The day that my husband posed this question I felt extremely proud, for it was his first open admission that the information I brought to him had intrinsic value. I had just won my laurels so to speak, as super secret agent to Mussolini, one of my various pursuits which few people know about even to this day.

But the curious thing is that to acquire my items of intelligence I never directed any kind of police force; it was essentially a product of my feminine instinct and my peasant good sense; I had noticed since 1926, on my first visit to Rome, that certain people in the Duce's entourage failed to inspire the least trust in me. And so I decided to keep them under surveillance.

Later, in 1929, when the whole family moved to the Villa Torlonia, I came up against the snags of protocol: as the wife of the head of government, I was not expected to lead the kind of life I had previously adhered to – even in Milan after my husband came to power. I couldn't, for instance, take the children to school, go into the big stores to buy shoes for them, or, more simply, stand over the stove and do the housework. This didn't suit me one scrap because I'd never been accustomed to a lazy life and I found these limitations a real burden.

On the other hand, I was soon to discover that few people knew who I was. My photo appeared in the Press a few times but hardly anyone could describe Rachele Mussolini's features – especially as I had rarely been seen at official public functions. I remember at the wedding of my daughter, Edda, some journalists expressed astonishment on seeing what I was really like. Some days later Benito brought me some foreign papers – mostly English and American – observing: "You've been a hit with the reporters, Rachele. They all thought you were marvellous. They were even more amazed because they thought you were old and ugly."

The compliment flattered me at the time, but it didn't make me any more eager to emerge from the shadows in which I'd decided to live. At the Villa Torlonia, or at certain ceremonies that I couldn't avoid, I was Her Excellency Rachele Mussolini, wife of the head of government; for the rest of the time my name was Rachele Guidi, my maiden name, and I had complete freedom of movement.

And yet there was a minor obstacle. Whether I was Rachele Guidi or Rachele Mussolini I still remained the Duce's wife and as such came face to face with security problems. In all, three or four policemen were assigned to me personally as bodyguards and because I couldn't get rid of them I resolved to employ them as secret agents. At least in that way I could keep them occupied so that they didn't bother me much.

Besides, like every wife of an eminent personality who wants to make some useful contribution and isn't just looking for honours, I helped certain people in various ways, and before long I'd formed an information network with offshoots all over Italy. That, and the thousands of letters I received each week, demonstrate how I soon acquired more information than probably anyone else in Italy.

My husband was quick to appreciate that he could exploit this situation to his advantage. Every now and again he would send me to "take the temperature" of the man-in-the-street or perform some special mission – as, for instance, in 1931 in the Alto Adige. The local Fascist Party secretary had been sending derogatory reports criticising the official authorities, the governmental representatives in that region, for alleged incompetence. In return the Prefect denied these accusations, blaming the branch secretary for meddling in other people's affairs; in short, exhibiting too much zeal.

The whole problem was much more ticklish because, since my husband had come to power, he had endeavoured to separate the party from the State, so that the Fascist Party could not identify itself with the State. In this way, he hoped to avoid corruption and maintain respect for the establishment; so much so, that every time any kind of dispute arose between representatives of party and government, he almost always found in favour of the Prefect. This not unnaturally caused some resentment.

In the Alto Adige, however, it appeared that both sides were not blameless and the Fascist secretary's arguments worried the Duce. Seeing that I had to go to Merano for a course of treatment, he asked me to "ferret about" up there. I stayed for a month and when I came back to Rome, he had my completely objective reports to guide him: neither the Prefect nor the local secretary were fulfilling their duties as they should. Both were moved to other posts.

This was one of the few extra-mural jobs which I carried out by the Duce. Because of his beliefs about what a woman's rôle ought to be, he thought my activities should be confined to picking up rumours and passing them on to him. And they were not to be "old wives' tales" either, for then my reports would annoy rather than interest him.

I, on the contrary, had no desire whatsoever to stop there. From what Benito told me, backed by my own intelligence sources I was becoming daily more convinced that the whole truth never reached him. Some people in whom he placed trust were definitely misleading him, assuring him that no problems prevailed when the reverse was the case. In normal peace-time conditions, this attitude would have no serious impact, but I wondered what these people would do if Italy was beset by crisis or involved in war.

My fears were all the greater because not a single facet of my husband's nature was hidden from me. I knew, for example, that he was susceptible to persuasion in that the last speaker usually left the most indelible impression. He was trusting to the point of naïveté, thinking that anyone who agreed to work with him could never betray him. Basically kind-hearted, he was opposed to hurting people, always finding an excuse to forgive whether it was his children or his Ministers. His philosophy of man was such that he felt a more intimate bond with someone like Gandhi or Saint Francis of Assisi (whom he worshipped and had made the Patron Saint of Italy), than someone like Stalin or Hitler (whom he admired to some degree but whose brutality and violence he'd always condemned).

I should imagine that this trait in Mussolini is virtually unknown, for the world has stopped short at the false image of the dictator, the despot. There are many people who, sincerely or not, will give the lie to my words but I can prove my arguments with two official and historical facts.

The first is connected with the list of war criminals which the Allies drew up at the end of the Second World War: Mussolini's name did not appear on it, any more than the name of any other Italian, soldier or politician. He was Adolf Hitler's major ally but no one could accuse him of any crime against international ethics.

The second is Hitler's own personal view, as stated in September 1943. When Otto Skorzeny rescued my husband from the Gran Sasso, where his successor, Marshal Badoglio had sent him, the Führer received him at his general headquarters in Rastenberg. During conversation he summed up Benito Mussolini's paramount weakness. "Duce you are too kind-hearted," he told him. "You'll never make a dictator."

Nowadays such words are a source of comfort to me, especially as not a day passes without someone saying to me: "You remember how good the Duce was, Donna Rachele. He did this, that and the other." Yet for a logical reason, at the time I thought that all these fine qualities were the worst faults a dictator could have. Take, for instance, a strong and forceful man who is firmly in control. Give him all the equipment of command and you'll make him a dictator. But for such a man to do everything himself is physically impossible.

He therefore chooses trustworthy associates who have sworn their loyalty and who may even have proved their love for the cause which brought them together before they reached the heights of glory.

Supposing this dictator makes a mistake, or that his colleagues – driven by ambition and corrupted by the desire for advancement, riches and titles – decide to betray the man who has put his trust in them. Cunningly, they refrain from telling him that they're no longer what he thinks they are. Therefore all that they can do is to spin a web of lies in which they'll try to trap him. That way they'll hide the truth from him – the truth about themselves because it's not attractive and the truth about the outside world because it might disturb their tranquility.

Then, with the passage of events, they begin to move from "omissions" to deceit and from deceit to treachery. One might forgive all this while things are going well, but I think they should be punished when the moment of truth arrives.

Finally, if the dictator is an easy-going rather than a stern Victorian father figure, then one day he is bound to lose control of the situation; by the time he realises that he's been deceived, it'll be too late! That is what I always feared and wished to avoid by keeping watch on some of the "faithfuls" who were faithful only by name. I might as well say at the outset that although investigation exposed a deterioration that went from bad to worse, the end result was always the same: my husband would punish the man who had erred simply by appointing him to another post or sending him away. But this was feeble compared to the severe punishment or purges like Stalin's.

But it was still true that my activities as a female James Bond were often useful and they had an edge to them. For instance, on one occasion I learnt that my husband drove to a farm on the outskirts of Rome every morning. At first I was somewhat sceptical but when friends who told me about it described the car, driver and passenger I had to admit they were talking about the Duce.

In the end I decided to get an explanation. One afternoon while we were taking a stroll in the garden of the Villa Torlonia – as we often did after lunch – I asked him point blank why he went to the farm. I had caught him nibbling at some peas he had just picked. He stood open-mouthed, the shell in his hand and looked at me wild-eyed, as if I had suddenly gone mad. I didn't make an issue of it. Obviously the key to the mystery lay elsewhere.

I quickly put my "secret police" to work and soon wrested the secret. True, the car was my husband's, the driver was Ercole Borratto, our chauffeur, but the Duce wasn't the Duce. Let me explain. As it was wartime and there was rationing in the country, our chauffeur had devised an ingenious plan for trading on the black market without being caught. He found an accomplice who was bald and of the same stature as my husband. The perfect double would sit in the back of the car – the ideal decoy – while in the boot were the goods which Ercole could distribute quite freely.

I considered the matter serious enough to tell Benito about it, yet all he did was grumble and give his driver a drubbing down. He didn't take the matter any further because he was fond of Ercole Borratto, for he had been through some trying times with him. He therefore forgave him and when I told Benito that Ercole might be capable of more harm some day, he began to laugh. But he was wrong, although I had no proof of Borratto's treachery until much later when my husband was already dead.

During the time when Benito was still head of government, I had often noticed Borratto jotting various things down in a little notebook when we were in the car. I told my husband about it, expressing my fear that any conversations he might be having with other passengers were being passed on.

"While there's only the two of us talking," I said, "it doesn't matter, but any indiscretion about a political conversation could be more troublesome."

"You think so, do you," he exclaimed. "You see danger everywhere, Rachele. The honest fellow is only making a note of the mileage. That's all!"

Some years later, at the end of the war, a book was published, written by Ercole Borratto. In it the "honest" chauffeur described the discussions he said he'd heard between my husband and other people. That was the very thing I had feared. But I am sure that Borratto wasn't acting alone because his revelations weren't confined to conversations in the Duce's car. Under remote control from various quarters he agreed to take part in a small campaign to blacken Mussolini's name, for at that time those people made continual efforts to drag my husband into the gutter.

If someone else had been involved I wouldn't have been surprised, but that it should be Borratto, whom my husband had trusted for twenty years, made me sad; it was further proof that a sense of gratitude is something which not all men possess. I knew that Borratto had recorded a tissue of lies. He did so again, a few years ago, when he wrote another book containing another series of lies as foul as the first.

If such disloyalty had been confined to chauffeurs, the tale of my exploits would not be very interesting. But there was much more serious treachery afoot than Borratto's.

In 1935, during the Abyssinian War, the Villa Torlonia, had a permanent telephone line to the general headquarters of the Italian armies. That was how my husband was able to follow operations hour by hour, to receive reports and to give orders. One evening he got the distinct impression while he was actually speaking that someone else was on the line though they hadn't said anything openly. One should remember that in those days telephone lines weren't as clear as they are now. This interference which lasted throughout the conversation, reappeared with such regularity that eventually the Duce tore out the telephone wires in a fit of temper. "This really is too much! Who on earth has the nerve to listen in on my line," he burst out.

He ordered an inquiry but the mystery went unsolved, and so I decided to meddle in the affair. Without saying anything to my husband, I instructed a couple of my agents who were familiar with the workings of the telephone to make some tests. In no time I learnt that our line was quite simply being tapped by Marshal Badoglio, the commander-in-chief of the Italian forces in Ethiopia, the very man whom my husband most trusted from a military point of view.

It cost me 5,000 lire which was quite an appreciable sum at the time, but my men cut the line which enabled Badoglio to tap ours and paid some of Badoglio's agents to keep quiet about it.

However, we didn't have peace for long because after Badoglio there were others. And astonishingly enough, the Marshal managed to listen in to the Duce's conversations even when he was no longer chief of general staff. Stroveglia, one of my private policemen, had to go into action again before we could put a stop to Badoglio's chicanery.

Now that I am on the subject I could refer to Badoglio for hours. To sum him up, I think he was a typical example of the man who is prepared to do anything to slake his thirst for honour and titles. When my husband made him chief of general staff in 1925, many people advised him against the choice, criticising Badoglio for not being entirely trustworthy. During the First World War he hadn't been noticeable for his brilliance. Moreover, he was a Freemason and well known for his lack of concern for anything other than his own interests.

The Duce, however, thought that someone who had pledged his honour by agreeing to take on an important command could not betray him. So strong was this belief that he paid no attention to other people's opinions of Badoglio.

He would have done better if he had heeded them, for Badoglio had time to commit quite a few lapses before the Duce realised his blunder. Of these lapses I shall give just one example, for the record, which concerns his endless delays to the start of military operations in 1940, under the pretext that the army wasn't ready.

But there were two more serious instances which, in any other country, would have meant a court martial at least for the offender. First, Badoglio never kept the Duce up to date with the exact state of the Italian army before the Italians entered the war. Neither did he do so when it came to the French and Greek campaigns.

I know it is hard to make such accusations stick thirty years later when the archives have vanished – at least some of them, anyway – and when the two men most closely involved, Mussolini and Badoglio, are no longer alive. But trying to argue logically, if Badoglio really did warn the Duce that the army was unprepared and the Duce didn't consider his opinion, then why did he agree to uphold such a far-reaching decision? In his position as chief of general staff, Badoglio could then have resigned or asked the King, as supreme head of the armed forces, to arbitrate. But he didn't.

The second instance is even more compromising. Three months after Italy went into the war the Fiat factories designed a 30-ton tank. While it had become clear to the whole world over the past few weeks that German strength lay essentially in this kind of armoured vehicle, Badoglio ordered the weight of the machine to be reduced to 27 tons. The Fiat engineers worked frantically and the 27-ton tank was soon ready. But then the chief of general staff asked for further modifications, and they'd to reduce the weight again from 27 tons to 24.

Such stupidity – assuming that it was never more than that – would have meant a council of war anywhere else. Not only did Badoglio go unpunished, but he went on seeking honours and sinecures until the Duce's eyes were finally opened and he relieved him of his duties during the Greek campaign.

Just for the record, I would mention that one day a telegrapher passed on to my husband a cable from General Ubaldo Soddu, commander-in-chief in Albania, who had wired that the situation there was causing grave concern. But he specifically ordered that the Duce was not to be told. Ubaldo was also relieved of his post.

Since I am on the subject, I would point out that these treacherous acts began as soon as Italy entered the war. I wish to make this point quite clear because one might assume that in the face of defeat and with the prospect of total disaster, the military leaders were changing sides. In actual fact allegiance was violated right from the start when Italy was still powerful and her ally Germany was marching from one victory to the next.

The truth is much more depressing and nauseating. The King, some of the military leaders and various Fascists had irons in every fire, using Mussolini as long as he could serve some purpose but consolidating their position, even if they had to betray him, for what the future might bring.

They were forgetting that before destroying Mussolini, they'd be destroying Italian soldiers – young men who could laugh at life, who trusted them and who believed that they were dying under enemy fire when in fact their fellow Italians had been their undoing. And nobody can convince me that these persons were prompted by idealism. If there had been one leader ordering them to fight Fascism, they could have assassinated Mussolini. At least that would have been honourable, if more dangerous. And danger makes for fear, especially when one lacks courage.

The only attempt on my husband's life – if it really

was one – took place in Albania in 1941, when he went to the front line to watch our forces make what was intended to be an offensive but which finally never materialised. While his car was crawling to an observation post at the top of a hill, he heard a voice say to him in Romagnol: "Don't go any further, Duce! Don't go! I'm speaking to you in dialect so that no one can understand."

Benito told me that he disregarded the warning seeing that he couldn't cancel the offensive. He merely looked round to see where the voice had come from, if for no other reason than to show how glad he was to hear Romagnol, but no one came forward.

Staying at the observation post for a while, he left a quarter of an hour earlier than arranged. He had only just gone when a shell came straight down to explode on the very spot where he had been, a splinter even penetrating the binoculars he'd just used. I kept them as a souvenir. Whether it was chance or whether the soldier who shouted the warning to him was right, we never knew.

The worst of it all was that after a certain time Benito was well aware of the treachery, but all the inquiries he set in motion resulted in nothing. It was as if some irresistible and invisible force was driving him off course. In fact those reponsible were various influential army leaders who were acting partly out of blind fanaticism, partly because the Duce – having meddled in sacrosanct customs – had disturbed the comfortable tranquility of the officers' existence, and partly out of opposition to what they called "Mussolini's war".

Once, in 1923, Benito and I went round some of the high-ranking officers' quarters, and he was horrified to discover how they treated their batmen. While ordinarily they were only meant to help their officers in the performance of their duties, my husband found that they were used as all-purpose servants. The poor soldiers who had been "picked" as batmen were helping madam to do the shopping, doing the housework, wiping the children's noses and so on. The Duce kicked up a great fuss, though I need hardly say that it was all to no effect.

Sometimes he could be ironic about the acts of sabotage. On one occasion he said of the Abyssinian war: "We were so quick that even the traitors haven't had time to betray us." But most of the time he was sadly upset by what he learnt, always after the event. He used to groan: "Who can I trust?"

It grew so bad that when the Italian secret service first reported, in May 1943, that an Allied landing might take place in Sicily during the next few months, the Duce said to me one evening: "I'm sure they won't be able to land, unless everyone is lying to me. I trust the soldiers, but as for the others . . . !" Unfortunately that was precisely what I feared, for I too, had my informers, and my private police force were reporting nothing but alarming news.

During the winter of 1942, for instance, a Carabiniere brought me a rocket made by our Terni munitions factories. There was no powder inside, but sawdust. Yet again my husband ordered an inquiry. The mass of evidence was all there in black and white and the report was put on his desk, then suddenly nobody could find it; it was as if it had been spirited away.

There was worse to come. On our way home from Terminile, the winter sports resort where we sometimes stayed, the Duce paid an unexpected visit to an air base. According to the lists provided by the general staff, there should have been squadrons of fighter planes, but Benito was astounded to discover that there were no planes at all. After giving him the figures, a general had conceived the idea of keeping up the deception by moving various squadrons from base to base to be ready for inspection. Fortunately my husband had discovered the ruse in time. I was so angry about it that I was ill for several days.

Similarly, on another occasion Benito summoned the Under-Secretary for Aviation to Rocca delle Caminate, instructing him to visit the Caproni factory which was manufacturing new planes. This time, because the factory was close to Predappio, it meant that we would have no great difficulty exposing any fiddle that might ensue. The Secretary made his inspection, noted the quantity of raw materials required and promised delivery of several hundred aircraft. Some time later my husband was advised that hundreds of this new type of plane had been produced and were actually ready to fly, yet I soon discovered that in fact the raw materials which had reached the factory were only sufficient for two planes – yes, two planes, not one more.

I passed this staggering piece of news on to Benito and I must admit I seldom saw him get into such a state. Harsh measures were taken, but as I've already said, he would have had to sack many people to put the situation right. Once again he had to give me the credit, which at any other time would have made me happy. "Ninety times out of a hundred," he admitted, "Mamma is right."

Even more depressing than the deliberate acts of treachery was the passive attitude of some people and, after the early defeats, the criminal habit of not daring to tell the Duce the truth. Consequently, those who had the courage to do so were immediately discovered and removed so that they couldn't make the same mistake of reporting to Benito again. Once my own son Vittorio, an officer in the air force, came to see his father, informing him that the radio receivers on some aircraft just weren't working at all. Indeed, the pilots were reduced to using sign language to communicate between themselves, which wasn't very easy during combat.

Benito summoned the Under-Secretary at the Air Ministry and I don't know how many generals and demanded an explanation. He got one: the receivers were working perfectly. He soon realised he was just banging his head against a wall.

I even wondered about the death of our son Bruno. On August 7, 1941, his plane crashed to the ground on the verge of the runway at Pisa aerodrome, for some reason which has never been explained. Bruno was a distinguished pilot who had totalled an impressive number of flying hours. Even at the last moment, he managed to avoid inhabited areas though his plane was in distress. I shall never be quite free of the idea that Bruno, who was also in a position to find out discrepancies and discuss them with his father, paid for his powers of observation with his life. Whatever anyone says to the contrary, I saw evidence of too much wickedness to believe it was only an accident.

In the same way, I don't think it was chance that the *Duilio*, the *Cavour* and the *Littorio*, three of the finest cruisers in the Italian fleet, were sunk by English bombs in the middle of Taranto harbour in November 1940, and only four months after Italy went into the war. "Without some treason, it's impossible to score such a hit," the Duce was forced to admit. Even then, in 1940, treason was already at work.

So, contrary to my husband's hopes, I was worried about our chances of beating back an invasion force in Sicily. But even I, who was well known for my pessimism, could never have imagined that the Italian defences in the area would be so weak.

When Admiral Pavesi, the commander-in-chief of the fortress of Pantelleria, insisted that the supreme commander of the Italian forces – that is the Duce – should allow him to surrender because, he said, he hadn't a drop of water left and was in an impossible position, my husband was dubious. He gave Pavesi permission though out of concern to save human life.

It was not until a few days later that he came home blind with rage. He had a bundle of papers under his arm and threw them on his desk, saying to me: "Read that, Rachele! They're English radio messages which our listening services have intercepted. He may say he's come out of it with honour, that Pavesi! He hasn't lost a single man. He just threw in the sponge. The English say so."

Unhappily it was all too true. In these messages the English had reported to their general staff that the base at Pantelleria surrendered without having suffered any casualties. The same applied to the fortress at Augusta, a highly fortified naval base, where the commander-in-chief hadn't fired a shot. As soon as he saw the enemy, he burnt his papers then opened his gates and his arms wide in welcome.

What could I say to the American officer who, when it was all over and I was in a concentration camp in 1945, asked me: "Can you explain, Excellency, why millions of Italians who worshipped Mussolini for twenty years should have made a complete turn around in this way?" Could I tell him that the Italian people hadn't changed sides or committed treason. When my country entered the war the soldiers did their duty with enthusiasm. When the time of defeat and sacrifice arrived, the civilian population showed themselves capable of self-denial and courage. The people had behaved irreproachably even when they longed for peace in 1943. Thus, the Italian people made no contribution to the fall of Mussolini, any more, by the way, than did the anti-Fascists who boasted of it after the event.

Even so, I couldn't admit to this officer, who had been our enemy, that the Fascist régime had destroyed itself; that some officials had weakened through fear of the future or through ambition. After 1943, as part of a well organised propaganda campaign, we were led to believe that these officials had turned against Mussolini. This is untrue, for even among those men who voted against my husband during the meeting of the Grand Council just before his removal from power, there were many Fascists who, while they wanted peace, didn't wish the Duce to go.

But I couldn't tell him any of that. So my answer to his question was a silent shrug of the shoulders.

CHAPTER 19

The true portrait of the dictator

One day during the Second World War, while we were at Rocca delle Caminate, I exposed a fine scandal. After that I acquired some notoriety as Mussolini's adviser. It all started when Benito was receiving some Fascist dignitaries in the hall of the Grand Council. I had sneaked in behind them and when – as was the custom – they rose, arms outstretched, to salute him with the cry "At your command, Duce!" I echoed loudly, "Yes, to betray you."

Far from being furious with me, Benito asked me to be present at further talks with other notables. He wanted to know if his visitors spoke the truth or not. I would sit on one of the wooden benches padded with cushions, which stood under each window, and follow the conversation without speaking.

Such was the case – again at Rocca delle Caminate – the day Mussolini received the Minister of Agriculture. He had brought sheaves of paper covered with figures and graphs to justify the corn quota he intended to allow the peasants. Perhaps I should explain that during the war food rationing applied to both urban and rural populations. After long explanations as to why the Minister thought these quotas should be limited to 100 kilos for adults and 150 for children, Benito turned to me and said: "You know about these things, Rachele. What do you think?"

By chance, some minutes before the Minister arrived in a special coach, an agent had informed me that

217

people in the vicinity were annoyed with the big-wig. His personal cook had been requisitioning stocks of biscuits from local tradesmen. Since he had come to discuss rationing, this seemed rather curious, to say the least.

So, before I said anything else, I eagerly told the Duce about it. Then I looked the Minister straight in the eye, and said: "One hundred kilos of corn would be too much for you, because you don't need bread. You've your supply of biscuits. But do you realise that to peasants, bread is everything? In Romagna they even kiss it before putting it on the table. Country children eat twice as much as adults because they're always hungry."

Turning to Benito, I asked him if he would guarantee that adults received 150 kilos and children 200. From behind his desk he nodded his approval, while the Minister, now on tenterhooks, would have agreed to anything. All he wanted to do was leave – in a hurry.

That is how biscuits and my private police gave a little more corn to the Italian peasants during the war.

I could achieve such things only at Rocca delle Caminate, however, for in Rome I never made a habit of going to the Palazzo Venezia. Affairs of state were conducted much more formally in the capital than in Romagna; the whole atmosphere was different. But I didn't abandon my self-appointed mission to keep a watchful eye on the administrative hierarchy to prevent them from deceiving the Duce. Besides, I began to establish a reputation for fairness and was beseiged with appeals to right other people's wrongs.

This could be risky seeing that nothing is more misleading than hearsay. For every ten items of information which came my way, one or two might be reliable – sometimes none at all. It was wise to be cautious, because if some accusation reached the Duce's ears and was later proved to be unjustified, the swindlers went straight into action.

I had to check every detail meticulously, especially at this time, and if I thought the affair serious, I did not hesitate to investigate it myself. That is why, when I heard rumours that an official had changed the facade of his stable to resemble the frontage of the Duce's villa at Riccione, it took me a while to believe that so foolish a whim could be true. But I went to check. It was false. Then I was told that a Minister had paved the road leading to his house and erected a statue of himself in the village square; I saw red. I could not tolerate anyone who held a position of high social responsibility behaving in this way. That sort of vanity infuriated me, especially as my husband had always refused even to tarmac the stretch of road leading to the Villa Carpena, although it was only about three quarters of a mile long. So I went to see for myself and found that all the rumours were absolutely true. I took action at once, I can assure you.

I was just as painstaking when I learnt that one of Mussolini's own secretaries was building himself a magnificent villa at Rocca di Papa on the outskirts of Rome. There were even reports, untrue as it turned out, that Mussolini had given it to Clara Petacci, though luckily they never reached my ears. As far as I was concerned the owner of this sumptuous property was the secretary, but I had to have proof that it belonged to him.

I went there with Irma and one of my investigators and found that there was indeed a building site. I urged Mussolini to ask his secretary for an explanation. The man swore that the allegation was untrue and, to prove it, produced a photograph of a small farm which belonged to him to show his good faith.

Not satisfied with this, I returned to the site some days later disguised as a peasant woman desperately seeking work to support her six fatherless children. As I stood chatting to the man on the gate, both full of admiration for and indignant about the cost of this structure, Romano – who had accompanied me – tactfully filmed the whole scene. Indeed, I still have the reel.

A week later I suggested that Benito should come and see a little film his grandchildren had made. My scheme worked to perfection and he followed me into the hall prepared to admire the children's handiwork. Benito sat amazed, though whether his secretary's guilt or my system of detection surprised him the more, it is hard to say.

In the face of such evidence, he asked for a further explanation from his secretary. This time he excused himself on the grounds that his wife had inherited some money. My husband dismissed him.

It was after enquiries of this kind that Bocchini, the director-general of the police force, once said that he would gladly use my services if I were not the Duce's wife, for he could do with someone who stuck to the scent. Romano, on the other hand, seeing how tolerant his father was, suggested with childish spontaneity that there should be a coup d'état and I should be made dictator.

Some readers may find these stories disrespectful or even offensive. Others may think that I'm exaggerating and trying to turn Mussolini into a simple man who was deceived by everybody, preached to by his wife occasionally, and most emphatically under Hitler's thumb. I wish only to give an objective account of the Duce, neither for nor against him as his biographers have been.

From the day I first met him to his poignant farewell telephone call 45 years later, Mussolini always kept his humanity and his good qualities along with the bad.

It's all too easy to say that Mussolini was ruined because he was Hitler's ally, that his fate was no more than what tyrants deserve, and that he was guilty of every imaginable crime. This book is not intended to make him appear to be a greater man, but only to restore him to his real stature, his true aspect.

I think it is right to censure my husband for pardoning his "faithful" supporters. I held it against him as well. But very few people know that the man who assassinated him owed his liberty, if not his life, to Mussolini.

Walter Audisio says that he was the instrument of

justice when, under the pseudonym of Colonel Valerio, he executed Benito Mussolini – as a beast is slaughtered – against a wall.

But he never tells the story of how he found freedom in 1934 after being arrested and interned as a Communist. He quite simply wrote the Duce a letter asking how long his internment would last because his family were in need. And what did Mussolini do?

He freed Walter Audisio and even authorised him to work in a Fascist agricultural co-operative. Obviously Fascist money was not tainted then.

The Jews are supposed to have suffered racial persecution in Italy. Against this, one would do well to view the situation of the coloureds and the Indians in America, as well as the life of Russian Jews, before criticising Mussolini's attitude towards the Jews.

I do not mean that there was nothing against the Jews on paper during the Fascist régime. But there is a wide gap between what is said to have happened and what actually did take place.

One thing is certain. Benito Mussolini was never hostile to the Jews. He was an enemy of Zionism, whether in Italy or on an international scale, because he thought it made for a conflict of loyalties. Perhaps I should explain this. An Italian Jew could not be wholly Italian in that, as a Zionist, he might be tempted to make over capital to the Zionist movement – capital he had withdrawn from the Italian economy. And if he ever had to define his position – that is, make a choice – he could not be sure that he would reject Zionism. If he held an important position in his native country, there was no reason to suppose he might not harm Italy.

In this sense, the Duce's attitude to Zionism was more defensive than fundamentally hostile.

But I can give several instances of his feelings towards the Jews, whether Italian or not. I should begin by saying that in 1940 the Italian Jews could not be considered a serious problem, for there were only about 50,000 of them, if I remember rightly.

Having made this point, I return to the illustrations

I have mentioned. The first concerns my husband's dentist. He was called Piperno and was an orthodox Jew. The Duce could have had his teeth attended to by another dentist of another faith, but he never even considered it and carried on going to Dr. Piperno. What is more, my children had several Jewish friends. Our doors were always open to them and, as far as I know, we never made them conscious of their race in our home.

On a very personal level, two of my husband's mistresses were Jewish. There was Angelica Balabanoff who, according to some people, was my daughter Edda's real mother – an idea which greatly amused us – for I know better than anyone whether she is my daughter or not. Margherita Sarfatti was Jewish too.

There were Jews among the founder members of the Fascist Party and in Parliament under Mussolini's regime; for instance, Aldo Finzi, one of the members of Mussolini's first government, and Guido Jung, for several years Minister of Finance, were Jews.

On the other hand, while the Duce didn't persecute the Jews after 1938, various notorious anti-Fascists were Jews, though nothing had been said about their running the risk of retaliation, nor on which side the enmity began. And Mussolini was one of the first and, at times, the only man to attack Hitler for his racial policies. In March 1933, less than two months after Hitler had come to power, Mussolini did what no other religious or political bodies thought to do. He instructed the Italian ambassador in Berlin to make representations to Hitler about his policy towards the German Jews. There must be documentary evidence of this since everything was conducted on an official level.

In June 1934, when my husband met Hitler in Venice, he persisted in making it quite clear that he was against any kind of racial persecution. And though the Führer never gave them a second thought, my husband made continual efforts to improve the lot of German Jews. Sometimes he facilitated their departure from the

Reich on a large scale, with Italy as the first halt on the road to freedom.

It is true that the Fascist Government passed certain measures against the Jews. For example, non-Italian, as opposed to Italian Jews were debarred from attending Italian schools.

In September 1938, it was decreed that non-Italian Jews were forbidden to take up residence in Italy, Libya or the Dodecanese. These two measures followed Hitler's desire for vengeance on German Jewish refugees. But the Italians never returned these Jews to Germany – and certain death. Indeed, my husband actually told the children when these measures were imminent so that they could warn their Jewish chums.

Many Jews quit Italy. One of Vittorio's friends went to Argentina. I admit it was hard to uproot a family yet again, but surely it was better than the concentration camp – and death – awaiting the Jews in Germany, Poland, Holland and France. There is another historical fact about which few people know. When the Germans occupying France asked for information about the Jews living in the Italian-controlled zone, Mussolini gave written instructions banning any communication on the subject. And he also ordered that there should be free access to and freedom of movement in this zone for Italian Jews fleeing from German-occupied France and for Jews of other nationalities, though they were not the responsibility of the Italian administration.

I remember seeing a letter from the prefecture at Nice acknowledging receipt of these instructions and saying that they had been obeyed. The Vichy Government objected strongly to the Italian attitude and Laval even protested that the Italians had no right to concern themselves with the fate of Jews who weren't Italians.

There must still be documentary evidence of all this. If it were published, it might not whitewash Mussolini, but it would give an accurate picture. If an old woman may digress, assuming that historians one day recognise Fascism to have been a political doctrine like any other – not unrelated to Nazism – and that they clear it of its alleged crimes, then anyone who cries down Fascism will have to find another name to vilify.

In effect, Mussolini introduced measures against Italian Jews also, after the Pact of Steel had been concluded, but never of the extreme kind taken by other régimes. There were some anti-Jewish laws, and violently anti-semitic articles appeared in papers like the *Tevero* and the *Difesa della Razza*, but there was little concrete persecution.

Officially, Italian Jews were prevented from marrying Italians of another faith, to own or direct enterprises employing more than one hundred people, to own more than 50 hectares of land (about 125 acres) or to serve in the armed forces. That was all.

These measures were not enforced until 1938. And even then I can give a personal instance of how rigorously they were enforced. In April 1938, Vittorio took part in the *Mille Miglia* motor race with an Italian Jew as his co-driver. This person didn't try to conceal his origin but even if he had wanted to, he would never have succeeded with his surname.

I myself was at the centre of an incident which conveys something of Mussolini's attitude. It happened in July 1942, when there was no sign of defeat on the horizon. By that I mean that it was not my intention to make a public stand to save Fascism. The Duce was then in North Africa and I was spending the holidays with some members of the family at Riccione.

Farinacci, a former first secretary of the Fascist Party, who no longer held an official post, organised a conference in Milan during which he was even more violent and extremist than usual. In his case, that meant a great deal. But what infuriated me was to see that the following day's *Popolo d'Italia* had given this conference full coverage. It was a crazy thing to have done, for everyone knew that the newspaper belonged to my husband and by giving such space to Farinacci's utterances it could be interpreted that Mussolini agreed with them. And that just wasn't the case.

I called the editor or someone in a position of responsibility and they listened to me right enough. Whoever answered got the rough edge of my tongue.

I adopted this attitude because, in my opinion, the Duce's paper should never have approved a call to violence, nor supported any kind of extremism. Few heads of government can have had wives who meddled in this way. But I never hesitated because I knew my husband would have agreed with me.

Anyone who wishes to moralise – and many do in retrospect – may think that whatever Jewish persecution prevailed in Italy was still enough to bring condemnation of the Duce from the enemy nations. It makes no difference whether I agree or not – and, I repeat, I am not an apologist – but I am only trying to give things their true perspective and explain the whys and wherefores of events. One need only consider the Nazi persecution of the Jews in Germany and the occupied countries to realise that it was no small matter for Mussolini, Hitler's main ally, to diverge from his policy in this area.

And any Jewish people reading these words will be aware that the Duce afforded effective protection as long as he was in power, since from 1943 (when he was dismissed by the King and the Badoglio clique) to 1945 – that is, until the end of the war – the Germans applied the same harsh measures in Italy that they'd enforced elsewhere. Even though he was not influential enough to oppose all their activities, my husband continued to try to save the Jews.

Before ending this chapter there are two points I would like to shed some light on.

Nobody has ever disclosed until now that Mussolini almost founded the State of Israel after the conquest of Ethiopia. During several secret meetings with Chaim Weizmann, who later became the first President of the Jewish State, their talks were about to bear fruit – since Weizmann and Mussolini were in agreement – when they encountered a financial stumbling block. The American Jews were refusing to finance any such project, though God and the American capitalists alone know why.

A training camp for Jews was set up near Rome on my husband's orders, and it was there that the nucleus of the Jewish terrorist organisation against the English occupation of Palestine was created. Some of the main leaders of the Irgoun were schooled by Mussolini's Fascists. That surely must have been some help to them.

In Israel there is an Israeli admiral who was one of the leading commanding officers in the Italian fleet under Mussolini's régime. It is significant that he was never victimised for being a Jew.

One might suppose that Mussolini did all this to harass the English. It is quite possible, but one should appreciate that he could also have turned to the Arabs.

I believe it was a tactical manoeuvre, but one which also sprang from his respect for individual peoples. This is borne out by the specific orders he gave to Italian forces in the Ukraine and all along the Russian front.

The second point I would like to clarify concerns the role of Victor-Emmanuel in all this. If it is true that he disagreed with Mussolini about the racial policies, one might wonder why he never declined to countersign the anti-Jewish laws in Italy. All decrees had to be signed by the King. If he had thought them immoral, or at least contrary to his own standards of morality, he could have refused his assent. As far as I know, never did Mussolini on his twice weekly visits to the Quirinal force the King to sign at revolver point. Victor-Emmanuel might have risked dethronement but he, too, had his responsibilities to bear.

Moreover, once the King had signed, the Ministers enforced these laws. It is noteworthy that none resigned because he disagreed with Mussolini. It is curious, too, that no amendments were drafted when the laws were passed by the Lower House.

I would like to think that Mussolini had faithful friends, but the men who raised the first cries of "Monster!" were the very men who had always said

"Amen" to Mussolini, while it suited them, and that included the King.

There is one other point which I must expose, and that concerns the Nazi extermination camps.

In all conscience, I can say that Mussolini never knew anything about these vile centres. He knew that there were internment camps, where the Italian labourers in Germany were imprisoned as enemies of the Reich after the Badoglio Government signed the armistice in 1943. Indeed, he made strenuous efforts to bring 600,000 Italians back from Germany during the Salo Republic, when Badoglio had abandoned them to their fate. It was not until some of them came home in 1944 that he heard rumours of certain special camps, but there was never any precise information. In any case, it was 1944 and too late to try and find out.

I have said that my husband respected peoples. He also respected persons, even his enemies or political opponents like Nitti and Pietro Nenni, who benefited from his humanity and generosity. And one must not forget the Matteotti children, whose survival was solely due to Mussolini's financial help.

It would have been easy for him to arrest his opponents even those in German-occupied France. Indeed, after the Germans arrested Pietro Nenni and handed him over to the Italian authorities, Mussolini could have arranged a fate far worse than surveillance on the island of Ponza. It may not have been freedom, but neither was it a concentration camp, or the death sentence carried out on Mussolini.

It was when I saw how my husband was killed that I began to think that his fine, humane qualities were really defects. Nobody remains a true dictator for long unless he ruthlessly strikes his enemies down.

The men who killed Mussolini in 1945 knew only too well what they were doing.

CHAPTER 20

Betrayal

Before going into details, it would probably be as well to give an idea of the background against which the conspirators planned and carried out the plot against Mussolini.

The first consideration is the Duce's state of mind and health in 1943. Physically he was not in very good shape. The nervous ulcer which had already given him some trouble, particularly in 1926 when I was living in Milan and he in Rome, was again causing him terrible pain. Sometimes it was so unbearable that he would roll on the floor trying to ease it. Most of the time he sat on the edge of his chair and fell back bringing up his knees to his chin and holding them there with his hands. This extraordinary position gave him some relief, so he said.

When he returned from the North African front on July 22, 1942, the pains were fiercer than usual and as a man who was accustomed to having only two colds a year – one between winter and spring and the other between summer and autumn – he found this ordeal particularly trying.

On my own initiative I began trying to nurse him by deleting all fat in his food but soon had to call in one of his medical practitioners, Professor Castellani. Then followed an infernal round of prominent medical men and every conceivable diagnosis was put forward: an ulcer, cancer, a virus, a nervous infection and heaven alone knows what else.

So in 1943 my husband was in no condition either

physically or mentally, to withstand the critical news arriving from every front. There was no military defeat as yet though that hovered on the horizon. In Africa, all hopes of recovery which my husband had cherished had gone up in the smoke of scuttled boats, British and American offensives and in the wrangling between the Italian and German commands; both persisted in conducting the war as if the other didn't exist. North Africa was falling in May 1943 and the Axis front shrinking away to nothing.

Since April, the Italian secret service had been reporting that the Allies were preparing to land in Sicily at any moment. My husband was therefore in a dilemma, for he could only recover the military situation with support from the Germans who alone could provide him with the materials Italy needed. But Hitler himself was having to face serious difficulties in Russia and the German generals, who distrusted the Italian high command and our government, were unwilling to take the risk of trapping troops in Italy unless they had total control of the country. The Führer couldn't agree to this because of his confidence in Mussolini and his regard for him.

That state of affairs could only be to the advantage of the British, the Americans and the traitors. There were also a number of Fascist leaders who wanted to fight or to put an end to the war, but not to stay where they were. They wanted to fight; that was all very well, but the morale of the troops was low. A break with Germany and withdrawal from the war was a solution the Duce had entertained but, as in 1940, there was always the vision of Marshal Kesselring's troops just marching in and occupying the country.

It was this fear, a human fear, which made some people say that Mussolini was weak and indecisive. And in the face of impending disaster, strength of will was weakening, emotion taking over and the leaders were fast losing their sense of responsibility.

On February 25, 1943, when we returned to Rome from Rocca delle Caminate, the news was becoming so alarming that the Duce had chosen to leave Romagna though his health demanded he should stay there. From then onwards he spent hours at the telephone, both day and night, organising relief work for the civilian populations of Milan, Turin and Naples – the victims of air raids – never stopping until he knew that shelter had been provided for the homeless. I, meantime, was making lists of any clothes and provisions I could accumulate to send to the local authorities. Benito, naïvely imagining that everyone who had a duty to perform in the overall defence of the country was actually on the job, said to me: "I must ask for complete information about the towns which have borne the brunt so that we can make amends to them. It's encouraging to see how resilient and patient the Neapolitans are. It's at moments like this that I feel I'm not alone."

But I can recall his anger and bitterness when one night, after a boat loaded with munitions had exploded in port, he had to take sole charge of the relief organisation; the Duce himself was compelled to work on his own for the Prefect was simply not there.

There was even one evening when he'd to call various Ministers at their homes some twenty times or more to settle urgent business or was unable to reach them. One or two had the effrontery to reply that they weren't in.

It was with this kind of laxity that my husband was struggling. Obviously he could have worried a little more about his political future, started a witch-hunt and paid attention to the information I brought him of plotting in Rome, but he said: "It's not the conspiracies that worry me, Rachele, but American tanks."

And yet the conspiracies were ripening. Since January 1943, since the first real rumours had started, several plots had taken root, but three of these presented a more serious threat than the rest.

The first was an intrigue among the general staff with Cavallero, Ambrosio, Roatta and Vercellino, the second with Badoglio and Acquarone (who had the support of the Court) and the third among the Fascist authorities.

It was this last conspiracy which succeeded in eliminating the Duce, if for no other reason than because the part played by the Grand Council enabled it to conform to constitutional requirements. Let me explain. I have already said that one of the quarrels between Victor-Emmanuel III and my husband arose from the assignment of constitutional prerogatives to the Fascist Grand Council. The King of Italy, who was very down to earth, remembered about these prerogatives at just the right moment and took advantage of the councillors' majority vote against the Duce on July 24, 1943. The conspirators who planned to arrest Mussolini had found a legal pretext for doing so.

Ironically, just as he had taken power through the most lawful means, the Duce lost it in the same way. But that point in the story is yet to come. I was discussing one of the intrigues which a lady of the Court told me about. She was at the very hub of the conspiracy since I was soon to learn that Victor-Emmanuel III had given his blessing to it.

Among the most dynamic of the conspirators was Dino Grandi, president of the Chamber and a former Minister of Justice, who had once been ambassador to London and Minister of Foreign Affairs. I can give an idea of how deceitful these people were by mentioning that Grandi, even while he was plotting against the Duce, had no qualms about asking for his support to obtain the Collar of the Annunziata from the King.

There was also Giuseppe Bottai, a Fascist from the early days and Minister of Education, the very man my husband had referred to in his indignant comment on the massacre of Röhm on the night of the long knives: "It's as if I had killed Bottai, Federzoni, etc., with my own hands."

Luigi Federzoni, president of the Italian Academy, was also involved in the group, as was Bastianini, Under-Secretary of State at the Foreign Ministry. I knew that these unexciting people were not the only ones, but I never expected to hear that my son-in-law, Galeazzo Ciano, was with them. So when I was told about this I couldn't really believe it until I'd had confirmation of it from various sources.

Eventually, amazed that I knew so much and yet saw the police doing nothing, I decided to have a chat with Carmen Senise, the chief of police. This interview, which I asked to be secret, took place at the Villa Torlonia and was fairly lively.

"How can the police be ignorant of everything I have managed to find out without going to a great deal of trouble?" I asked him. He was sceptical until I produced an impressive number of documents and photographs. Then he seemed shaken but I didn't know if he was being sincere or just play-acting.

"Are you a friend or an enemy?" I asked him, in an attempt to break his resistance. Naturally he swore he was loyal to the Duce and to Fascism, but that he didn't know any of the details I had told him. This provoked an acid comment from me about the efficiency of his forces.

"This kind of ignorance is hardly to the credit of your force nor of your professional rating." In one last attempt to convince him it was serious, I added: "I have spoken to you as a mother and as an Italian woman who has given a son to the country, not as a Fascist or as Mussolini's wife. Just think of it, the fall of the Duce in the present situation can only lead to total collapse for Italy."

It was pointless to go on. From the moment I started, Senise had avoided my eyes and had been looking for loop-holes. He was familiar with everything I had told him and, what is more, he was one of the conspirators.

The people, meanwhile, were showing evidence not only of courage and patience but also of self-sacrifice, accepting their ordeals and suffering without protesting. There was never any mass demonstration against the régime in Italy before July 25, 1943, and even afterwards there were no mass movements, but rather localised and skilfully organised outbursts.

Altogether the foundations held better than the leaders, as was also the case in the army. But the people could not agree to shilly-shallying when they had to bear the cost of it while the men in charge lined their pockets. When it came to a choice between war and peace in July 1943 the ordinary Italian wanted peace but if he had to go through with the war he wanted everybody to be in the same predicament.

The Duce knew all this. There were daily reports to the Palazzo Venezia, but they didn't tell him everything, for I could fill in the gaps with what I knew. The total picture was not a very happy one.

Finally, on February 5, 1943, my husband decided to take action. He reshuffled the government from top to bottom, taking over various key ministries himself as he had done before at times of crisis. He called this great upheaval "the changing of the guard".

The Duce formed a Ministry of War. Younger, more dynamic men came into it and were a symbol in the eyes of the public that the Duce had decided to stand firm. At the same time he unwittingly broke up one of the lesser conspiracies led by Marshal Cavallero, while giving other men like Ambrosio, a new chief of general staff, and Castellano more opportunity to carry out another plot, the decisive one.

Several Ministers learnt of the loss of their portfolio by listening to the radio or opening the newspapers. There was immediate panic, firstly among the conspirators who, thinking they had been discovered, were expecting the wrath of Mussolini to descend on them and bombarded me with 'phone calls to assure me of their loyalty.

Those who were not plotting were equally scared, for it was dangerous to be caught up in a political whirlwind at that time. They also 'phoned endlessly for reassurances that they wouldn't suffer any repercussions.

One would need to have known Rome in 1943 to realise just how much anything seemed possible there. The capital was a gigantic laboratory where the most surprising mixtures were being concocted, where everyone was plotting against everyone else. Besides, the climate, the character of the city and the general atmosphere had a softening effect on the people who were most implicated. This meant that it was difficult to see clearly and the best bloodhounds in the Gestapo couldn't find their way around. They simply thought that everything could be sorted out, when they themselves weren't in the process of concocting something. In fact, although the Germans were on the alert for the slightest sign of weakening in the Italian régime, they never realised that Fascism was in danger.

I remember on July 16 I even had an interview with Colonel Dolmann, Himmler's confidante in Italy and gave him my honest opinion of the situation. I derived the impression that, although he told me he shared my views, he wasn't as loyal as he made out to be; indeed, he hadn't the slightest concern for the fate of either the Duce or the Führer.

However, it was not this government change which brought a new twist to events, for in April 1943 – and even more so after the loss of Tunisia in May – the number of conspiracies increased.

Each one had its own answer. The only point in common to all the "combinazione" was the necessity to remove Mussolini. More seriously, an evergrowing number of Fascist leaders were beginning to think, in all good faith, that they should invite the Duce to resign, surrendering his powers to the King so that Victor-Emmanuel could try to bring Italy out of a dead-end situation without Mussolini having to suffer loss of dignity. They were victims, poor things, of the propaganda of Radio London and the Voice of America which stressed continually that the Allies were not making war on Italy but on Mussolini and Fascism.

These officials thought that peace would be within their grasp if Mussolini was willing to go.

It is important to clarify this point because it has since been suggested that the attitude of all the Fascist leaders who contributed to the fall of Mussolini was hostility directed at the Duce himself. To a large extent that is inaccurate. Acquarone, Grandi and Badoglio, the arch-conspirators who sought to eliminate Mussolini for personal aggrandisement, played on this ambiguity and misled most of the other Fascist dignitaries.

The ambiguity was all the more criminal in that it wholly ignored Italy's predicament at the time. Whatever were my husband's faults, he was no fool, realising quite well that everything revolved around himself. Perhaps contrary to general belief, he was not particularly in love with power. If his departure would have enabled Italy to steer clear of chaos, he would have resigned of his own accord. He even said once in private that when weapons could no longer determine the outcome of the war, the next step should be diplomacy. But he also knew that nobody other than himself could negotiate with the Allies.

"These gentlemen are in a hurry to talk about peace," he said, thinking of the conspirators, "but they don't know that the British and Americans want unconditional surrender. What Italy must do, even now, is to stop the Allied advance, win a victory; and then I know the only man capable of negotiating with them. If Mussolini goes there will be chaos, for one way or another, whether the war carries on or grinds to a halt, there'll be disaster. If war persists, the people who clamour for peace will see that Mussolini's going has changed very little. If Italy leaves the war, what will the Germans do? They'll just trample Italy underfoot. Nearly everything I've done so far has aimed to prevent that happening."

The Duce had not overlooked the threat of Kesselring and his Nazi troops. Besides, there were the 600,000 Italians scattered all over the territory controlled by the Germans. These Italians had gone out trusting in the word of Mussolini who was sending them to allied areas. If their government yielded they would suffer and become prisoners; which is precisely what happened after September 8, 1943.

It's always easy to say what must be done. That's bar-room strategy for *scopa* players but not for the serious-minded who are conscious that hundreds of thousands of human lives depend on what they do.

Therefore at this time the Duce's chief concern was to stem the Allied advance, achieving this with as many reinforcements as the Führer could provide by withdrawing German units from the Russian front and arranging a possible truce with the Soviet Union.

Against this, there were the conspirators, the men who saw themselves as the saviours of Italy, yet in fact were doing nothing but pave the way for the final tragedy. The Badoglio-Acquarone-Grandi triumvirate waited for the strategic moment to act, having been joined by Bottai, Federzoni, Ciano, de Bono and Ambrosio, who had himself collaborated with the Court in search of a "military solution".

Meanwhile the King, lurking in the gloom of his palace like a cat stalking its prey, bided his time for a sure-fire opportunity. He delayed until June 15, but the next day he gave the conspirators the signal to go ahead once he knew that the Grand Council would be meeting. Like Pontius Pilate, he could then wash his hands and say that he hàd only adhered to the wishes of the Fascist Grand Council which Mussolini himself had convened.

The conspirators, who often assembled at Castelporziano within the very walls of royal property, met more frequently as the days passed. I received regular news about this and every shred of evidence which reached me only served to excite my fears.

Victor-Emmanuel III had intrigued with the politicians in 1922, deserting them when he turned to Mussolini at the last moment to save his throne. But now the Fascist boat was taking in water and it was time to make haste and quit before it foundered. The King was looking for a means to save the House of Savoy, and so my worst fears were justified.

Duke Pietro Acquarone was the head of the Royal Household, the King's evil spirit in the sinister affair which strove to remove Mussolini. Acquarone, another wretched victim of self-delusion, foolishly aspired to the heights of glory.

Badoglio, a collector of statues – especially of himself

– had always managed to make capital out of a situation as, for instance, in 1935 when he stole the credit for the victory in Abyssinia from Marshal Graziani and, according to some rumours, the treasure of Haile Sellassie. Badoglio, who could only come into his own at the centre of the group, pictured himself loaded with honours and invested with the highest offices of responsibility for personal gain. The interests of Italy came second.

Grandi was a lawyer whom my husband had brought out of obscurity, making him ambassador after teaching him how to take his place in society. An eternal chaser after titles and honours, he would have adopted a jaundiced attitude if he hadn't been involved in the affair.

As I have said, a range of events, a convergence of varied interests and mistaken sincerity in some quarters all meant that the Duce was in a particularly solitary position in July 1943. He knew that these people were conspiring against him, but there was one person in whom he placed consummate trust, believing he could count on him in the final resort. That was the King. I think that if Benito Mussolini had known for certain that he could not rely on Victor-Emmanuel III history would have followed a different course on July 25, 1943, for there would have been no reason to remember it.

I wrote at the beginning of this chapter that it was my husband who upset the conspirators' plans. In fact all that he did was to anticipate their wishes. When various officials asked him to convene the Grand Council, he immediately agreed and even fixed the date of the meeting for July 24. For the plotters this was too early. Because they were not ready, Grandi asked the Duce to change the date, but he refused.

I remember on July 22 he seemed more preoccupied than usual. There were any number of reasons why he should be, so I respected his desire for silence. But after some minutes he spoke to me and, as if he had come to some conclusion after debating with himself, he commented on Grandi's attempts to delay the meeting of the Grand Council. "They want this meeting of the Grand Council. Well, they'll have it. Now everyone has got to recognise his responsibilities. This Grand Council business is some idea of Grandi and Federzoni. If there's any disagreement they're always at the head of it, those two. But they're satisfied with words."

On July 18, chance brought the conspirators a final upset. Hitler had told the Duce that he wished to talk to him immediately, and that the rendezvous should be at Feltre, near Venice. There could have been inherent dangers in this meeting for those intriguing against my husband, for if he had given Hitler the slightest hint of his suspicion of loyalty, the Führer would have taken measures for his friend's security thus frustrating the conspirators' intended scheme. If, on the other hand, the Duce succeeded in persuading Hitler to provide him with further resources, he would be less vulnerable when the Grand Council met.

Thus the conspirators had one overriding aim: to prevent by whatever means Hitler and Mussolini from talking at length. Therefore the last discussion between the Führer and the Duce was sabotaged, and by the easiest and least controversial method, because the security of the two men called for special measures. They were to travel by train and then by car to the villa where the meeting had been arranged.

All these unexpected delays nibbled away a major part of the schedule before the meeting had even begun. Nobody thought to wonder why at such a critical moment Mussolini and Hitler were frittering away their time in planes, trains and cars to get to Feltre when for the journey home they travelled direct to Treviso aerodrome. Indeed, they could have held their talks quite easily at Treviso.

All these complications were intentional, as may have been the air raid on Rome which was reported to the Duce at about midday, hardly an hour after the meeting had begun. Altogether the two men spent a maximum of four hours together while Hitler was prepared to stay indefinitely to settle the question of

Italy's defence. That day the conspirators ensured the success of their own venture, but they also made way for Italy's later tragic days.

Incidentally, I would add that my husband 'phoned from Feltre to Rome, checking that relief work was well underway. He was assured that this was the case, but once he returned to the capital the truth stared him starkly in the face: none of the things he had been promised had taken place. So now, on July 20, 1943, there were no further obstacles to the removal of Mussolini.

That evening the Duce and I quarrelled at the Villa Torlonia. He was dressing and Irma was buttoning his collar when I tried to pass on the news I'd received that day about the evil machinations of Badoglio, Grandi and company. My information was clear and explicit: they would stop at nothing, not even murder. I knew, for example, that because I was an embarrassment, they would dispose of me before they dealt with my husband; that they would hand him over to the Allies or kill him if he tried to resist or escape; that the meeting of the Grand Council was to be the constitutional excuse the King was waiting for.

I had also learnt that from then onwards, our telephone lines were to be permanently tapped by the army's general staff which was also embroiled in the plot through its chief, Ambrosio, Cavallero's successor. Finally, I had indisputable evidence that Giuseppe Bastianini had delivered eleven passports to the men implicated in the Cavallero plot. This was serious because Bastianini was Under-Secretary at the Foreign Office which my husband had taken over in February. It was evident that Bastianini was not to be trusted either.

I had already told my husband about the matter of the passports. He had asked Bastianini for an explanation only to be given a vigorous denial.

That evening I brought up the subject again, but the Duce brushed me off with the words: "Rachele, I'm telling you again, it's the American tanks I'm worried about, not Badoglio's activities or other people's intrigues." Then, when I reminded him of the case of Bastianini, he cut me short with the terse comment that I was the one who was plotting.

Angrily I grabbed the telephone and promptly 'phoned Bastianini himself, telling him of all my suspicions, and giving him the names of the people for whom he'd obtained passports, adding that I had told Mussolini about it myself. My husband was beside himself, cutting the line because he had heard enough of the home truths I'd told to Bastianini.

It was just four days before the meeting of the Grand Council. I knew that that would be the day of judgment, but I couldn't persuade the Duce to take prompt action because he had won a last reprieve by upsetting the conspiracy when he arranged for the Grand Council to meet on July 24. Originally the officials involved had planned everything for August 7, thinking that the meeting would be held on that day. If he had gone all out to destroy them, by making use of this snag, later events might have been very different.

But he declined to listen. Having reached his decision, he stubbornly refused to budge an inch. Indeed, in his view, the meeting of the Grand Council could only clarify the situation since everyone would have to face up to his responsibilities. Besides, my husband believed that, should the King's intervention prove necessary, it would doubtless swing in his favour. I was confident that the very opposite would be the case but he didn't want to know. He had put implicit trust in the monarchy because he could see nothing on his, Mussolini's, side to warrant betrayal and he wouldn't give the matter another moment's thought.

Neither my daughter Edda, who tried in vain to warn her father about Grandi, nor Carlo Scorza, the new Fascist Party secretary who hinted of possible surprises, nor I could make him change his mind. It was maddening. I wasn't counting days any longer, but hours.

On the morning of the 24th, I rose earlier than usual, not having slept that night. I couldn't even converse

241

with one of my children and express my anxiety because Vittorio was on a mission and Romano and Anna-Maria were with my grandchildren at Riccione.

I pushed open the door of Benito's room. He, too, was already up. "Is this evening's convocation really necessary?" I asked point blank. He looked at me in surprise. "And why not? It'll only be a discussion among comrades – at least I think so. I don't see why it shouldn't take place."

At the mention of "comrades", I burst out: "Comrades? Is that what you call that bunch of traitors who are deceiving you? There's Grandi, for a start. Do you know that nobody has been able to find Grandi for the past few days?"

At Grandi's name he looked uncertain, as if he'd suddenly remembered something. Then he calmly tried to explain that he wasn't expecting anything serious.

We said good-bye to each other that morning without either of us having made any concessions, but I was distraught. I knew that in a matter of hours the final curtain would fall and that my husband had only been looking on the bright side to allay my fears.

I was also sure that the men who had sworn to ruin my husband wouldn't make it easy for him, because they couldn't – if for no other reason than because I had received a detailed report a few days before the Feltre talks about various secret meetings between Ciano and other members of the Grand Council. Benito had 'phoned Ciano, asking if he had really met these people, and he admitted as much – saying that it was for private reasons.

In spite of my counsels, my husband had summoned Scorza to the Villa Torlonia and given him back the report requesting him to get an explanation from Ciano. My son-in-law went to see the Duce and declared his loyalty once again, but the harm had been done and the masks were down; the conspirators now knew that Mussolini had knowledge of the treachery.

Several times during the morning I was surprised to find myself thinking about what my husband was doing at that particular moment. "Now he is holding such and such a meeting," I thought. I felt as if I was living out a nightmare and that the following day Benito would say, as he had before: "You see! You were wrong!"

I hoped with all my heart that this would happen, but deep down I was sure of the opposite.

At lunch he wasn't visibly nervous, but from his pale face and the way he kept putting his hand to his back I knew that his ulcer was giving him pain. It was hardly surprising after the life he had led during the previous year.

While the Grand Council usually opened its proceedings at ten in the evening, on July 24 the session was due to start at five since the debate was expected to be long. Twenty minutes to five Benito left the Villa Torlonia, carrying a brief-case full of the papers he had gathered in his office.

I went out on to the steps with him and while he was getting into his car, I couldn't help saying: "Have them all arrested, Benito. Do that before you even start." He made a gesture which could have meant that he would, or that it was too late. Irma had asked him if she should send the usual thermos of milk and he told her not to do anything unless he 'phoned himself.

I would mention that the Duce himself decided to give leave to the militia that day and not to reinforce the guard at the Palazzo Venezia. Yet again, the man was overriding the dictator; Mussolini didn't want to force anyone's hand.

CHAPTER 21

Mussolini dismissed

Is there any point in describing the meeting of the Grand Council yet again? I doubt it. Firstly, it has now found its niche in history. Secondly, virtually everyone who was present has given his own version – each varying the nuances that best suited his personal situation. Finally, I wasn't there myself and my account of the facts would not be very enlightening since it would be based on what I have heard or read.

I can say, however, that Mussolini's own safety was never under attack. Though criticism was levelled at the political system, the alliance with Hitler and the recent course of events, most of the nineteen councillors (of whom fourteen were Freemasons) who supported Grandi's motion aimed merely to relieve the Duce of some of his responsibilities, thus enabling him to devote more time to straightforward political activity.

The men who aimed to destroy Mussolini – Grandi, Albini, Bastianini, Bottai, Ciano and Federzoni – spent the whole eight hours of the meeting casting blame on my husband. But even when the vote went against him, Mussolini continued to command respect.

In fact, the Duce's democratic attitude actually led to one councillor voting with Grandi. This was Gottardi who was sitting on the Grand Council for the first time. He had understood hardly any of the debate, but he'd assumed that Mussolini must have agreed with Grandi once he allowed the motion to be put to the vote.

There was another cardinal factor: two hours before

the meeting began, my husband had suffered acute stomach pains while he was working in his office at the Villa Torlonia. He'd remained silent about it, not wishing to give me any additional worry. But through the debate, as he later confided to me, he had been floating in a kind of mist.

Even if he'd been in perfect health, he would have acted as he did. For he wanted to clear the field once and for all. Moreover, he was sure the King would support him through this new time of trial. And after thirty years I am sure that, even if he had known that Victor-Emmanuel was to desert him, he would have done nothing to militate against the wishes of the Grand Council. It may have been only a consultative body, but the Duce had no wish to minimize its importance for all that.

As I write about it now, it occurs to me that Benito may well have thought there was no other way out; not that the situation was hopeless but that once something gets off to a bad start it cannot be recovered. By midnight, that evening, I was in a terrible state of suspense. I called De Cesare, the Duce's secretary, who told me that the meeting was still in progress.

I 'phoned the Palazzo Venezia again at one in the morning, at half-past one and at two. It still had not finished. I knew just how much was at stake and I hadn't expected to see him home after only an hour or two but I couldn't control my anxiety.

I became the prey of bizarre thoughts, as always happens in moments of crisis – and I even began to regret our early and exacting years together. I wondered whether, all things considered, they hadn't been happier.

In the silence of that house, as if to forestall disaster, I determined that once it was all over I would drag him away – forcibly if necessary, but I would make him forsake politics.

It came graphically to the mind that ordinary, unimportant people can be really happy. They may not climb as high as the great men, but they don't fall so low either. We are like that, we always seek more and we are ready to fling everything overboard when the game is over. For during those twenty years in power, our effort and sacrifices had outweighed the glory. And it seemed a sad irony that Mussolini should be accused of self-seeking. He'd had one immovable aim: to make Italy a great, strong and respected country, and it looked as if all this might be swept away in one snap of the fingers by people who put self-interest before Italy.

And, paradoxically, while I was thinking about my husband's future and ours, my thoughts turned increasingly towards the future of my country which was to be tossed in the wind of personal ambitions and shady dealings. The men who were to die as the result of others' egoism would be sacrificed for nothing. All the crosses which stood as a sign of our children's sacrifice, over marked or unmarked graves in Italy and elsewhere in the world, would have lost their purpose. I was afraid that their parents would even be denied the consolation of having lost them for the honour of their country.

At about three-thirty, a message from the Palazzo Venezia informed that the Duce was on his way. It was about four when I heard the sound of the car. I ran down to meet Benito on the stairs. He was with Scorza. I could see from the signs of fatigue and tension on his face how the meeting had gone. Before he could say a word, I exclaimed: "You've had them all arrested, I hope."

Scorza looked at me in surprise. My husband murmured tiredly: "No, I haven't yet, but I will tomorrow morning."

"Tomorrow morning will be too late," I said despairingly. "Grandi must have covered some distance already."

He shrugged, released Scorza and handed me his brief case. We went up to his study and there utterly exhausted, he fell into an armchair. With his head in his hands, he sat staring at me in silence for a long while, as if my presence was proof that he was not dreaming. Then, holding the telephone out, he said: "Call the general headquarters for me, please. I want to know if there have been any alerts and air raids."

I knew already of the incidents that evening, because while waiting for Benito, I'd 'phoned several people in various towns and learnt that there had been raids and alerts in Bologna, Milan and other centres.

However, I now called the general headquarters and – expecting to hear the same reports – passed my husband the receiver.

I overheard the answer – "All quiet, Duce; there's nothing to report anywhere on the home front," – and my patience snapped.

I snatched the telephone out of Benito's hands and shouted: "Liar! Practically the whole of Italy is on the alert. Bologna has been bombed. Do you have to lie to the Duce about that too? Even now?"

Benito replaced the receiver and said: "Calm down Rachele. There's nothing you can do, not now. There's nothing to be done at all. They want a show-down whatever it costs. I'm afraid even my own wishes count for nothing now."

Then he began to tell me how the meeting of the Grand Council had gone. I realised he needed to get it off his mind so I let him talk for about twenty minutes without interrupting. I only broke in once when he told me that Galeazzo Ciano had voted against him.
"Even him," I exclaimed unhappily.

We always feel that life has caused us enough suffering but it seems as if fate, in its cruelty, keeps one blow in store to test us when we are least able to withstand it. Ciano's vote was that kind of blow.

I remembered the day when I'd entertained him for the first time and had told him that I wanted him to be completely aware of Edda's true nature. I had played my cards on the table.

It was nearly five o'clock when we said goodnight, though the words were meaningless, for I knew all too well that neither of us would be able to sleep. Before going to bed, I watched the dawn breaking over the garden – a day which could have been like any other.

And, once in bed, I found myself looking round my room as if I'd never seen it before. I wondered how many more nights we would spend there, before falling into a few minutes' restless sleep.

When I got up I found Benito already dressed. Doctor Pozzi arrived soon after to administer the daily injection, but Benito would have none of it, explaining: "My blood's boiling over today." In fact, he was in a hurry to go and was in his office by nine.

Carlo Scorza 'phoned quite early, telling him that Cianetti, who voted for Grandi's motion, was retracting his vote. He had even written a letter, which he'd given to Scorza to forward to my husband, begging the Duce's forgiveness.

Then Benito sent for Grandi, but he was not to be found. At the time my husband thought that he was too ashamed of the previous day's dealings to face him.

Next he 'phoned his private secretary, De Cesare, asking him to obtain an audience with the King. Surprisingly there was no immediate reply. Only later did I learn that Benito's request had upset the conspirators' plot, since the Duce usually went to the royal palace on Mondays and Thursdays. It was Sunday and Victor-Emmanuel was at the Villa Savoia, his private residence. Before agreeing to the meeting, the King had to change the nefarious plans for Mussolini's arrest and abduction. The Queen was also faced with a moral problem, for the Duce would be arrested under their own roof, which was contrary to any code of honour.

But my husband was totally ignorant of all this. In due course an answer came from the King granting him an audience at five that afternoon, but rather oddly, the head of protocol asked that the Duce should attend in civilian dress. This last point surprised Benito, but with so much else on his mind for the moment, he forgot about it.

At eleven, Albini, Under-Secretary of State at the Ministry of the Interior, went to the Duce's office for the daily report. Albini, by the way, had voted against the Duce the night before and could easily have tendered his resignation because of political differences with his Prime Minister and Minister of the Interior, since my husband had retained this portfolio and that of Foreign Affairs. But, without any qualms and as if nothing had happened, he continued with his duties.

Benito asked, sarcastically, if he thought he'd made good use of his first vote in the Grand Council – "Seeing that you are a guest in the Grand Council, thanks to the position I have given you; you're not a titular member."

Blushing with shame, Albini answered that if he had made an error of judgment in voting for Grandi's motion nobody could doubt his devotion to the Duce. When he told me about it over lunch, Benito summed Albini up with the words: "When he left, he had the face of the self-confessed traitor."

I knew Albini and had taken his measure from the moment he'd been appointed to his post some months before. He had asked to see me, having heard of my opinion of him and knowing, besides, that I was well aware of various irregularities he'd committed while he was Prefect of Naples. His appointment had been followed by adverse reactions in several quarters.

I had discussed it with my husband, but he'd replied: "Men are like apples, I buy them by the box. There may be several good ones and one rotten. But I am hoping his new duties will give him a chance to make amends and clear his reputation."

So Albini had come to see me and had spent the entire interview repeating the stereotyped flatteries of the well-trained official. "But, Excellency, for us the Duce is everything. Excellency I am ready to give my life for him." I had no illusions about Albini, any more than I had about the others, but that was little help by then.

About eleven o'clock, I received a 'phone call from Guido Buffarini, Albini's predecessor at the Ministry of the Interior, who asked to see me without explaining why. We arranged a meeting for five that afternoon.

At midday, as if nothing had happened, the Duce welcomed the new Japanese ambassador, who asked on his government's behalf for information about the military situation in Europe. My husband gave him a clear picture of events, emphasising the point that his government should impress upon Hitler the need for a settlement with Russia. "When arms no longer afford a sufficient means for tackling a situation, a political solution must be sought," he said.

These words, which came to my ears only later, were Mussolini's last pronouncement on the war as head of government. They demonstrate that he was completely lucid and conversant with the situation.

If the Japanese diplomat is still alive to read these words (I understand that this book is to appear in Japan), he will surely remember that my husband gave no impression that he was a marked man, living his last hours of freedom, but that he was as clear-headed as ever.

At about two, I learnt that Benito was leaving the Palazzo Venezia. When he had not arrived at the Villa Torlonia half an hour later I began to grow anxious. Finally, he arrived at three, after driving round Rome with General Galbiati to see the extent of the bomb damage. He had distributed money to the unhappy people who had lost everything, giving all that Galbiati and his police escort had with them. Even then he was more concerned about the sufferings of his fellow countrymen than his own safety.

All this time Badoglio was celebrating with champagne, for he had been head of the Italian Government since the end of the morning. The crowds cheering my husband at San Lorenzo had not the faintest idea that he no longer counted for anything.

For that matter, Benito had no idea either. And thus it was that for a few hours Italy had two heads of government. Only in Rome could such things happen.

For the sake of history, I would add that Victor-Emmanuel had visited the same quarters in Rome some days before and had been given quite a different reception. And when I say "different", I am being extremely kind.

I still remember nothing of that fateful afternoon

except that Benito told me he was going to see the King at five. I sprang to my feet as if I'd been bitten, and pleaded: "Don't go, I beg you not to go." We were sitting at table, though in fact we'd sat down quite mechanically, for Benito would not eat anything; he only took a few mouthfuls of soup.

"I must go and see the King," he replied. "For we have a treaty with Germany and we must honour it. The King signed it, as I did, and we must discuss the whole business. If necessary, I shall stay in command to keep our side of the agreement. Otherwise I shall resign on condition that he gives me the means to arrest the traitors. We're going through a difficult time, like we did at Caporetto, but we'll survive this one, too."

Benito was not thinking of himself or talking about his predicament. His whole concern was for Italy. As we talked, there were three telephone calls from the Court. The King wished the Duce to go to the Villa Savoia, his private residence, and somewhat strangely to wear civilian – not military – dress.

This emphasis on the arrangements made me uneasy again. I was increasingly certain that Victor-Emmanuel would not want to tackle the moral problem raised by arresting the Commander-in-Chief of the Italian forces to whom he – the King – had delegated his powers because of the war.

I went to join Benito who was dressing in his room. As I entered, he asked: "Which suit shall I wear?"

I didn't even answer. Wringing my hands, I tried desperately to dissuade him from going. I began by reminding him of something which he had told me himself and which he had found amusing. One of the keepers at the royal hunting lodge at Castelporziano, where the conspirators had met, wrote him a letter warning him to beware of the King. "He is not to be trusted," he wrote, and after various graphic phrases about the Sovereign, the letter ended: "His Majesty is afraid you are becoming too powerful because the people love you."

Benito had forgotten this warning. I had not, since I had also received a confidential report from one of the ladies of the Court on May 8 – just over two months before. She'd given specific details about the development of the conspiracy and the part each of its members was to play. Acquarone was the heart of the treason, Ambrosio was to arrest my husband in due course, and so on. As my husband dressed, I reminded him of this, but he said nothing.

I added that I'd every reason to suppose that the whole royal family, apart from the Queen, was hostile to him. True, Princess Maria-José had written him two cordial letters after meeting him at Castelporziano when the Empire was declared. And Crown Prince Umberto had reason to thank the Duce for having hushed up some minor personal scandal in which he'd been involved. But were they grateful? Rather to the contrary.

As for the King, he'd never forgotten the various "attempts" on his rights made by the Duce's measures. At the same time, he knew that my husband had chosen to ignore the transfer abroad of royal capital and securities at the very time Italy was struggling in Ethiopia and in Geneva against the League of Nations.

Poor Benito assumed that all these factors could not outweigh twenty years of loyal collaboration with the House of Savoy. "If you think about it, Rachele," he concluded, "the King can't possibly act against me because by doing so he'd destroy not only me, but the monarchy and Italy itself."

When he was ready to leave he took from his desk a bundle of documents, including that section of the constitution which laid down the prerogatives of the Grand Council, and also drew out the letter from Cianetti that Scorza had sent him that morning. He asked me to take care of it, and that is how Cianetti emerged from the Verona trials with his life.

It was nearly four-thirty when De Cesare arrived, since as the Duce's private secretary he was to go with him to the Villa Savoia. As I greeted him, I said: "I'm very afraid you may not be going home this evening."

253

But, like my husband, he thought I was being over-anxious.

When Benito was about to leave, Scorza 'phoned advising that Marshal Graziani offered his services if they were needed. Benito answered that he would see Graziani after his discussion with the King.

I add this detail to illustrate that not once had it occurred to my husband that by going to the Villa Savoia he was putting his head into a noose. However important this meeting might turn out to be, he never thought it would end in disaster.

It was just before five when, in a blue suit and his bowler hat, Benito Mussolini got into his car. Ercole Borratto was driving. I cannot convey my emotions as I watched the car disappearing down the drive. It was not until he'd gone that I realised we hadn't even said good-bye.

Buffarini arrived at five as arranged, still stunned by the session of the Grand Council. As he told me his version of what had happened the previous night, he handed me a sheet of paper which my husband had covered with the kind of doodles one makes when one is bored.

We were talking about Scorza when the telephone rang. I literally leapt towards it and heard a breathless, almost inaudible murmur from the other end of the line: "They have just this moment arrested the Duce."

I stood frozen, still holding the receiver but no longer listening to the repeated hellos from the other end. Buffarini came over, took the telephone and asked: "Who are you? Tell me who you are."

The voice, distorted with emotion, could only mutter: "There is nothing else I can tell you. That's all I know. Be quick and warn the children at Riccione." Then the line went dead.

Less than half an hour had passed since I had begged my husband not to go and see the King, fearing he'd be arrested. And now I had proof that I had been right. Mussolini was a prisoner.

CHAPTER 22

Ten minutes to wipe out 20 years in power

It was July 25, 1943. I had to wait until September 13 to hear from my husband's own lips the precise circumstances of his arrest. But at that time, the thought that I would some day see him again was far from my mind. It took me a few minutes after I had heard the telephone message to grasp what had happened.

I had told Benito so often that he was going to be arrested that, logically, the knowledge that it had finally happened shouldn't have upset me. But no, I was standing there in the drawing room looking at Buffarini, Irma and the caretaker without really seeing them. I had one thought throbbing through my head – that Benito was no longer with me. I didn't even know where they had taken him.

In Forlí or Milan I had known if he was in prison, for someone always came to tell me and bring some hastily scribbled message. This time the rules of the game were different. The treachery came from the top; there was nobody to whom I could appeal.

And, like a complete idiot, my whole mind was concentrated on a single idea: if he was alive where would he get his medicine? Would they think to cook him fat-free meals?

Having overcome the initial panic, I began to fight back. I called the headquarters of the militia, the German Embassy, the Palazzo Venezia and the home of General Galbiati who had left my husband at three

255

o'clock. But everywhere I got the same reply: "They've lied to you Donna Rachele. Nothing's happened."

I was almost beginning to wonder whether the whole thing hadn't been some tasteless joke when I heard the sound of running engines. Going to the window, I saw some trucks stopping in front of the door and Carabinieri getting out of them. I immediately grabbed the telephone but the line was dead. I couldn't even get through to the caretaker any longer.

Any last doubts I may have had were dispelled when I saw the Carabinieri sending our security police away. Some of them looked as though they wanted to come towards the house, presumably to say goodbye to me, but I saw the Carabiniere officer barring their way.

In the end everyone went, leaving the Villa Torlonia in the care of two agents and a telephonist, none of whom were armed. I would have been at the mercy of the first maniac who wanted to use me for his own ends. Worn out, I went into the garden and sank onto a bench. Buffarini, who was beside me, had been following me around because I was his last and only hope, drinking cognac after cognac to keep his spirits up.

It was then that I realised how strange the pattern of history can be. Less than an hour after Benito's arrest, I myself had informed everyone who might have been able to free him by taking prompt action, even if it were only the German Embassy. Everyone had thought the news so absurd that nobody had made a move.

Suddenly I thought of Vittorio who had been flying the previous night and was now sleeping peacefully in the villa he used to stay in at the other end of the grounds of the Villa Torlonia. I sent a message for him to come, he arrived, his eyes puffy with sleep, whistling in an offhand way, and asked: "What's the matter, Mamma? Is the house on fire?"
"They've arrested your father. You must find refuge quickly."

Vittorio didn't waste time. Leaping into his car, he left the Villa Torlonia without difficulty through a gate opening on to the via Spallanzani which he invariably used.

The telephone rang some moments later. It was Romano calling from Riccione to ask my permission to go to the cinema. My daughter-in-law Gina, Bruno's widow, who was with both Romano and Anna-Maria, had told him he couldn't go because she was afraid of air raids. I knew that our line was tapped, and I couldn't warn him about what had happened. Besides I didn't want to alarm the children. When I was non-committal in my reply, Romano thought I was refusing to let him go. So, as he always did when I wouldn't agree to something, he told me to ask his father for him because he was sure he could force agreement out of him.

How could I shout down the line that his father was a prisoner and had been kidnapped? I wasn't even with my son to comfort him. Therefore I chose to say nothing, but it was a terrible strain.

After Romano, it was Vittorio's turn to telephone, calling me several times to find out how I was. These calls were the only link I had with the outside world.

Vittorio admitted later that he was convinced his father was already dead. It wasn't until about ten that I managed to talk to the Quaestor Agnesina and the Prefect Stracca who had been responsible for the Duce's security right up to that day. But I extracted little news except that, according to Agnesina, the Duce had arrived at the Villa Savoia at five o'clock and had been arrested soon afterwards. His car having stayed in the grounds until the evening, it had led the Quaestor to suppose that Benito was still at the Villa Savoia. Soon after the two officials left, I listened to the news bulletin, hearing for the first time the announcement that Badoglio had succeeded Mussolini.

That night I had a guest. Terrified by the thought of what might happen to him if he fell into the hands of the mob, Buffarini asked me to put him up. I had never valued Buffarini very highly and was to show him so later, but at that time we were both in the same boat and it would have been churlish of me to show him the door when he had come to try and cheer me up.

As if one ordeal a day wasn't enough, fate dealt me another blow on July 25. It was then that Irma, whose nerves were in a terrible state, told me about Benito's relationship of several years with Clara Petacci. The special editions of the newspapers announcing the Duce's dismissal were already talking about it. Poor Irma, who had looked after us so kindly, suffered the consequences of her admission there and then, for her husband slapped her in my presence.

In the street, groups of people were gathering in front of the main gate and shouting: "The war is over." Unhappily they had to retract their words very soon. Meanwhile, there was also the chanting of anti-Mussolini slogans. An anti-Fascist – and who wasn't one that evening – who had once been told by a guard not to sound his horn in the vicinity of the Villa Torlonia, took his personal revenge by parking his car near the entrance and jamming his horn.

It was not until two days later, in the morning of July 27, that the caretaker informed me that someone wanted to speak to me. It was Princess Mafalda of Savoy's maid, who had brought me a letter from her mistress assuring me that the Duce was alive and in no danger.

"God be praised," I murmured, closing my eyes for a few moments so that I could concentrate all my heart and soul into these few words of gratitude.

According to Princess Mafalda, her maid told me, a lively tension existed between Victor-Emmanuel and the Queen. She had refused to allow the Duce to be arrested under her roof since for her such an action would have been both treacherous and a breach of the most elementary rules of hospitality.

At any other time I would have taken violent exception to their villainous behaviour but that day I didn't care what anybody said about the King, the Queen or anyone else. The earth could have stopped turning on its axis, I wouldn't have minded, because now I knew that Benito was alive.

Of all my experiences during that harassing time, only a few are still as vivid in my mind as if they had happened only yesterday. My husband's first letter was one. A certain General Polito brought it to me at the Villa Torlonia, ceremoniously escorted by two high-ranking Carabiniere officers. When he held it out to me I read it diagonally at first, jumping from the first line to the last trying to take in the whole contents at once. "Dear Rachele," he wrote. "The bearer of this letter will tell you what has happened to me. You know what my state of health allows me to eat, but don't send me very much, just a few clothes because I haven't any and some books. I can't tell you where I am, but I can assure you that I'm well. Keep calm and kiss the children for me. Benito."

General Polito also gave me another letter to read, this one signed by Marshal Badoglio. But he took it back once I had read it through. Roughly speaking, Badoglio was asking me to send my husband some clothes and money, otherwise – he had the audacity to tell me – he couldn't provide for food. I was incensed. "For twenty years," I flung at him, "Mussolini has disclaimed every title, even his salary. All the presents that he received from Italians and from abroad, he gave away. That Badoglio, with his pockets full of the millions he earned through my husband's régime, should now dare to refuse a crust of bread to a prisoner like Mussolini is an outrage."

To hear me, nobody would have thought I was the wife of a man in hostile hands. But grief and anger lower the gates of caution, and I could see myself showing Polito the door.

The officers with him could appreciate my sentiments and one of them, a colonel, took me a little to one side and said: "Madam, you are perfectly right. Unfortunately I can't do very much to help you but you can rely on my loyalty. However, you must keep cool because these people are prepared to do anything." And with these last words, he pulled back his tunic to show me the Fascist badge pinned to the inside.

For that reason, I put on a bold face and packed a parcel with some presents for his birthday (it was July 29), some handkerchiefs, a pair of socks and a tie. Then I put in the items I'd always sent him in prison, from the days when we were living in Forlí: a chicken, some really fresh tomatoes, fruit and tagliatelle. And I slipped in a bottle of oil because the doctors had forbidden him to eat anything cooked in butter (I later found out that this bottle never reached him) and a book which I found open on his bedside table with some notes in the margin, entitled *The Life of Jesus* by Ricciotti.

When Polito took his leave I couldn't help letting fly with a final barb when I saw the brand new general's star on his cap. "My congratulations," I said. "1 see that July 25 has helped more than one person."

From the hate in his eyes I realised that I had made myself an enemy. I couldn't have cared less because I had just recalled this brilliant General Polito. I had met him in Bologna in the days when my husband was in power. As a Quaestor, he had never missed a chance to proclaim his admiration for Mussolini and his fervent faith as a Fascist who was ready to go through fire for the Duce. At that time he'd been waiting to make his way in the world and glad to have the honour of carrying Donna Rachele's suitcase. It was less risky than walking through flames.

On August 2, I left the Villa Torlonia forever. Polito again came to fetch me and drove me to Rocca delle Caminate where, he told me, I would find my children.

I wanted to pack my bag in his presence to show him that I wasn't taking anything of value. Giving away everything except Benito's little chest and decorations, I gritted my teeth not to show how flustered I was. But when it came to making a quick round of the house, I couldn't hold back the tears though nobody saw them. I formed the impression that the furniture took on human form and that everything looked fondly at me, as if to say: "Go in peace, we'll protect what you have entrusted to us." As I passed, my hand brushed over the back of a chair, a table and they seemed warm to the touch.

In a few minutes I took my leave of what I had built over fourteen years. Even the animals, suddenly quiet, seemed to be murmuring: "And what's to become of us?"

I scolded myself: "You mustn't give way; you, after all, are still free, while Benito is a prisoner."

It was about eleven at night when I got into the car. Through the open window, I shook hands with the few people who had served us over the years. We didn't say anything but I could feel the emotion. If I had any doubts about Polito's hostility, our journey to Rocca delle Caminate removed them. It was torture – both physically and mentally; physically, because the journey which we could have completed quite easily in six or seven hours, lasted more than twelve. The Carabiniere colonel was sitting beside the driver and in the back Polito sprawled beside me.

He had closed the windows and doors making the atmosphere already polluted by the cigars he chain-smoked even more unbearable. Even when we stopped, he locked me in the car as if I had the plague. I pointed out that the detours he made the driver take were only wasting petrol. He burst into smug and mocking laughter. "Don't worry about that," he jeered, "we've enough petrol. We've always had enough, for us."

Utterly hateful, after nauseating me with his very presence he went on to the mental torture of humiliation. There were no more tremulously respectful murmurs of "Donna Rachele". He was very familiar now, that cardboard soldier. Taking advantage of the situation, he even dared to suggest that my husband's fate depended on him alone and that my attitude would decide his treatment of him. He actually ventured to put his hand on my knee, but the way I looked at him even in the gloom stopped him short. If he'd gone any further I think I would have killed him. I don't know how, but I would have done.

In the end he thought it more prudent to give me his visiting card so that I'd know where to find him, for he was sure that I'd rush to throw myself at his feet.

It was eleven in the morning when I saw the tower of Rocca delle Caminate standing out in the distance. I breathed a sigh of relief; at last I was going to be rid of my odious companion. In spite of everything I'd had to bear, my journey had given me one satisfaction: the ever-conceited Polito had disclosed all the police conspiracies in minute detail. If he hadn't done so, some of them would never have come to light.

When the car stopped I heard the voices of my children. They were the sweetest sounds I had heard for nine days.

CHAPTER 23

The rescue of Mussolini

"When I drove into the grounds of the Villa Savoia, I saw an ambulance parked not far from the door and naïvely imagined that some member of the royal family must be ill. I told myself that I only hoped it was nothing serious."

Only Benito Mussolini could have entertained such thoughts while the King, who was waiting for him on the threshold, corseted in his impeccable uniform, made ready to play out the final scene of the conspiracy.

I heard this on September 13, 1943. At about two o'clock I saw my husband for the first time since July 25. He'd arrived at Munich in an aircraft provided by Hitler, and when I saw him emerge from the plane – in a broad-brimmed Romagnol hat, his face pale and wasted, and so thin that his black overcoat seemed to swamp him completely – I felt my heart miss a beat.

As he kissed me, he said: "I thought I'd never see you again." But no words could have said more than the few moments' silence while we gazed at each other.

For the time being, we went to my hotel room in the Karls Palast. My husband had intended to continue his journey to Rastenberg where he was to meet Hitler, but unexpected bad weather had forced him to spend the night in Munich.

I took the opportunity to run him a much needed bath. His socks were full of holes and sticking to his feet, his shirt was dirty and creased, and his underpants –

which were much too big for him and fastened with a big black button – took me completely aback.

"Who gave you those?" I asked.

"A sailor on board the corvette *Persephone*. The Germans were looking for me, so they dodged about from port to port. While we were sailing towards the island of Ponza, some sailors came up to me and asked if I needed anything. One of them offered me 400 lire and the other these pants. I took the lot seeing that I had nothing of my own."

Although we had separate rooms, Benito decided to sleep in mine. "I'll sleep with you," he said. "My room's too big and I've had enough of being alone."

We were both happy with this arrangement and my husband took the opportunity to tell me what had been happening to him.

"The King greeted me in an extremely agitated state," he explained. "His speech was very clipped and he could not keep still. As soon as we had gone into his office, he said: 'My dear Duce, there's no point in going on. Italy is on her knees, the army has been completely defeated and the soldiers no longer want to fight for you. The Alpine infantry even have a song which says as much.'

"And with total disregard for the seriousness of the situation," my husband went on, "the King began to hum a few words of the song in Piedmontese dialect. Then, chewing nervously at his nails, he reminded me of the meeting of the Grand Council. 'At this moment you are the most hated man in Italy. You haven't a single friend left, Duce. There's only one man who is still your friend and that is me. So you needn't worry about your safety. I have decided to ask Marshal Badoglio to take over as head of government. He will pick his own officials to administer the country and continue the war. We shall have to see how it goes.' "

"And what about you, what did you say?" I asked.

"Very little. I tried to remain calm and dignified but it was a hard knock to take. I suppose there are bound to be repercussions after twenty years in office and going to war. I wished my successor good luck, but added: 'Your Majesty, you are making a very serious decision which is going to have disastrous consequences. You are going to excite a crisis which will mislead the people and may even cause a tragedy. For they will suppose that if you've dismissed the man who led the country into war, it is because peace is in sight. If you deceive the people there will be terrible after-effects. Army morale will feel it. If the soldiers don't want to fight for Mussolini any longer, then that's that. But will they agree to go into action for you? Your Majesty, the crisis you are about to cause will simply mean victory for Churchill and Stalin.'

"All this took no more than some twenty minutes, at the most. We then walked towards the front door and as we crossed the hall the King said in a matter-of-fact way: 'It's hot today.' 'Yes,' I answered, 'it's more close than usual.' In the doorway, De Cesare was presented to him for the first and only time. Then when it came to shaking my hand, the King asked: 'Where would you like to go now, Duce?' 'I've only one house, Majesty, Rocca delle Caminate and I'd like to retire there.' "

Events followed thick and fast. When my husband went to get back into his car, after the King had gone inside, a Carabiniere officer, Captain Vigheri, came up to him and said: "His Majesty has ordered me to see to your protection, since we've learnt that you may be in danger. I'm to escort you."

"I don't need an escort. I have my own," replied Benito.

"No, it is essential that I escort you myself."

"In that case get into my car."

"That's out of the question. We have provided an ambulance for better security."

"You must be joking! What is all this? You must be exaggerating anyway."

"I'm sorry, Duce, but it's the King's orders."

To put an end to this absurd conversation, and out of respect for the royal command, the Duce went over to the ambulance.

"I was surrounded by armed men," he went on. "De

Cesare was in front beside the driver. At the time I really thought that it was an actual security measure and I didn't worry. The streets were quiet like any Sunday. There were bands playing, people strolling about, going in and out of cinemas. The ambulance was going so fast and rolling about so much that I couldn't help saying to the officer: 'If this is how you always handle your patients, you must make the doctors' work easier.' As soon as I said it, the driver slowed down."

Even a night spent in the School of Carabinieri did not suggest to Benito that he was a prisoner. It was not until the following morning, when he saw sentries in the corridor outside his room, that he began to suspect he'd been tricked.

Now that I had him with me, what concerned me most was his health.

"And your stomach? Who looked after you?" I asked.

"The same evening we reached the School of Carabinieri, Major Santillo of the medical corps came to see me. I wouldn't let him examine me, and refused to eat." Remembering one point, Benito interrupted the story to say: "Ah, Rachele! I've just thought. I owe the price of a shave to the barber who came in for me. I couldn't give him anything because I hadn't any money on me. But I must find out his name so I can thank him." Then, returning to the story, Benito told me what had happened that first night in captivity.

"At about one in the morning I had a visit from General Ferone, who brought a letter from Marshal Badoglio. While I was opening the green envelope, stamped from the War Ministry, General Ferone, whom I'd already met in Albania, smiled contentedly as if he was enjoying the sight. In Badoglio's own hand, the gist of the letter ran: 'The undersigned head of government wishes to bring to your Excellency's attention that the measures taken concerning you are due only to the interest taken in your personal safety. We have precise information gathered from various sources to show that there is a serious conspiracy against your person. I regret all this, but I wish to inform you that I shall be glad to arrange for you to be driven, in total security and with the consideration you deserve, to a place of residence of your choice.' And it was signed 'Head of Government, Marshal Badoglio.' "

"And you believed what that traitor wrote?" I burst out.

"Why shouldn't I? On the one hand, I'd heard about the King's proclamation – and about another from Badoglio – that fighting was to continue. On the other hand, as far as the whole world knew – and that meant the Fascists as well as our enemies – Badoglio was one of the most prominent Fascists in the public eye, a registered party member and his family too."

"But a registered Freemason as well," I added. "He's even one of their leaders."

"You know, he's not the only one. But I couldn't believe that a man who'd acquired so much glory, so many titles and so much wealth through Fascism, could betray me in such a despicable way. He had even agreed to become president of the National Research Council. Do you remember, Rachele? Admittedly he only set foot in the building occasionally to read his newspaper. But at that time, I'm telling you, I really thought Badoglio – although he was restructuring the government – had decided not to change Italy's general political position. And more than that, I thought he was carrying out the King's instructions for my safety. If I'd thought there was anything else, I would never have dictated a letter for Badoglio to General Ferone, saying that I was ready to go to Rocca delle Caminate. And if I'd thought for one moment that he was discontinuing the war on the side of the Germans, I, Mussolini, would never have written assuring Badoglio of my support and good wishes. I assumed he was acting out of respect for our commitments – to keep Italy's honour bright."

The following day, despite Major Santillo's entreaties, my husband refused to eat. In the end, he accepted a hard boiled egg, a little bread and some fruit.

By the evening of July 27, all further doubts about his situation were removed when General Polito – that man seemed to be everywhere at once – arrived to take him, so he said, to Rocca delle Caminate.

"Through a gap in the car's curtains I saw that we weren't travelling north at all, but south. 'So we're not going to Rocca delle Caminate?' I asked General Polito. He merely answered: 'No, there's been a change of plan.' "

The first stop was Gaeta, when Benito commented: "You are doing me too great an honour. This is where Giuseppe Mazzini, the famous patriot, spent his exile. I am overwhelmed." But it was only a stage in the journey. "I embarked on the corvette *Persephone*, which sailed to Ponza where I spent ten days or so in total isolation. I used the time to translate Carducci's *Odi Barbara* and to finish the life of Jesus you sent me."

During this time, Benito was surprised and comforted by the obvious sympathy and respect he encountered everywhere. On the *Persephone* the sailors asked him if he needed anything – a gesture which compensated to some extent for the order to stay in his cabin. It was the same in the garrison at Ponza and at la Maddalena where he spent about three weeks.

"When I arrived," he told me, "two Carabiniere came forward and gave their names – Avallone and Marini. Their eyes were full of tears, Marini dared to give me the Fascist salute, saying that he wished he had met me much earlier so that he could have told me everything he'd seen and heard. 'You've achieved your ambition now,' I answered, 'but in the oddest circumstances.' "

For some moments my husband was silent, staring at a point on the wall, then he went on as if he was talking to himself. "The amazing thing is that the people who were supposed to hate me, according to Badoglio, Polito and their colleagues, couldn't have been kinder to me. When we docked at la Maddalena, for example, the admirals and generals went off to dine without giving me a thought, leaving me in a room where the furniture comprised a dirty, rickety table, a chair and a metal box bed with no mattress or covers. I rolled up my jacket for a pillow – as I used to when I came back tired from some meeting in Romagna in 1909 and lay down in a ditch by the roadside to rest – and fell asleep. The islanders and the Carabiniere woke me. Some of them had brought fish, others fruit, and the soldiers had got their wives to cook soup and eggs. And these were the people who were anxious for revenge! On August 1 I finally heard from you – receiving the 10,000 lire you sent and the parcel of clothes with Bruno's plate, Edda's letter and yours. Then I began to feel I wasn't alone."

On August 28, leaving la Maddalena in a seaplane, Benito alighted on Lake Bracciano, about forty miles from Rome. Again in an ambulance (he hadn't been in one since the First World War), he was taken to a little village called Assergi, near Aquila, spending three days there in a specially requisitioned villa. His jailers were in a quandary, not knowing what to do next to prevent the Germans – who were acting under Hitler's personal order of July 26 to rescue Mussolini – from finding a clue as to his whereabouts.

Finally on August 31, he reached the last stage of his travels at the Gran Sasso. "You can imagine how well Badoglio organised things," said my husband, with a touch of sarcasm. "The only place he could be sure to keep me was in the highest prison in the world, nearly two miles up."

If our "cousin" Badoglio had organised things well, he had been equally liberal with the security measures. Both my husband's guards and the men watching us at Rocca delle Caminate had orders to shoot if one of us tried to leave.

"Just once," said Benito, "I managed to leave the hotel at the Gran Sasso. There was a guard with me but he was having a struggle holding the four wolf-dogs which strained at the leash. They'd been detailed to watch the 'prisoner' too. At one point the guard was dragged a few steps away from me, and it was then that I saw an old shepherd coming towards me. He cut a proud figure in that imposing landscape, with his fur waistcoat, velvet trousers and a long beard.

" 'So it's true you're here, Duce,' he whispered. 'The

Germans are looking for you everywhere to free you. I'll go and tell them, don't you worry. When I tell my wife I've seen you, she won't believe me.' Before he went, he took my hand and kissed it."

I can now confirm one point: Benito Mussolini would never have allowed Badoglio to deliver him into Allied hands. When he heard on the radio – on September 10, I think – that one of the clauses of the armistice Italy had signed specified that he would be surrendered to the Anglo-American forces, Benito decided to kill himself.

"In spite of this solemn promise, the commander of the place, Lieutenant Faiola, swore he would never hand me over to the English," added Benito. "Faiola told me in tears that he had been a prisoner of the English himself, that he knew what it meant and that he would never give up a fellow Italian. I think that if Skorzeny had not arrived on September 12, I would have killed myself."

There seems no point in relating the details of Mussolini's rescue yet again. It was one of the great exploits of the latter half of the Second World War.

It might be interesting to mention, however, that as he watched his own rescue from the window of his room, he was more concerned about the Italian soldiers; he was afraid they would fall under the fire of Skorzeny's commandos. As they were about to shoot, he shouted from his window to the Carabiniere: "Don't open fire. There's an Italian general with them. It must be in order.

It was no trick. The Germans had taken General Soleti as a hostage, though I think he would have gone of his own accord.

"I've had some adventures in my time," said Benito, "but nothing to equal taking off from the Gran Sasso in that Fieseler 'Stork'. Just imagine an overloaded plane, tipping from side to side, and lumbering forward to the edge of the precipice. Suction seemed to keep us there. We nose-dived, but the pilot managed to regain control. He's an ace that Gherlao. Skorzeny was with us. He thought it better to risk being killed with me than to appear before the Führer without me."

"And what are you going to do now?" I asked, no longer able to hide my anguish.

After a pause, he replied with a note of bitterness in his voice: "Start again from nothing."

"There's nothing left Benito. In the last six weeks everything you built has been destroyed."

I didn't know if I should hide the truth from him, too; if I should omit to tell him that all his former supporters had joined the rush to forget him, to trample him under foot after raising him to the skies. Had I the right to blurt it out all at once? I decided to lie by omission and merely gave him to understand that he'd find Italy remarkably changed.

Then, as if he'd guessed what I was thinking, Benito said: "I know I may die for it, but whatever the cost I must honour our agreement with Germany. It's the only way to prevent the Italians paying for the armistice of September 8. If I don't stay with them to deaden the blow, the Germans will take terrible vengeance. In any case, I must have talks with Hitler and then we'll see.

Once again, on September 13, 1943, Benito had sealed his destiny. He could not hope to gain by his attitude. The Allies were bound to win sooner or later as everyone now agreed. Mussolini had his family with him in safety. He could have gone to some neutral country and the Allies themselves would have welcomed that decision. But there were still Italians in Germany and Italians in Italy caught between the Allies and the Germans.

As in 1936 and 1937, several paths were open to him and my husband chose the hardest. Who could suggest that he was aiming at anything other than the safety of hundreds of thousands of human lives? The members of the Liberation Committee? What a grotesque joke!

CHAPTER 24

My husband's secret dream

"You were right, Rachele. There's nothing left. It's as if a hurricane had destroyed everything in its path."

This was Benito's first comment to me when he returned to Italy at the end of September. He'd decided to come back as soon as he could after he heard that the Badoglio Government had declared war against Germany. "What Badoglio has just done is absurd," he said. "It's going to cause a confrontation between the Italians and the Germans."

My husband would have liked to settle in Rome again but the proposal failed to rouse German enthusiasm mainly because the capital had been declared an open city and might therefore be difficult to defend. Besides, geographically Rome was too far from that part of Italy governed by the Social Republic.

Milan was also out of the question, for otherwise the Milanese might have had to suffer the problem of additional bombing, especially as the air raids had never seemed so heavy as in August – that is, while Badoglio was in power.

It was finally decided to set up the various ministries in any of the small towns around Lake Garda where buildings were available. So the Italian Social Republic later became better known as the Salo Republic since the Foreign Ministry was situated in the village of Salo.

It was no easy task to form the new government, for my husband wanted men who were new, trustworthy – at least so we hoped – and trained in affairs of State. He finally managed to do this and was glad to have Marshal Graziani as Minister of War. This was the same Graziani who had assured the Duce some minutes before he left for the Villa Savoia on July 25, 1943, that he was ready to serve him. It was he, too, who had been truly responsible for victory in the Abyssinian campaign, as I've already mentioned. That he should be a member of government in the Italian Social Republic gave it considerable weight.

To keep in touch with Hitler, the Duce had the services of Rahn, the German ambassador for political affairs, of General Wolff, commander of the SS in North Italy for security matters, and of Kesselring, who was to prove a worthy marshal for military operations.

One sunny afternoon in November 1943, I arrived at Gargnano on the shores of Lake Garda where my husband was already staying. The countryside had something grand about it. There was the lake with its shimmering surface which I suddenly glimpsed at a bend in the road and snowy Mount Baldo overlooking it.

We were to live in the Villa Feltrinelli which belonged to the family of Giacomo Feltrinelli, the extreme Left wing publisher. There was a fixed rent of 8,000 lire a month to pay and this meant that the Duce wasn't treating the house as captured territory but respecting other people's property. Altogether it was an attractive house, with slender colonnades and a floor of pink marble inside and surrounded by olive trees in the grounds. Yet it looked cold and sad, and just as I had done for the Villa Torlonia, I was anxious to give it more warmth and welcome. With the help of Pierina, who arrived after us, and of some faithful Romagnol friends who would have stayed with me at the gates of hell, the Villa Feltrinelli soon became a real home, which was just what Benito needed to keep his sanity.

While it wasn't hard to do the decorating and rearrange the interior, it was quite another matter to persuade the officials and soldiers to decamp.

I should say, in their defence, that the Villa Feltrinelli

was originally intended to house both the private residence of the Duce and the offices of head of government and chief of State, since Mussolini held both these positions in the Italian Social Republic. And after the events of July 25, 1943, Hitler's orders were extremely strict: there was to be no chance of the Duce running the risk of a kidnapping or an assassination attempt. This meant that the Villa Feltrinelli was less like a home and more like a barracks and a ministry with all the military and official comings and goings.

I went straight to work on this task, too. My husband helped me a great deal, for he didn't particularly like all the measures taken for his security.

In less than a month we got the offices moved to another building, the Villa delle Orsoline, then the officers and men of the SS went elsewhere. Soon the Duce's guard was reduced to about thirty men, some of the best fighters in Romagna, and a small unit of SS. The Germans also had to leave because Benito considered it a point of honour that there should only be Italians to protect him. The only people I couldn't get rid of at once were some SS officers who were under orders to protect the actual person of the Duce. Admittedly they were very polite and faultless in their behaviour towards my family, but they were so suspicious. More than once our maid Maria had the fright of her life when she realised there was someone behind her. It was one of the SS who, following her like a shadow, only left her when she went into our private apartments or into the kitchen. Finally, I appealed to the Duce and, before this surveillance came to a halt, he had to tell General Wolff that he trusted our staff completely and asked for them to be left alone.

And so our daily life at Gargnano gradually fell into shape. My husband resumed the precise and organised work patterns that he'd followed in Rome, and his daily schedule was still equally full. He divided his day between the Villa Feltrinelli, where we were living, the Villa Torlonia in Gargnano, and the Villa delle Orsoline, where he housed all the offices of the Presidency of the Italian Social Republic, a State which he had to piece together himself.

Without going into great detail, I can say that my husband had first to put together all the machinery of this State, obviously on a smaller scale than when he was ruling the whole of Italy, except Rome. Yet the Italian Social Republic was possibly even more important seeing that it covered the area containing the largest industrial plants and the economic activity vital for the whole country; moreover, until September 8, 1943, Rome was also under its administration.

But the Italian Social Republic had no flag, no uniforms, no constitutional structure. Everything had to be done. Designed by Vittorio and some friends, the colours of the new flag were the green, white and red of the traditional Italian flag but instead of the arms of the House of Savoy, they now drew an eagle holding the fasces in its claws. During the first few months the soldiers chose their uniform themselves, giving the army of the Italian Social Republic both colour and a whimsical effect. This, however, was also brought into line and before long there was a uniform common to all.

Some tidying up was imperative on the political side. From the beginning, everyone agreed on the need for a Constituent Assembly, but my husband postponed any meeting, claiming that the Italian Social Republic ought first to take its place in the theatre of operations. "What we need are fewer words and more action and we ought to be doing more fighting than parleying," he once declared.

An army of 500,000 men was assembled and by September 1944, the Italian war effort on the German side amounted to 786,000, including men at arms and paramilitary workers serving with the Todt organisation. In addition, there were several squadrons of fighter and bomber planes and the submarine base of Bordeaux which the Italian navy had retained. Small, fast and efficient boats for chase and surprise operations completed our arsenal. Finally, there was the "decima MAS", which famous for its sabotage activities under the command of Valerio Borghese, was a constant source of anxiety to the Allied general staffs. I should also mention that factories like Fiat, which were making trucks, continued to supply vehicles which the Germans used to great advantage.

All this meant that the Italian Social Republic was not the puppet State which enemy propaganda took such delight in ridiculing. If that had been the case, the Italian front would never have held for 600 days.

My husband was particularly keen to reform the army into an efficient, fighting machine because he had not forgotten a hurtful comment of Marshal Keitel: "The only Italian army which can't fail the Reich is one which doesn't exist." But in 1943 the Duce found himself in a paradoxical situation. Up to that year he'd had to battle with the Royalist Italian generals to force through his ideas for modernising the army, but now that he no longer had this problem he had to contend with the German general staff. After the betrayal of July 1943, they were reluctant to have anything to do with an Italian army of some size, making no attempt to conceal their suspicion and their desire to act in isolation without any concern for Italian sovereignty. More than once the Duce had to intervene personally so that the Italians would not have to tolerate the ignominy of German forces in their midst.

From September 1943 until 1945 Benito Mussolini took a solitary stand against the generals, the diplomats and the Führer's closest advisers to drive home his viewpoint and prevent what would otherwise have been an inevitable clash between the Italian forces of the Social Republic and the Germans. Luckily, Hitler's friendship and esteem and the German generals' trust in himself enabled him to avoid this calamity.

It was a question of the Duce having to heal the wounds inflicted by the senseless armistice that the King and Badoglio, shirking their responsibilities and feeling no concern for those who hadn't sheltered with them behind Eisenhower's guns, had handed to the Allies.

I'm proud to say that due to my husband's skill, the

territories controlled by the Social Republic never had to use the "mark of occupation" whereas the Americans distributed large amounts of "Am-lire", or American lire, in the zones that they occupied. Furthermore, there was no inflation, goods were cheaper in the north than in the "liberated" areas, and the Government of the Italian Social Republic repaid a huge loan contracted before July 1943. Faithful to his principles, my husband paid off his debts even when they no longer concerned him.

Anyone who doubts my words has merely to consult the archives – that is, if they haven't been hidden away by people trying to disprove that Mussolini served some purpose to the end.

Meanwhile, there was our ordinary family life. That, too, returned to a normal routine, less frenetic and more intimate than in Rome, if only because we were geographically and spiritually closer to each other. As at the Villa Torlonia, I set up my farmyard and my rabbit hutch, and even possessed a cow which supplied milk to others as well as my family. Our children and grandchildren soon joined us – to the great delight of Benito who needed this family circle more than ever.

My husband had changed psychologically, due chiefly to the shock of his arrest and abduction. It was not so much his dismissal which distressed him as the vindictive treatment he'd received from generals who owed their careers to him.

When, between July and September 1943, they were dragging him from one place to another, he said to one of them: "Why are you behaving like this? I've been a man who respected even his own enemies. I've turned them into senators or found some way to show my regard for them. I've never scorned or reviled them."

Apart from these memories, he also feared German intentions for the future of Italy. Most important of all, after July 1943, Benito Mussolini, my husband, thought that his star had completely faded; from that time he spoke of himself solely as "Mussolini defunto", or the late Mussolini. He was conscious, as head of the Italian

Social Republic, that he was merely protecting the Italians from German revenge. He had accepted this role – an act of sacrifice so that he could at least leave something positive to his successors after he had gone.

Generally speaking, surely he – and no one else – drafted the birth certificate for the present Italian Republic. On November 15, 1943, when my husband drew up an 18-point manifesto with social measures that were later christened the "social storehouse", nobody could accuse him of acting in personal interest. As in the early days when he expressed his Socialist beliefs, he dreamed of founding a popular State which was truly Socialist, but of a different Socialism from the chameleon one sees today.

As for journalism, he sold his newspaper which had given him impetus along the road to power, doing so because he could never have tolerated his own creation being published under German control. Just as Mussolini felt that he had reached the end of his journey, so the *Popolo d'Italia* had to close its doors.

I never heard about the sale until it was accomplished, for Benito, aware that I too would be sad, didn't wish to talk about it beforehand. In the main, the money that he realised was shared among the children and the family, but part of it was used to defray everything he owed to people who had worked on the *Popolo d'Italia*.

That completed, he began to write *Storia di un anno*, an historical account of one year from November, 1942 to November 1943, as well as articles for various newspapers; briefly, towards the end of his life my husband returned to his first love.

At home his favourite relaxation was to engage in cycling or read and play with the children. Even the noise that they made, which had once annoyed him, was now a source of amusement. The great change that came over my husband left him indifferent to the material things of this world, more sociable, more human than before, more kind in his relations with the people he saw.

CHAPTER 25

The moment of sacrifice

Though neither he nor I suspected it, it was to be our last Christmas together. Moreover, it may have been the thought of the pending meeting in Milan, but Benito was now particularly relaxed.

Four months later the inevitable happened. I don't know why, but when, on April 17, my husband left for Milan, I felt that the separation wouldn't be like the rest. I had urged him to stay at Gargnano, a view shared by an SS officer, but he refused to go back on the decision he'd reached.

To calm me, he said: "I'll be back in two or three days," adding that he'd to take some very important decisions in Milan, mentioning Cardinal Schuster.

I still recall his departure on that April day. It was early evening. We were standing by his car which he was about to enter, when suddenly he turned round, stared at me for a while then walked back to the house. From the top of the steps he looked out over the garden and the calm blue waters of Lake Garda, then raised his head towards the window of his room and listened for some moments to Romano playing the piano in the drawing room.

Then, as if he regretted having yielded to a moment of weakness, he strode towards the car, banged the door and said to the driver: "Let's be off, we're late." Behind him two escort cars revved up.

That was the last time I saw my husband alive.

For me the end of Benito Mussolini's life consisted of

a short letter, a whirl of events which lasted four days and, the day before his death, a voice full of emotion – his voice – saying: "I must follow my destiny, Rachele. You must start your life again."

After he left on April 17 I received no news until the 23rd, when he 'phoned explaining that he would be back at about seven that evening. Some hours later he 'phoned again, saying that he couldn't come home because the road from Milan to Gargnano was blocked, the Allies having occupied Mantua.

"It's not true," I shouted down the telephone, "they're lying to you again, Benito. A military truck has just arrived from Milan. I've been chatting to the soldiers myself. They didn't encounter a single obstacle on their route."

Then he cut in, ordering me to leave at once for Monza, where arrangements had been made to help us.

At Monza I found Gatti, his secretary, who hadn't eaten for two days and so I gave him a little chicken and a bowl of soup. Benito called me twice; first to ask me how we were, then to tell me that he couldn't join us and that we must leave for Como. It was April 24. That was the last time I heard his voice before the final telephone conversation of our life together.

I spent the 25th and 26th trying to reach him without ever managing to do so. I was alone with Romano and Anna-Maria, listening for the slightest noise behind the door or leaping to the window whenever the sirens began to whine.

During the night of April 26-27, I heard someone knocking on the door of the villa where we had taken refuge. It was a soldier. "I have a letter for you from the Duce," he said.

I opened the door quickly and took the envelope. I recognised his writing. "Who gave it to you?" I asked. "His Excellency Buffarini."

Buffarini? What could he be up to now? He was no longer a Minister and, since my visit to Clara Petacci I had stubbornly refused to see him. I wondered how the letter could have got into his hands.

Awakening the children, we began to read the few lines he had written, and from his first words an icy feeling swept over me.

"Dear Rachele," he wrote. "We may never see each other again. That is why I am sending you this letter. I ask your forgiveness for all the harm I have unwittingly done you. But you know that you have always been the only woman I have really loved. I swear it before God and our Bruno in this supreme moment. You know that I must go to the Valtellina. You must try to reach the Swiss border with the children. You can make a new life for yourself there. I don't think they'll refuse to let you through because I have always helped them whatever the circumstances and because you have never been involved in politics. If it isn't possible, give yourself up to the Allies. They may be more generous that the Italians. Look after Anna and Romano for me, especially Anna who has so much need of affection. You know how I love her. Bruno will help you from heaven. Kisses to you and the children. Your Benito."

I wasn't able to keep this letter but I remember every word, every comma, written in blue crayon. The signature was in red. So the end had come. In less than two minutes, 35 years of life together had drawn to a close. No one could understand what I was feeling, and I couldn't begin to explain.

I wanted to hear his voice again – just one last time. It was too stupid to say good-bye for ever in that way, both so close and so far from each other. Hoping for a miracle, I lifted the telephone which had been dead for two days. To my joy, we had a line again. I spent half an hour trying to reach him, and finally, I heard his voice.

"Do what I wrote to you, Rachele. It'll be much better if you don't follow me into the Valtellina. Save yourself and save the children." I felt the tears coming to my eyes and couldn't speak, and so I handed the receiver to Romano.

"You must be organising some defence for yourself, at least?" Romano said. "Who is with you?"

"There's nobody any longer, Romano. I'm alone. Everything is lost."

"But where are the soldiers – your personal guard?"

"I don't know, I haven't seen anybody. Even Cesarotti the chaffeur has abandoned me. Tell Mamma that she was right not to trust him."

With the sudden realisation that he would never see his father again, Romano began to sob. I therefore took the receiver from him. I would have liked to go on talking for hours, hoping that I could cheat fate of something.

"You must start a new life, Rachele. I must follow my destiny," he murmured in a muted voice. "Go, leave quickly." With that he broke off.

There is no point in describing how he died. The whole world knows, and hardly a month has passed over the last twenty-three years without some fresh revelation killing him all over again. All that remains of Mussolini is a skeleton wrapped in a cloth and crammed into a white-wood box, with the kind thoughts of numerous people all over the world to watch over his last sleep.

To be perfectly frank, some years elapsed before I was able to pray by Benito's grave because his corpse had vanished and then, when it was returned, I discovered to my horror that the Americans had taken away half of his brain. Presumably they wanted to know what makes a dictator. I had to ask the American ambassador in Rome before I could recover this piece of my husband who had not been able to find peace even in death.

I never worry whether or not Mussolini will ever be commemorated by a statue in his own country. It would serve no purpose, and there is something much more encouraging than a statue; that is, the memorial one leaves in men's minds. If ever I thought that all the people – however famous or insignificant – who came to the little cemetery of San Cassiano at Predappio do so out of curiosity, something that happened a few years ago would assure me that the opposite was true.

It happened in 1969. One Sunday I went to lunch with some friends in a restaurant in Milano Marittimo, a small resort on the Adriatic. At the next table a group of men were celebrating, noisily singing the odd song which left no doubt as to their political ideals: they were Communists. Aware of my ready temper, my companions began to look for a place elsewhere, but I told them not to bother; it was a lovely day, I was relaxed and I had no wish to make a scene.

We were eating the *hors d'oeuvre* when one of the nearby men said in a loud voice: "Even with all the ones who were killed, there are still just as many Fascists. You'll see statues going up to the glory of Mussolini before long. All things considered, we were the idiots."

I stiffened at these words. Did he know who I was? Was he trying to start a scene? In 1946, that would have been feasible; in 1969, it was a stupid and unwarranted piece of provocation. Embarrassed, the waiter went over to my noisy neighbours, explaining tactfully who I was. Silence fell on the room, and while every eye was turned in my direction, a man left the table and came over to us.

"Are you Signora Mussolini?" he asked.

"Yes, why?"

"Because I'm a former partisan."

"Well? Should that make any difference to me? Don't you know that the war is over?"

"I know, but I wanted to meet Benito Mussolini's wife."

"Well you have. Now would you please let me eat my lunch with my friends."

"I haven't come to annoy you, Signora. On the contrary, I want to ask your forgiveness. I was one of the 52nd Garibaldi Brigade."

"Ah, you were with the men who used the purge as a cover to kill women and children. Aren't you ashamed of what you did! And you have the nerve to stand here before me, Mussolini's wife!"

Trembling with suppressed rage, I nearly shouted these last words in spite of myself. I was re-living the apalling scenes I had witnessed in 1945 after my husband's death. Vividly in my mind was a young man, wounded and fleeing, shouting something about a hospital, and whom I'd seen slaughtered like a beast. In normal circumstances I would never have willingly thought about that period again.

Leaning towards me, the man gently took my hand, raising it to his lips and, looking me straight in the eyes, said: "Signora, in the resistance they called me Bill. I was the one who recognised your husband in the German truck at Dongo. It was I who made him get out, who searched him and arrested him."

My heart beat wildly. There in front of me, holding my hand, was the man who had made my husband take the first steps towards his terrible death. What a strange turn of fate to meet this man twenty-four years later! He must have been very young then.

Clearly Bill wished to ease his conscience. As if he had guessed my thought, he went on: "I asked Mussolini if he had any money on him, then he looked me straight in the face and replied in a strangely calm voice: 'You can search me, I have nothing. In the truck I've a brief case. There isn't any money in that either, but something which may save Italy – some documents.' Signora, I went to check and it was true. Your husband was arrested. Since 1945, I haven't had any peace of mind. I can still hear his voice and see the way he looked at me. Signora Mussolini, I was 18, now I'm a man but I can't go on living until you've forgiven me. Chance has brought us together. Perhaps it's a sign of fate. Please, Signora."

So in the silence of that restaurant room in Milano Marittimo, twenty-four years after the tragic event, I made the sign of the cross over his forehead as he leaned towards me and forgave the man who arrested Benito Mussolini the day before his execution. What use is there in keeping hate alive? He was 18. Later, I learnt that the Communist Party had sent Urbano Lazzaro, called Bill, to the Argentine. Victims can forgive, the victors must not forget.

Now, at the age of 83, peace prevails in my heart and soul. I have gathered my family round me, and those whose work prevents them from living under my roof come often to see me. I am a contented mother, grandmother and great-grandmother. But at my age I expect the inevitable to happen any day. If someone asks to meet me, I answer that I can accept only for that day, since I don't know whether I shall still be here tomorrow.

That is not the opinion of my good doctor Gentile, however. He finds me sound in wind and limb and still the same by nature. May God grant that it is so for a long while yet – not for my sake, but because every day that passes brings fresh proof that my husband was not entirely wrong.

His work still stands, whether in stone or in men's minds, and an increasing number of people are discovering that, basically, Mussolini did more for his country than all his successors. This is some comfort to lighten my old age.

I am certainly not commenting as a Fascist, for even when Benito was at the height of his glory I always thought of myself as an Italian and then as a Fascist. And today my position remains the same; I am Italian first and foremost.

So what can an Italian hope for? To live as long as possible to see her country strong, happy and peaceful.

I would have been so glad if the Italians and their leaders had said to themselves after the war: "Well, all that is over now. Let us respect the dead but let us ensure that the living may benefit from their good and generous example." Instead of that the political parties saw fit to continue widening the gap which was already dividing the Italians. Rather than make roads, build houses and put the economy back onto its feet, they allowed the situation to deteriorate; a bid for popularity ruined everything. It is so bad that now, in 1973, Italians have to resort to a medieval system of private messengers to sent a letter rather than entrust it to the postal service, in which it has one chance in a hundred of getting there quickly if a strike breaks out.

So, whatever their age, to everyone who comes to see me or writes to me, or seeks advice, or complains about the present situation, or for nostalgic reasons, I say: "Think first of your country. You must love Italy as if she were your own mother. We're always ready to run down our country, but when we're far away we miss it and think it the loveliest in the world."

To all of them, to the young people who are inspired by generous and impetuous ideals, I, Mussolini's wife, say: "Don't forget that everything you do, you must do for your country because your country is your family – is yourself."

To the rulers of Italy whoever they are – Leone, Andreotti, Fanfani and so on, all of whom I knew in their youth – I say: "Be generous, be ready to forgive. Bring unity to the Italians and don't let them tear each other to pieces. The Italian is a great big well-meaning baby, but he doesn't like to be made a fool of."

From the leaders of the political parties – Left-wing, extreme Left-wing, Right-wing, or Centre – I ask that they should give a little more thought to Italy which needs all its energies to confront a world which has lost all sense of morality and respect for the human being.

I beg the parents not to stand aside. They are the foundations, for they support the first steps of their children. If they are never given this guidance, they will grow twisted like untended trees.

If I want to live a little longer, it is because I can see the gradual realisation of this marvellous dream. It was also the dream of Benito Mussolini, my husband. That is why I do not regret the life I lived by his side.

In this index, the Duce is referred to as Benito, and his wife as Rachele, to avoid confusion with their sons, Bruno and Romano. Under Mussolini, the relationship shown is that to Benito.

292

293

Printed in Great Britain by
ROBERT MACLEHOSE AND CO LTD
The University Press, Glasgow